D1739341

The Political Calypso

The Political Calypso
True Opposition in Trinidad and Tobago 1962–1987

Louis Regis

The Press University of the West Indies
Barbados • Jamaica • Trinidad and Tobago

University Press of Florida
Gainesville • Tallahassee • Tampa • Boca Raton • Pensacola •
Orlando • Miami • Jacksonville

Published by The Press University of the West Indies
I A Aqueduct Flats Mona
Kingston 7 Jamaica
ISBN 976-640-056-3

Published simultaneously in the United States of America by
The University Press of Florida
15 NW 15th Street, Gainesville, FL 32611
ISBN 0-8130-1580-4

03 02 01 00 99   5 4 3 2 1

CATALOGUING IN PUBLICATION DATA (The Press UWI)

Regis, Louis.
The political calypso: true opposition in Trinidad and Tobago, 1962–1987 / Louis Regis.
p. cm.
Includes biblographical references and index.
ISBN 976-640-056-3
1. Calypso (music) – Trinidad and Tobago – Political aspects. 2. Popular music – Trinidad and
Tobago. I. Title.

M1681.T7 R45 1999   781.63

03 02 01 00 99   5 4 3 2 1

LIBRARY OF CONGRESS CATALOGUING-IN-PUBLICATION DATA (UPF)

Regis, Louis.
The political calypso: true opposition in Trinidad and Tobago, 1962–1987 / Louis Regis.
p. cm.
Includes bibliographical references and index.
ISBN 0-8130-1580-4 (cloth: alk. paper).
1. Calypso (Music) – Trinidad and Tobago – History and criticism. 2. Calypso (Music) – Political
aspects. 3. Trinidad and Tobago – History. 4. Trinidad and Tobago – Social conditions. I. Title.
ML3565.R46 1999
781.64–dc21   97-37804

Set in Adobe Trident
Book design by Errol Stennett
Cover art Errol Stennett

This book has been printed on acid free paper

. . . as sure as Calypso is the culture of this Land
The calypsonian is the only true opposition

Bro Valentino, "True Opposition" (1980)

Contents

List of Illustrations

Preface

At 0001 hours on Friday 31 August 1962, the red, white and black flag of the infant state of Trinidad and Tobago replaced the British Union Jack atop the standard on the front lawn of the Red House, the parliament building in Port of Spain, the nation's capital. Two weeks before this signal event, however, the achievement of independence had been celebrated publicly in song at the finals of the first Independence Calypso King competition staged at the Town Hall, Port of Spain.

All things considered, it was fitting that the calypsonian be the herald of independence because he had long championed the national forces and movements agitating for self-rule and statehood. Over the following 25 years, and beyond, he continued commenting on happenings in the political domain, communicating his views about politics, politicians and power sharing. Twenty-five years of his song have left us a priceless archive of social history which is at once the saga of independence viewed from the perspective of the urban, largely Afro-Trinidadian underclass, and at the same time, the dynamic story of a popular folk urban song form as it developed in a volatile time.

Sadly, many nationals do not accept the calypso as the national song. Some despise it as "rum music" (to quote Stalin's "Wait Dorothy" 1985); others, remarking its intimate relationship with the carnival bacchanals, divine in it the hand of the Devil; still others decry its seasonality; while there are those who dismiss it as an Afro-Creole expression. To all these objectors, the calypso cannot qualify as "The voice of the People" much more (and here the conscientious shudder) "The voice of God".

It cannot be disputed, however, that the calypso enjoys national hearing although the calypsonian does not profit from this and is hardly aware of it until, paradoxically, he is engulfed in controversy. Stalin, in an afterword to the "Caribbean Man" controversy which raged over his "Caribbean Unity" (1979), commented: "In one sense I was happy because we was conscious even though we wasn't getting support from certain areas, people listening who we didn't even know was listening."

True enough. A few hundred Trinis buy records; these and others patronise the tents, competitions and shows; thousands more crowd carnival fetes; but others listen in the privacy and secrecy of their homes and use calypsoes in much everyday discourse, so too do politicians and other social leaders.

This declared, the next order of business is to rationalise the role of the political calypso in national life. It makes good sense to start with a definition provided by the calypsonian himself. Gypsy's "Respect the Calypsonian" (1988), which details the several social roles and functions of the calypsonian, asserts that: "I could write a song to make government strong/I could write a song to bring government down."

This couplet warrants close examination. The "I" of the first line is generic. Gypsy clearly refers to the role that Sparrow, Striker and others had played in propagandising the People's National Movement (PNM), a role acknowledged by no less an authority than the party's founder, Dr Eric Williams, in his career autobiography Inward Hunger (pages 201 and 248). The PNM regime, however, did not succumb to the calypso pressure of the roaring 1970s and early 1980s. When it was swept from office in 1986 it was to the tune of Gypsy's "The Sinking Ship" (1986) and Deple's "Vote Dem Out" (1986), but one hesitates to declare that those two calypsoes were responsible for the PNM's defeat. Reviewing the period 1956–86, it seems safer to conclude that while the calypsonian contributes to the legitimisation and delegitimisation process, he may not necessarily make the difference in national politics.

Arising from this is a thought on the nature of the relationship between calypsonian and politician. They seem to form uneasy informal alliances: the politician welcomes the calypsonian into his camp but not into his councils; the calypsonian, for his part, supports but hardly ever signs up. Stalin's "Sing for the Land" (1984) crystallises the calypsonian's attitude to the politician:

> If your party like the things wha' I saying
> We could put platforms together and do a little protesting
> But when the moment reach and we both start to disagree
> To go we separate ways we all must be free
> Because I doh owe you nothing, is the land I owe
> And how you serving your Country I doh want to know
> Because for the love of my Country my motto is to do my best
> And as the old people say, 'Do yuh best and forget the rest'.

Unfortunately for us, no politician has chosen to respond in song, leaving us to wonder if the man of politics is comfortable with the "man-talking-to-man" familiarity which allows the man of words to openly criticise and chastise the politicians he admires and supports. The calypsonian is his own man and does not need the politician's permission to make statements in song. On the other side of the coin, there is the reality that his audience may quite comfortably agree with him and still vote for the man he is 'pounding' in song. Even so, the politician tries not to antagonise the man whose public ridicule from a calypso stage is something to make a politician cringe.

As far as group relationships are concerned, the calypsonian has been able to force society to look at itself honestly – if only briefly. Although we lack instruments to measure the impact of a calypso like Stalin's "Caribbean Unity" we cannot deny that songs such as this act like what Stuart Hall calls "maps of meaning" into the geography of a complicated political culture. Race is a taboo subject in public polite discourse in our society but not for the calypsonian. All but one of the major calypso controversies since independence have had to do with race relations. They have caused much bitterness – or rather, they have exposed the bitterness secreted behind the smiles of tolerance – but they have involved the national community in discussion which, unfortunately, hardly ever reaches the platform of dialogue. Apropos of this, I remark that several songs have been condemned as being disrespectful, divisive, insulting, mischievous, misleading, prejudicial, prejudiced, racial, racist, sexist, any or all of the above. Happily, these negative designations do not hold good for most calypsoes.

One final consideration needs to be made. The calypso continues to articulate deep-seated aspirations for the nation. If we compare the independence calypsoes of 1987 to those of 1962 we realise that although the notion of model nation took a beating during the first 25 years, it is still a cherished illusion, at least in the mind of the calypsonian. He, at least, has not despaired of Trinidad and Tobago.

In conclusion, then, I wish to affirm that the calypso is our national song. Within six short years of our achieving independence, Duke's prize-winning classic "What is Calypso?" clarified the fundamentals of what is considered to be nation song, defining it as "an editorial in song of the life we undergo". It is the readiest reference to our history and the medium which best allows us to make contact with our secret soul. Our most distinguished novelist, V.S. Naipaul, writes in *The Middle Passage* that, "It is only in the calypso that the Trinidadian touches reality." The art form belongs to us all and invites all to participate. It speaks to us all in a language we all understand. We may not always like or agree with its messages but it is impossible to imagine Trinidad and Tobago without it.

The survey period for this study is defined quite tidily by two Independence Calypso King competitions, the first held on Wednesday, 15 August 1962 and the second on Saturday, 22 August 1987. In the interest of understanding attitudes fully formed by 31 August 1962, I have had to review the calypsoes of 1956–62 which embrace the PNM's first six years in office. The period before this is sufficiently documented in what are universally considered the three most comprehensive and responsible studies on the calypso: J.D. Elder's "Evolution of the traditional calypso", Raymond Quevedo's *Atilla's Kaiso*, and Gordon Rohlehr's *Calypso and Society in Pre-Independence Trinidad*.

SOURCES AND METHODS

In any study of the calypso, the primary resource remains the calypso text itself. It proved impossible to gather in all the calypsoes composed and performed in any one year, therefore I had to rely on phonograms, tapes, live performances, videos, accounts of performances and songbooks. The much maligned Dimanche Gras Calypso King (Monarch after 1976) competition proved invaluable because it is the calypso show which is most viewed and recorded – not to mention discussed – and in many ways it is the best calypso show of any given year. Competitors there, fully aware that they are being tested on a national stage before an international audience, refine all their performing skills, costume themselves appropriately, sometimes write new stanzas, and even introduce dramatic adjuncts, all of which taken together impress meanings which may have been lost in the hurly-burly of the tent. The Calypso Fiesta, the qualifying semifinal for the Monarch Competition, is also very useful for the researcher because it is generally agreed that the 48 songs performed there are among the best of a given year, save for those performed by those calypsonians who have either forsworn competition or can only manage one good song. This latter group still enjoys a hearing thanks to competitions like the Young Kings, the National Calypso Queen and the regional competitions. Thus, a good look at the competitions and the tents indicates what were the major songs of a particular year.

Sadly, it was not possible to consider all the calypsoes performed at the National Junior Competition, the various school competitions and those organised by institutions and firms. One regrets this omission because these competitions unearth a wealth of composing and performing talent. Also, they provide viewpoints which centre stage professionals may not consider. A child of retrenched parents, say, singing a calypso composed by one of these parents, or a white-collar career wife and mother may respond to the budget in ways that the professional calypsonian may not consider. Their viewpoints contribute to the spectrum of song on given issues of national importance and one sorely misses this.

This brings us to the all-important point of approaches to the study of the political calypso. A calypso is the sum of personal forces which define a calypsonian, and is the product of social contexts which allow him to write and/or sing or record as the case might be. A political calypso is an expression of an individual's feelings, given his political affiliation – or want thereof – and other personal circumstances. Secondly, it is a marketable good in an overcrowded entertainment industry, a fact which threatens to make the community versus market debate a life or death situation. I have therefore paid some attention to singers' background knowing that this allows for two kinds of comparative study: (1) responses of different singers to the same stimulus and (2) differing responses of the same singer to the same kind of situation. Walking with the calypsonian from idea to performance gives unusual insight into the art form. It helps us to appreciate the artiste as a human being, and it ushers us into the magical private world of creativity and into the robust public world of performance. We see how the calypsonian adjusts his tune and tone to conditions within his home circle, within calypsodom and within the larger society. Above all, we see how the calypsonian is moved by the part-time loving on the part of a public to which he is committed; how he deals with his society's massive expectations and meagre rewards; how he wears his laurels and his crown of thorns; how in spite of all this, he still creates.

The material presented in this book was approved in 1994 by the University of the West Indies (UWI) as a thesis in fulfilment of the Master of Philosophy Degree in English under the title "Popular music as communication: The political calypso in Trinidad and Tobago 1962–1987". It is largely unchanged, except that a preface and an afterword replace the introduction and the conclusion, and a chapter named "Ars Poetica", which illustrates the calypsonians' literary technique, has been added. Also, I have presented the calypsoes on the 1961 general election as a separate subsection, and in a few cases I have added several explanatory passages and lyrics.

Acknowledgements

I owe so much to so many people that I can only mention those whose immediate influence and assistance can be seen and felt in the production of this book:

Eustace Ward who so kindly provided all but one of the photographs used in this book;

the Guardian newspapers for permission to reproduce the photograph of Dr Eric Williams and the Mighty Sparrow on page 194;

Professor Gordon Rohlehr, who introduced me to the study of the calypso and encouraged – if not nudged – me into serious work; and also for permission to use material from *Pathfinder* and from *Calypso and Society in Pre-Independence Trinidad*;

Squibby and his many friends, including Warrior (deceased), and Tenderspot (now Kinte), who gave me the calypsonian's perspective on the calypso;

Zeno Obi Constance, my brother-at-arms, who put his collection at my disposal and whose ear is ever attuned to discourse on the calypso; and for permission to quote from *Valentino: Poet and Prophet*;

The 84 calypsonians whose work I used in the study, and the many others whose work I did not quote or allude to but found useful in terms of perspective on the period;

Sparrow, Stalin, Valentino, Composer, Short Pants, Rawle Aimey and Glen Roach, who kindly consented to be interviewed;

Anthony des Caires, James Baisden and Irwin Barry who allowed me the use of their collections,

Mrs Donna Coombes-Montrose and Mr Jerry Kangalee of the OWTU library, who brought to my attention material which I didn't even know existed;

Dr Hollis Liverpool, for permission to quote from *Kaiso and Society*;

Pat McNeely of COTT for permission to use calypso lyrics;

Professor Selwyn Ryan for use of material from *Race and Nationalism in Trinidad and Tobago*, *The Disillusioned Electorate*, *The 1970 Black Power Revolution* and from ISER publications;

Eugene Norville, Carlyle Ledgerwood, Krishna Samaroo, Oliver Henry and Kenneth Glasgow, all of Pleasantville Senior Comprehensive, whose discussions with me proved invaluable;

Gerard David and Novack George who programmed my computer and walked me through the fundamentals of computer literacy;

and my family, who understood and supported.

List of Abbreviations

STE and FWTU	All-Trinidad Sugar Estates and Factory Workers' Trade Union
CDC	Carnival Development Committee
COLA	Cost of Living Allowance
DAC	Democratic Action Committee
DLP	Democratic Labour Party
ICFTU	Islandwide Cane Farmers' Trade Union
ISA	Industrial Stabilization Act
NAR	National Alliance for Reconstruction
NCC	National Carnival Commission
NJAC	National Joint Action Committee
NLTRA	National Land Tenants and Ratepayers' Association
NUFF	National Union of Freedom Fighters
ONR	Organization of National Reconstruction
OWTU	Oilfields Workers' Trade Union
OYB	Original Young Brigade
PNM	People's National Movement
SDLP	Social Democratic Labour Party
TIWU	Transport and Industrial Workers' Union
UNC	United National Congress
ULF	United Labour Front
UWI	University of the West Indies
WFP	Workers' and Farmers' Party

The Calypso
and Politics 1956–1962

After the 1956 general election victory, Dr Eric Williams, unsung before, became the darling of the calypsonians largely because he was their living legend who had destroyed myths of black intellectual inferiority by his own effort and achievement. Another valid reason was that he had presented himself as being totally committed to destroying the colonial system and to securing his people's welfare. The famous resignation speech when he broke with the Caribbean Commission and linked his personal struggle with the common historical destiny of the masses seemed proof of his earnestness in their cause.[1] On a personal level, he was friendly towards calypsonians and he is remembered kindly, at least by Superior and Blakie, for his ready, generous responses to their hard-luck stories.[2]

At the opening of the 1957 tent season, Cypher was billed to lead a chorus of his fellow Original Young Brigade (OYB) singers in rendering his "Balisier",[3] and at least six other prominent calypsonians (Sparrow and Bomber of the OYB; Spitfire, Viper, Striker and Radio of the Senior Brigade) performed songs in praise of Williams and the PNM during that season. Sparrow's "William the Conqueror" is perhaps the best known of these victory paeans:

I am no politician
But I could understand
If it wasn't for Brother Willie
And his ability
Trinidad wouldn't go neither come
We used to vote for food and rum
But nowadays we eating all the Indians and them
And in the ending, we voting PNM

Praise little Eric, rejoice and be glad
We have a better future here in Trinidad

P.N.M.
It ent got nobody like them
For they have a champion leader
William the Conqueror

This original calypsonian attitude towards Williams is crucial in that it established a complex of images ("visions") and an organisation of language ("voices") against which calypsonians of other persuasions would need to contend in their effort to dismantle the Williams myth.

One incident in particular testifies to the strength of support that Williams could count on. In 1959, The Growling Tiger, that indomitable ex-pugilist/ex-*chantuelle*, criticised Williams for his secret wedding and for his base desertion of his wife of several hours, an affair which had taken place in 1957 but had been discreetly hushed by all concerned until exposed in a headline story in the *Trinidad Chronicle* more than a year after.[4]

Although Ah read it
Ah don't believe it
He didn't do it
They got to prove it
Ah dirty propaganda
Saying that the Doc marry down Caledonia
A man of such high moral integrity
Wouldn't marry on the island there secretly

Chorus
No, no, not the Doc
No, no, not the beloved Doctor
I can afford to gamble my life
He'll never marry and next day desert his wife

(ii) After a year of gossip and rumour
We found out was Dr Mook Sang from British Guiana
She couldn't keep the secret much longer
She told the Press she married the Doctor
The two witnesses were Ministers of State
Yet they couldn't find the marriage certificate
Rev. McKean said 'Yes' without a doubt
But up to now not a word from the Doc mouth

(iii) The wedding full of thrills and sensation
The woman don't carry the name of her husband
Instead of cherishing one another

In fact they don't live in the same house together
He in Woodbrook, she in Frederick Street
Ah wonder what time in the night these people does meet
Don't think I'm inquisitive
But up to now he got her nowhere to live

(iv) The *Guardian* are responsible people
So there's something in the mortar beside the pestle
Doc, Ah wish you a Happy New Year
If you married or not is your own affair
But you are leader and I am one of the flock
Tell me if you married please, Doc
Ah wanted a piece of your wedding cake
So tell me if they lie or if it's a mistake

The implication here is that the incongruence between overt expressions of morality in public affairs and covert manifestations of immorality in private matters suggested that Williams was capable of deceit and deception. This hurt the image of integrity which Williams had been cultivating assiduously. Party faithful and Williams himself retaliated by boycotting the Senior Brigade at which Tiger was appearing. The consequent fall off in revenue brought about Tiger's constructive dismissal, "in obedience to an unwritten law", the tent manager explained elliptically.[5]

As chance would have it, Melody at the rival OYB was offering a different interpretation to the affair. His "Doctor Make Your Love" hurls defiance at all of Williams' detractors by declaring that Williams' actions were nobody's business but his own, and that the outcry and outrage were nothing but venting of jealousy for a man whose intellectual power was feared and hated. There may have been a hidden subtext in that Melody could also have been satirising the idea of Williams as lover, he being in appearance a contrast to the lean and hungry *sagaboy* ideal of lover personified by Sparrow and later by Shorty. The faithful, seduced by the line "We are the PNM", may have latched on to the main text and missed the *mamaguy*, a tendency that would show up time and again and especially where Williams was the subject. The fact that Tiger was pressured for his calypso and Melody lauded for his indicated that the largely urban tent-going audiences were willing to accept Melody's endorsement of Williams' sexuality. This was a most welcome prospect in an unabashedly heterosexual society which celebrated the machismo of politicians and other public figures but had yet to evaluate scholars in sexual terms. On the other hand, audiences refused to countenance the desecration implied in Tiger's reduction of their idol to the level of sinful, selfish man.

Sparrow's "Leave the Dam Doctor" (1959) silenced the critics and ended the matter for the while:

All of them that giving they verdict
'Bout the doctor getting me sick
I don't know why they doh mind they stinking business
Leave the boss in peace

Leave the dam Doctor
He ent trouble allyuh
Leave the dam Doctor
What he do he well do
Leave the dam Doctor
And doh get mih mad
Leave the dam Doctor
Or is murder in Trinidad

The other party is there
They can't handle they own affair
They stumbling with all their plans
But still they harassing the blasted man

The end result of this was a massive display of collegial solidarity on the part of calypsonians as far as the Williams cause was concerned, and by the next year *The Trinidad Guardian* reported that, "There was not an antigovernment calypso in sight." Indeed, Senior Brigade singers complained of the damage done them by a negative label earned because the tent manager was a campaign manager for the opposition Democratic Labour Party (DLP).[6]

THE SPARROW FACTOR

The case just discussed throws into relief the Sparrow factor in the politics of 1957-65. No one doubts the power of Williams' mass appeal or even the immense store of goodwill towards the PNM[7] but the Sparrow factor as one of the major planks of the PNM public relations campaign has been sadly neglected although it has been indicated by political scientists and by Williams himself.[8]

Before 1956, Sparrow was a 'Grade B' calypsonian, that is a hustler milking tourists on the beaches, on the Lookout overlooking the city and on the 'Gaza Strip' when not performing at the tent.[9] Late in 1955 he joined 'Gayap', a group which raised funds at home and abroad and otherwise prepared for the coming of Williams into the political kingdom.[10] Sparrow's stock soared with his 1956 Calypso King and Road March victories and was guaranteed by the voluminous output of his peerless genius to the point that he could declare, "If Sparrow say so, is so" and have many believe him.

His consistently brilliant and aggressive campaign for Williams gives one the impression that the PNM public relations thrust was dictated by Williams in parliament, at Woodford Square, at Balisier House (PNM headquarters) and elsewhere, and was supported magnificently by Sparrow in calypso and by C.L.R James, editor of the party newspaper, The Nation. Williams, for example, branded the parliamentary opposition a "pack of benighted idiots" and a "band of obscurantist politicians" and flayed them for their "ignorant declamations" in the parliamentary chambers.[11] Sparrow, no scholar himself, co-opts this intellectual snobbery in "Present Government" (1961):

> Some again have no education
> Is them does make the confusion
> Anything at all the Premier say
> They always standing in the way
> And like they suffering from a mental shock
> Talking one seta sewerage talk.

Stench better suits the unwholesome dealings in connection with the financing of an island wide sewerage scheme.[12] Sparrow's "sewerage talk" reduces attempts on the part of the opposition to initiate probes into those dealings, the first of a long series of allegations of corruption on the part of PNM hierarchs. By turning the matter round, Sparrow is able to suggest that it is the opposition and not the guilty government ministers who were the source of filth in parliament. He lumps the opposition with those labour unions whose many strikes seem to be a form of opposition to the PNM:

> No gas today, no phone tomorrow
> What next I don't know
> No drain digging, no rubbish cleaning
> Only corbeaux working
> The Island as you see
> Suffering politically
> Because the present government
> Have some stupid opponent
> Oh Lord man! they ignorant
> Because the present government
> Have some stupid opponent
> Not one is intelligent

James, citing the above as evidence of Sparrow's political maturity, comments: "I believe here he faithfully reports public sentiment. Things are in a mess and the reason is that the Opposition are objecting to everything." [13]

Sparrow's "William the Conqueror" celebrates the 1956 victory as a triumph of the new intellectualism ("Big Brains") over old-style leadership ("Big Belly"), jabbing viciously at Albert Gomes (the defeated opponent, being a man of massive girth). That very year, however, Sparrow sounded the first note of disenchantment with the performance of the months-old government:

Listen, listen carefully
I am a man does never be sorry (repeat)
But Ah went and vote for some Council men
They have me now in a pen
After promising to give so much tender care
They forget me as soon as they walk out of Woodford Square

Chorus
They raise up on the taxi fare
No, Doctor, no
And the blasted milk gone up so dear
No, Doctor, no

But you must remember
We support you in September
You better come good
Because Ah have a big piece of mango wood

(ii) Plenty people sorry
Sorry that they throw down Big Belly
But not me, I sticking mih pressure
When Ah cyar buy milk, Ah using sugar and water
'Support local industry' they done declare
They mean Vat 19 and Carib beer
The way they forcing we to drink Vat
Like they want to kill we in smart

(iii) Ah waiting for the other move
Is something Ah want to prove
My friends, I would like to know
If the Council business bound to be so
When a fellow is high and Honourable
That is the time to study your own people
And regardless of what, you ought to see
That I get a raise on my salary

(iv) I only hope they understand
I am only a calypsonian

What I say might be very small
But I know poor people ent pleased at all
We are looking for betterment
That is why we choose a new government
But they raise on the food before we could talk
And they raise on the fare so we bound to walk

Sparrow represents himself here as a supporter disgruntled at the sudden burden of price increases yet willing to submit to the superior knowledge of the party wise men. He adopts the pose of the humble calypsonian alienated from institutionalised power and needing to trust in the tested might of street rhetoric. He therefore unburdens his mind by means of a threat, which, downgraded somewhat in the final chorus, set the standard for the tradition of Williams criticism among the believers.

"No, Doctor, No" articulates political naiveté (Sparrow was only 22 years old in 1957) based on an unquestioning belief in politicians and informed by the desire for instantaneous gratification of his wishes. It also reveals that lingering distrust that the masses still had for the Creole intelligentsia and the uneasiness of their marriage of convenience. This last would surface later in the Melody couplet "Ah hear the Doctor married again/Socialism must be maintained" which, as Professor Gordon Rohlehr points out, attests to that continuation of the elitism and secrecy among the ruling caste.[14] Still later, when Williams lost popularity, songs like Maestro's "To Sir with Love" (1974) and "Dread Man" (1977) and Relator's "Our Children Deserve Better" (1981), plus a host of Chalkdust compositions, would reproach him with the failings he had always demonstrated but which an enthusiastic following had celebrated as evidence of his specialness.

As a consequence of "No, Doctor, No" Sparrow was called in "for consultations",[15] which immediately bore fruit in "PAYE" (1958):

It's a shame, it's a shame
But we have weself to blame (repeat)
Because we ask for new government
Now they taking every cent
Cost of living is the same
So it's really a burning shame

Chorus
The Doctor say to pay as you earn
But Sparrow say you paying to learn
And mih father say he sharpening the axe
So when the collector come to pay off the income tax

(ii) Plenty people want to cry
They miss the water, the well run dry
But they can't do a thing about it
The money ent going in the Doctor pocket
First of all we want better schools
So we children won't grow up as fools
Then work for you and me
That is what plenty of them cyar see

(iii) Everybody is in misery
But this tax ent bothering me
For I ent working no where
And I have no income to share
But Mr This and Mr That
Who accustom with they payroll fat
Is to see them shedding tears
Men like De Freitas and Fernandes

(iv) When the Doctor went up to England
They bluntly refuse to support his plan
So there is nothing more he could do
Than to get it from me and you
That's the law now in Trinidad
If you doh like it that's too bad
Take your things and clear out today
For all who working must pay

"PAYE" is a masterpiece of pro-PNM propaganda. Stanza one voices the universal outcry against the tax but stanza two begins the process of softening the impact of the impost by making it seem - as no doubt it was - an investment in education and job creation. Williams, the narrator assures us, is certainly not pocketing the money. In stanza three, Sparrow glibly passes himself off as unemployed, which, though true in the sense that he did not draw an emolument from State or private sector employer, certainly devalues the profession of calypsonian which he defended proudly and violently and from which he had begun to earn a livelihood. Stanza four anticipates the arrogance which Williams would unleash in the 1960s, and this tone indicates that the narrator, who may here be representing the calypsonian himself, is in full agreement with the tax. This is reinforced by the change in the penultimate line of the final chorus from, "Mih father say he sharpening the axe" to "Mih father say he selling the axe."

"PAYE" won the 1958 Road March. One really cannot say if the revelling public was more in love with the lyrics than with the melody or loved them equally. How far the calypso contributes to what eminent political scientist, Professor Selwyn Ryan records as stoic acceptance on the part of the Afro-Trinidadian,[16] is open to question. Sparrow reinforces the message in "You Can't Get away from the Tax" (1959), in which he projects himself, as indeed he was, as a widely travelled citizen assuring his sedentary compatriots that income tax is an acceptable universal reality and is more onerous elsewhere:

> In the Virgin Isles
> You got to pay taxes with a smile
> In Puerto Rico
> If you don't pay, straight to jail you go
> Well in Cuba and Haiti
> Taxes higher than salary
> Don't talk about New York and Caracas
> You have to tief sometimes to pay tax

Characteristic calypso hyperbole serves as the literary vehicle for Sparrow's appeal and this is drummed in by the litanic response "You can't get away from the tax." Sparrow's attitude, too, has changed dramatically from the aggressive "If you doh like it that's too bad" of "PAYE" to the persuasive "Sparrow wouldn't tell you no lie" and even to the fatalistic "So you see, Doctor or no Doctor/You can't get away from the tax."

Increasing criticism of Williams, prompted to some extent by his secret marriage to a Guyanese of Chinese extraction, forced Sparrow – himself under pressure for his own marriage to an American white – into the more aggressive defence of "Leave the Dam Doctor" which threatens Williams' detractors in the language of the streets, Sparrow's familiar world.

Sparrow's support for Williams during the crisis of the West Indies Federation was total and unquestioning. C.L.R. James recounts the impact of "Federation":

> I was in the tent the night he returned and first sang it. When it became clear what he was saying, the audience froze. Trinidad had broken with the Federation. Nobody was saying anything and the people did not know what to think, far less what to say. At the end of the last verse on that first night Sparrow saw that something was wrong and he added loudly: "I agree with the Doctor."[17]

By Dimanche Gras night substantial numbers of calypso-going fans had come to agree either with Sparrow or with the "Doctor" because "Federation" was greeted with tumultuous ovation as Sparrow recovered the crown he had surrendered in a shock defeat in 1961.[18]

RACE RELATIONS AND THE CALYPSO

Much ink has been spilt in the definition and explanation of Afro-Indian relationships, the most intriguing social phenomenon of twentieth century Trinidad. One
rejects equally the predictions of imminent race war as the protestations of racial
solidarity, and favours the plural disassociation theory and the latency out of which
"there has developed a sort of easy-going picaresque relativism that frequently
allows a considerable range of individual deviancy".[19] In the war of politics, however, bitterness and suspicion threatened the calm of mutual tolerance. The PNM's
"broad interracial appeal" attracted urban Muslim and Indo-Christians such as
Kamaludin Mohammed and Dr Winston Mahabir but Hindus distrusted it as the
dawning of a black millennium.[20]

The calypsonians supported the PNM, and their songs wore the racial tinges
characteristic of all political campaigning. Sparrow attacked the opposition on racial
grounds ("William the Conqueror" 1957; "Leave the Dam Doctor" 1959; "Present
Government" 1961) but defended Williams against charges of racism by drawing
attention to his good standing with world-respected leaders in India whose prestige
and authenticity would make the lilliputian sniping of the Trinidad-born Indian
("Balisier" 1961) seem like petty malice. This needed special pleading after Williams'
outburst after the defeat suffered by the PNM in the 1958 Federal Elections.[21] After
that poll, the calypsonian warned that the Indo-Trinidadian was aware of the need
for political power and was working towards maximising voter turnout to ensure
this (Striker's "The United Indian" 1959). Melody's "Apan Jhaat" (1959), which
purports to be a statement on the 1957 general election in British Guiana, claims
that a fictional Indian calypsonian Lall was mobilising the Indo-Guyanese
community with the chorus:

Vote Jairam ...   ...Ah-ha
Vote Seeram ...   ...Ah-ha
Vote Beharry ...   ...Ah-ha
Apan jhaat
Marsaray kay kilwili (Our own race/ Pound the Creole)

While the Indo-Guyanese found no difficulty in trekking miles to the polling
stations to "marsaray kay kilwili", the Afro-Guyanese abandoned their leader Forbes
Burnham:

Mr B shoulda come first
But Black people too conniving and pompous
They should have done like the Indian
Walk down to the polling station

But no! They want an aeroplane
Because the weather report say it will rain
And with that they sign they destiny
My people too stupid, believe me

The last line suggests that Melody may have been warning the Afro-Trinidadian that his attitude could precipitate a similar disaster. This calypso becomes more significant in the use of the coded message which, in the survey period, becomes the standard technique where race relations are concerned.

With respect to the vexing matter of race relations, one notes the comparative marginality of Dougla's "Split Me in Two" (1961), a calypso which should have enjoyed a level of communicativeness commensurate with its continuing relevance to the society and its high profile as a Calypso King song. "Split Me in Two" examines the precarious situation of a child of mixed race in a society in which the major ethnic groups seem bent on polarisation along the specious basis of racial purity. It is not unusual for an intelligent, well-written calypso to be overlooked, neither is it surprising that a Calypso King song should be quickly forgotten; the rare coincidence of these two minor tragedies constitute an anomaly that needs to be examined.

In the first place, Dougla may have been his own worst enemy because he invoked the absurd fantasy associated with the shadowy Spoiler by directing attention to an unlikely scenario made all the more improbable by the movement towards independence and a definite claim to permanence and consolidation of presence. The calypso begins:

Let us suppose they pass a law
They don't want people here any more
Let us suppose they pass a law
They don't want people living here any more
Every body got to find their country
According to your race originally
What a confusion I would cause in the place
They might have to shoot me in space

Well if they sending Indians to India
And Negroes back to Africa
Will somebody please just tell me
Where they sending for me, poor Dougie
I am neither one or the other
Six o' one, half a dozen of the other
Well if they serious 'bout sending back people for true
They bound to split me in two

Professor Gordon Rohlehr, the scholar who has pioneered the multidisciplinary approach to the study of the calypso, has explained that, "Spoiler's art was to start with the fantastic and suggest its closeness to the texture of reality."[22] Dougla, by beginning with the fantastic, destroys the credibility of a real and urgent appeal for sense on the part of the races, an appeal which, if heeded, may have spared the society much bitterness. Although succeeding stanzas of the song describe the traumatic isolation of the *dougla* in the midst of warring 'pure' Africans and Indians, the somewhat exaggerated predicament evoked laughter, a response perhaps provoked and reinforced by the burlesque "Lazy Man", the second member of the crown-winning tandem, and "Teacher, Teacher", Dougla's third song of that year. It is possible that Dougla was perceived as a funny man and so dismissed. It may also be that the calypso was seen as an attempt to communicate a personal problem to an audience which is not particularly interested in the woes of the suffering "I". It is also possible that in those tense days that society had decided, as Duke would later state in "Black Is Beautiful" (1969), that "There's no in-between in race/You got to find your natural place," thus forcing the *dougla* to choose the parent he seems closer to or the one who makes him more welcome.

Another significant reason that "Split Me in Two" may have been overlooked may well have nothing to do with that calypso itself and may well have been a function of the exciting developments in the Calypso King Competition of that year. One can hardly discount the fact that Dougla's victory was realised at the expense of the Mighty Sparrow, the hitherto undefeated Titan of the modern era. This defeat was eagerly awaited in the *Guardian* newspapers,[23] then in opposition to Williams, and when it materialised attention focused on the charismatic loser. Since his irruption in 1956, Sparrow had been a force to reckon with, whether on the streets, in the calypso tent or in the concert hall. He had offended many by his brashness and his uncompromising zeal in defining and promoting a new professionalism, actions which, he charges, were punished in the conspiracy to upstage him ("Robbery with V" 1961). His defeat was welcomed by detractors as a much needed lesson; one letter writer hoped that Dougla would "seek to avoid the pitfalls of braggadocio and flamboyance and forgo that hubris which has proved to be a bane and dethronement of many kings before him".[24]

The exacerbated racial tensions of the 1961 general election buried "Split Me in Two", and Dougla himself returned to the shadows. By a cruel irony, the OYB, home to both Dougla and Sparrow, dramatised the PNM victory by organising an in-house Elections Victory Competition at which the second and third place winners, Nap Hepburn and Cristo, both sang pieces celebrating the African character of the victory.[25]

THE 1961 GENERAL ELECTION

Trinidad nearly descended into race war in 1961. For weeks preceding that crucial general election the air was poisoned with report and rumour of violence and violation, of threat and counter threat.[26] Dr Rudranath Capildeo, the mathematician/ lawyer recruited by the DLP to checkmate the PNM's historian, grew frustrated with the PNM's control of state power and the conspiracy with the *Guardian* newspaper.[27] By nature a highly strung character,[28] he made several inflammatory speeches, the most infamous of which included the words: "Arm yourselves with weapons in order to take over this country . . . get ready to march on Whitehall . . ."[29]

In response to Capildeo's harangues, Dr Patrick Solomon, PNM Minister of Internal Affairs, counter threatened, "If Capildeo incites violence, I will slap him in gaol fast . . . and he would not get out again."[30] Thankfully, both sides stopped short of anarchy, and tensions subsided although one suspects that animosities still smouldered.

Nap Hepburn's "The Mad Scientist" (1962), which draws its title from Williams' derogatory designation of Capildeo,[31] is a strong statement on that election. A shouted dialogue between Nap and Laddy (Conrad Prescott, leader of the March of Dimes chorus group) captures the tense excitement of those days:

Nap: Laddy! Doh go up dey!
Laddy: Why? I ent 'fraid dem
Nap: Ah tell you, doh go dey, boy.
Laddy: I ent 'fraid dem
Nap: It have gun and iron bolt dey.
Laddy: I ent 'fraid dem
Nap: Alright, go up, go up. Is your constituency, go up
Laddy: Ah goin', Ah goin'

This dialogue, begun in the opening band chorus, continues apace through each succeeding break between chorus and stanza, and eventually, as expected, Nap shouts, "Oh God! Laddy geh he head bus'!"

The calypso itself castigates Capildeo and his following:

Well Ah glad the election over
And the Doctor come back in power (repeat)
It was a hard fight
Platform speakers saying what they like
One side was offering education
And the next side revolution

Chorus
He say to arm yourself with your weapons, in the Savannah
He say to burn up your ID card, down at Couva
He say to break up the voting machine
That was bought by my Government
Is the mad scientist as usual preaching violence.

(ii) From Trinidad and Tobago
The Doctor had the go
Only in the rural districts
Support the mad scientist
The election was at hot pace
Some deceitful people vote race
But all who vote race, I have one thing to say
That the Doctor come here to stay

(iii) Election campaign is fun
I doh like how this one begun
From that Sunday in the Savannah
My blood started to shiver
An intelligent man addressing a congregation
Here what he offering my son and daughter
Is murder and manslaughter

(iv) I am sure this man is a mad man
He threaten the trade unions
I am sure that this man is sick
Always insulting the public
Down at Indian Walk he exploit
One seta sewerage talk
How he go handle the Police when he take over
And he go fire the Governor

Nap's partisanship is best reflected in the line "Some deceitful people vote race," a thrust at the DLP supporters who, as the calypso implies, had they allowed themselves to be guided by logic and sense, would inevitably have rejected the party which preached revolution. The corollary to Nap's statement is that all the PNM's supporters are logical, rational and sane; Williams' public tantrums and threats to bulldoze the opposition into the hillside[32] would then become Orwellian doublespeak.

Cristo's "Election Violence" (1962) also chortles over the PNM victory:

> That was real suspense
> And plenty violence
> Electrifying suspense
> And a lot of ignorance
> Because I can remember
> On the fourth of December
> Trinidadians stand by
> For results to know if to do or die
> To the polls they went
> And return the same government
>
> Chorus
> Whip dem, PNM, whip dem
> You wearing the pants
> If these people get on top is trouble
> And we ent got a chance
> Now we faring better
> Since we got we Premier
> We living in contentment
> So who we want: PNM government

Cristo voices the fear that an Indo-Trinidadian victory would spell doom for the Afro-Trinidadian, a thought that would surface later in Chalkdust's "Clear Your Name" (1974) and "Shango Vision" (1977), Maestro's "Portrait in Black" (1976), Natasha Wilson's "Reincarnation Wish" (1985) and Cro Cro's "Allyuh Look for Dat" (1996).

Stanza four contains ideas which would come back to haunt the voters of 1961:

> So let us compliment
> We new government
> Far and wide
> Don't mind the other side
> Because many years ago
> You coulda come from Tokyo
> Put up a big business
> And walk out with your pocket full of interest

In 1970 the children of the "We" who were supposedly living in contentment protested bitterly against the PNM regime. Part of their fury was directed against the expatriates who waxed rich from the PNM's tax holidays. This, however, was years in the future. For the present of 1962 the Afro-Trinidadian was truly and deeply content that he 'owned' Whitehall.

THE 1962 INDEPENDENCE CALYPSO KING COMPETITION

With independence a certain prospect, the society seemed to regain the equilibrium of consensus that all parties beguiled themselves into believing was the attitude proper to the birth of a new nation. By the unwritten terms of this concordat, the Calypso, the music of the politically and numerically dominant majority (Afro-Trinidadians and Tobagonians numbered 358,588, 43.3 percent of the total population),[33] was 'declared' national music, and so a subcommittee of the grand Independence Celebrations Committee organised a competition, the finals of which were held at City Hall, Port of Spain, on the evening of Wednesday, 15 August.[34]

The dominant theme of the calypsoes performed was the universal optimism in the nation's future, and this was reflected in the unstinting praise of country, its bountiful natural resources, the beautiful nature of its cosmopolitan citizenry, and the sterling qualities of its leadership past and present. Sparrow's "Model Nation" encapsulates all the euphoric sentiments expressed in the calypsoes of the finals and perhaps of the entire competition:

> The whole population of this little nation
> Is not a lot
> But oh! what a mixture of races and culture
> That's what we've got
> Still no major indifference
> Of race, colour, religion or finance
> It's amazing to you I'm sure
> We didn't get Independence before
>
> Chorus
> Trinidad and Tobago will always live on
> Colonialism gone, our Nation is born . . . everybody
> We go follow our leaders
> They always do their best, oh yes
> We want to achieve, we going to aspire
> We bound to be a success
>
> (ii) It's a miracle all these different people
> Can dwell so well
> You see we are educated to love and forget hatred
> You know, you know it's so
> You people who are foreign

Ah got a message to give you when you going
Spread the word anywhere you pass
Tell the world there's a model nation at last

(iii) The revenue we make from oil and the Pitch Lake
Is great, but wait
We got cocoa and copra, bananas and sugar
Coconuts, citrus
We may be small but we wealthy
Pound for pound we beat New York City
We got beaches and hotel built by Hilton
Our Nation ent second to anyone

(iv) You may not believe this but we didn't achieve this
With floods of blood
It is leaders like Butler, Cipriani and the Doctor
They fight for what is right
So now I'm congratulating
All our leaders from the present back to the beginning
They have fought now the battle is won
Thanks for a good job well done

Despite this remarkable effort delivered with all the sincerity he no doubt felt, Sparrow could only place second in the final reckoning. Some felt that he had not been "up to standard"[35] although this calypso is clearly one of his best; others felt that the title was denied him because it would have looked odd to award the first national Independence Calypso King crown to someone who was not born in Trinidad and Tobago. However, the 'gate keepers' at the radio stations, the librarians, programme managers and those responsible for the music aired, compensated by playing "Model Nation", and their continued favouring of this song has helped to keep alive both song and concept.

While on this point, it is in order to note that there was disagreement over the judging; in other words, this was a real calypso competition. The *Trinidad Guardian* reported that hundreds in the auditorium at City Hall cheered, while the thousands gathered in nearby Woodford Square roared their approval,[36] but all were not convinced if one accepts the bona fides of the letters to the editor. Janet Reid, for example, wanted a Bomber-Pretender-Dougla finish although she did not quarrel with Brynner's victory. Still, she was able to salvage from the whole exercise the valuable lesson that "Calypsonians have proven well their ability to follow the country's watchwords, discipline in accepting the decision gracefully, production as they are undaunted by setbacks and will continue to compose more calypsoes, and tolerance to bear any indignities that they might have experienced through the results of the Competition."[37]

Returning to the sentiments expressed in the calypso, it is interesting to note that while Sparrow blandly affirms racial harmony, others with truer memory of the songs they performed earlier that year, appealed for an end to racialism. Nap Hepburn's plea is especially significant. In January he had castigated Capildeo as a "mad scientist"; in August, in a forgiving, forgetting mood induced by the onset of independence he commends the erstwhile "mad scientist" to a position if not co-equal to Williams at least worthy of mention in the same breath. These new sentiments form part of Nap's appeal for sense in the national service:

Let us sing, let us dance, let's all be merry
Let's forget who is PNM, let's forget who is DLP
Let's live in harmony
In racial solidarity
This is your place
Let's forget this nonsense 'bout race
("Discipline, Tolerance and Production")

Brynner, the eventual winner, advanced a radical formula for eradicating the problem of race:

Conscientiously and constitutionally
Forget all this lousy rumour 'bout racial equality
If you are an East Indian
And you want to be an African
Just shave your head clean like me
And then they can't prove your nationality

A simplistic and nonsensical statement, bizarre in the context of the Indo-Trinidadian's perception of himself vis-à-vis the Afro-Trinidadian, Brynner's unrealistic recommendation would remain unchallenged in public until 1971.[38]

It seems clear from the determined avowals of racial unity and the urgent appeals for racial solidarity that the issue of race relations was perceived as the greatest obstacle to national unity. Given the national paranoia on this topic, the secretiveness of private discussions as opposed to the insincerity of public statements, one must compliment the calypsonian for at least trying to establish an ideal to which the nation should strive.

The standard and style for the patriotic songs which abounded in the competition had been established decades before[39] and have been copied faithfully ever since. The major innovation in 1962 was the adulation of the nationalist leadership past and present. Captain A. A. Cipriani, Tubal Uriah 'Buzz' Butler, Eric Williams and Rudranath Capildeo were singled out but the calypsonian 'forgot' his former mentor and friend, Albert Gomes, who had defended the calypso and other indigenous forms, in print and in parliament, and who was an early critic of the calypso long before its literary worth was acknowledged. Gomes' turncoat defection while he was de facto chief minister (1950–56) and his later hostility to his former friend Williams, may have turned the calypsonian against him. Indeed, the calypsonian had picked up Williams' contempt (compare Sparrow's jibe "Big Belly" in "William the Conqueror" and "No, Doctor, No"), and no honour in song was forthcoming for this nationalist leader, who still remains a forgotten man.

Even more unforgivable is the omission of tribute to Raymond Quevedo aka Atilla the Hun. Articulate, fearless and committed, Atilla is the only person in the history of Trinidad and Tobago to feature in the roles of calypsonian, tent manager, calypso historian and professional politician. His numerous calypsoes against the colonial system, his defiance of the colonial authorities, his struggles in parliament to have the hated Theatre and Dance Halls Ordinance repealed[40] certainly qualify him for honourable mention at the very least, and this moreso if calypsonians are compiling the list. Yet he died in 1962, a forgotten man. This unkind obscurity may have been a consequence of his association with Gomes in political opposition to Williams. Curiously, *Williams* remembered him in death, and honoured his impoverished widow and ten children with a monthly pension, establishing a singular precedent.[41]

The leadership factor prominent in August 1962 recurs intermittently in election victory songs but it is noticeably absent in high profile nationalistic calypsoes such as Sniper's "Portrait of Trinidad" (1965) and Baker's "God Bless Our Nation" (1967).

The tremendous interest in the competition evidenced by the large number of entrants at the preliminary stage (180, a number well in excess of the number of practising tent calypsonians)[42] and the enthusiasm of the large crowd in the auditorium and in Woodford Square, remain a wonderful achievement in the history of the political calypso, the unique concurrence of politician, calypsonian and people. And yet, curiously, the competition was supplanted by the PNM Buy Local Calypso King Competition, a listless ineffectual affair which bored itself to death by 1977. One wonders why the original competition lapsed: did the calypsonian exhaust himself in 1962, or did society's Moor, duty done, depart the scene? Did he instinctively distrust the colour of the nationalism preached by his politician allies, or did they instinctively fear his unpredictability? Later events would demonstrate that the calypsonian had developed his own sense of independence, and that his suspicions of the politician were well founded.

The Model Nation
1963–1965

Independence Day celebrations over, the calypsonian returned to his traditional themes, and it is perhaps indicative of his loyalty to the PNM regime that he did not scrutinise the performance of a government which was showing unmistakable signs of decay and decadence after six years in office.[1] Certainly the capacity for mature political satire was there, as is evident in Sparrow's "Mr Robinson and Lockjoint" (1964), a song which satirises the social divisions of the society apropos of the setting up of an islandwide sewerage scheme[2] but the fashion of the day, however, as Sparrow himself would affirm years later, ironically on the eve of the February Revolution, was to refrain from criticism: "*Picong* is fine and most people like *picong* on the government. But there is very little to laugh at in this government."[3]

In 1963 the absence of *picong* and criticism can be construed as calypsonian agreement with the position articulated by Sparrow.

Safe in this belief, the calypsonian transferred his attention to the dramatic explosions in the former Belgian Congo, to the volatile Cuban missile crisis and to strife torn British Guiana. These three were nearer home than it seems: Africa has always retained a romantic attachment for the Afro-Trinidadian; Cuba is a Caribbean sister and the United States, our Big Brother, is the metropole on which most West Indians fashion their future; and British Guiana's ethnic pluralism mirrors Trinidad's; further, British Guiana was a favourite stomping ground for Sparrow and others and was one of the first places outside of Trinidad to produce genuine calypsonians.

But danger stalked the streets of the city and the urban villages of the east-west corridor as gangs of youths staked out their turf and their patronised preserves with an amorality born of survivalism and crystallised in the Applejackers' street caption: "No Law, No God".[4] Weapons used in these internecine wars included the traditional bottle and stone, cutlasses, iron bolts and razors, to which arsenals were added an assortment of handguns, some bought, sometimes from the police, others stolen and still others crudely manufactured, and the fearsome, because unpredictable, home-made Molotov cocktail. The more spectacular demonstrations of the violent restiveness of these youths were treated in the calypso as isolated incidents until, paradoxically, brought into sharp focus by a calypso which sought to minimise the seriousness of such unrest and to silence those who made much of the violence.

"Portrait of Trinidad", the superlatively popular Calypso King song of 1965, and the nation's anthem in calypso, sounds at first like one of the independence calypsoes:

Trinidad is my land
And of it I am proud and glad
But Ah cyar understand
Why some people does talk it bad
All ah dem whey running dey mout'
Doh know wha' dey talking 'bout
They will paint here black every day
And the right things they will never say

Chorus
Like our sportsmen being rated among the best
Our scholars have sat and passed every test
And they rank right along the best
And then our Pitch Lake is the greatest one of its kind
Our sugar and oil is really refined
So you see, friends, this is a real King Solomon's Mines

(ii) They does talk some nonsense
Meh ent know what they doing it for
'Bout so much violence
Man, you would swear that we fighting war
We have we delinquents to face
But just like any other place
Look the things they does say 'bout here
Is really too much for me to bear

Chorus
Because my people are daily making progress
Without any form of stupidness
And in this way we must gain success
For when we moving, we all move as one body
No bickering between you and me
And our policy stands for racial equality

(iii) Now when a stranger
Spending a little time in this lovely isle
Every day you see him, he always have a hearty smile
And when his time is up to depart
He would say with pride in heart,
'll be back, you could bet yuh life,
And if Ah doh come back, Ah go send mih wife'

Chorus
Now leh me tell you, he really want her to come
To drink a rum and have plenty fun
In this great island in the sun
For Trinidadians, as foreigners do recall
It doesn't matter whether big or small
Or if you rich or poor, friends, we cater for one and all

(iv) So all ah them who talking
They either drunk or they staring mad
Or maybe they forgetting
Mr. Universe belong to Trinidad
We have men with talent and skill
With high hopes of improving still
And if you think all this is a lie
The Mighty Sniper go show you why

Chorus
Now our steelband is the best talent in the world
By calypsoes our stories are told
With its rhythm to touch your soul
So Trinidad, this lovely Land of my birth
Small but overwhelming in worth
And as you know, Carnival is the greatest frolic on earth

Close listening reveals that, apart from stanza three which idealises Tobago as an Eden for a modern day Adam vacationing in the island without his Eve, the calypso is overly concerned with glossing over the extent and seriousness of the recurrent violence.

Thus directed, one returns to the numerous calypsoes on youth violence to note that the calypsonians generally considered this phenomenon to be a juvenile aberration to be eliminated by superior adult or state violence. One wonders how far this attitude derives from Sparrow's *badjohn* calypsoes ("The Gunslingers" 1959; "Ten to One Is Murder" 1960; "Don't Touch Me" 1961; "The Renegades" 1961; "Hangman's Cemetery" 1962; "Royal Jail" 1962; "The Rebel" 1966) which presented, in terms of musical energy and innovation, that embattled singer's own struggle to break free of a life of the streets whose denizens sought to return him to their level. The autobiographical element is well established in "Hangman's Cemetery" in which the general narrative sentiment corresponds to statements made by Sparrow to the press with respect to alleged verbal harassment meted out to him and his companion of the hour by idlers frequenting the corner of Bourne's Road, St James.[5] Whatever the truth, calypsonians from the gentlemanly Cristo to Blakie, The Warlord, all endorsed a Sparrow-type response to the issue of the *badjohn* in their Calypsoes of the day. Kitchener, returning home after 17 years in exile, was shocked at the state of the nation ("A Bad Impression" 1964) but banking on the success of his melodies with the steelband which was becoming the premier accompaniment for the carnival parade, he busied himself with the threat to the peaceful enjoyment of the festival. Accordingly, the protagonist of "The Road" (1963) presents himself as a law-abiding citizen whose carnival pleasure is threatened by the irresponsibility of the steelbandsmen who happened, by the logic of the times, to be prominent among the warring youths. Kitchener would focus on this aspect of the violence for a long time just as Sparrow would capitalise on his familiarity with the city *badjohns* as a source of inspiration until he composed "Badjohn" (1974), an epitaph for a dead breed.

Remarkably, all these calypsoes do not put the violence into historical perspective even from the point of view of localising it in a tradition of the Calypso on this theme. Except for Cristo's "Town Gone Wrong" (1960), whose recommendation of the "cat o' twelve" alludes to Caruso's "Run the Gunslingers" (1959), and beyond to calypsoes sung in support of The Flogging Bill (the cat o' nine),[6] the calypsonians surprisingly do not observe that the extent, duration and viciousness of the current phase of violence symptomised deep disorder in the social system and was far from being a mere celebration of gangster movies and others in the mould of the Hollywood-inspired 'tough guy' image.

But the theme of violence led the calypsonian into unexpected directions, into unexpected perceptions. It is the failure to defuse this tension that earns Williams his first stinging rebuke in calypso in the independence period, and this from Blakie, a self-confessed protégé.[7] Blakie's "Doctor Ent Dey" (1965) concocts the fiction that "Blakie" and "Williams" – to indicate the vital difference between the two persons and the two personae in the song – had formulated a plan to deal with the hooligans but that when the time was right to implement same, "Williams" could not be found. "Blakie" protests this irresponsibility by respectfully submitting a warning/threat:

Doctor please take this warning
Am giving you, and you better do something
Ah tired put this thing in your brain

But all Ah try is the bloody same
Me and you sit down and draft a plan
How easy we go trap these hooligans
But since the riot start back in the place
From that day I can't see the Doctor face

Chorus
Every day Ah ring where he living
The Doctor ent dey
Ah ring Governor House in the evening
The Doctor ent dey
Then Ah ring the White House
His secretary come to explain,
'I'm sorry, Blakie, the Doctor left this morning by plane.'

Stanza two mixes defiance, deference and the insouciance of the famous calypso attitude to social superiors:

Doctor, Ah find you getting on funny
Ah talking mih mind, believe the Lord Blakie
Ah believe is 'fraid you 'fraid
Of San Juan All Stars and Renegades
But remember, you is the leader
All you got to do is to pass an order
Before you see about your territory
You chartering plane and flying from country to country

Blakie here perceives Williams as a kind of street *badjohn*. It does seem incongruous that The Warlord, whose fistic prowess elevated him to the signal honour of flag bearer for the dreaded San Juan All Stars, should seek to involve a scholarly politician in sorting out violence among the unemployed urban underclass, but it has been pointed out that Williams used steelbandsmen as mercenaries in his political wars and further that his favouring some over others led to an escalation of the infighting.[8]

Stanza four is a criticism of Williams' efforts to establish himself as an international statesman:

Dr Williams, take Lord Blakie advice
If you want Trinidad to be really nice
To stifle my conscience that I can't do
Trinidad and Tobago depend on you
Ah doh want when Ah watch the daily paper
You talking and smiling with Nkrumah

Nk smiling, why? he have cause
He seeing 'bout he Country, you see 'bout yours

Rohlehr draws attention to the unusual places where "Blakie" sought his errant leader: he had called the Royal Gaol and the duty officer answered that "Williams" had not reached there yet; he also called the Mad House. This, opines Rohlehr, anticipated widely held rumours of the 1970s that Williams was corrupt and that he was mad.[9]

THE CALYPSO AND THE PROTECTIVE SERVICES

Inability or reluctance to arrest a deteriorating social situation was criminal negligence; even more culpable was the shielding of the guilty from their just deserts. This was the calypsonian judgement on decisions involving the state organisations of uniformed and armed youths and adults whose duty it was to protect and serve but within whose ranks sinister signs of institutionalised violence had begun to surface.

Tiger's "Don't Touch Them" (1964) looks quizzically at the protectionist attitude adopted by the minister of home affairs towards undisciplined soldiers who, on the evening of 10 May 1963, invaded Carenage, a sleepy fishing village close to their Teteron Bay headquarters, and assaulted villagers in retaliation for the knifing of two soldiers at a local bar.[10] The newly commissioned regiment had been admired partly because it was seen as a counterweight to an increasingly corrupt and arrogant police force, but the intemperate actions of the vengeance minded soldiers stained the colours and strained public credibility. Army officials, acting immediately, investigated the matter and arrested those implicated, but Dr Patrick Solomon, the Minister of Home Affairs, imperiously overturned this decision pending the results of a civilian commission of inquiry constituted to appraise the efficiency of the army and to evaluate its public relations with specific reference to the disturbances of 10 May.[11] "Don't Touch Them" criticises what Tiger saw as Solomon's pampering of the delinquent soldiers.

Co-temporaneously, attention focused on the growing caesarism of the other arm of the praetorian guard, the police force as it was then named. Calypso antagonism to the police can be traced to the nineteenth century when the police had tried on several occasions to impose English ideals of law, order and decency on the *demi-monde*.[12] The rivalry had been easy to externalise because the largely Barbados-born constabulary favoured their compadres, Barbados-born toughs like the band 'Newgate' in their skirmishes with the patois-speaking bands.[13] By the 1930s competition for women introduced a new element and the calypsonian regarded the policeman as a competitor with the unfair advantages of salary, influence and mobility, unbeatable assets in the survivalist context of food acquisition.[14] Thus was added a personal twist to an entrenched rivalry made all the more bitter by the fact that the police were supervising the calypso tents on the instructions of the expatriate inspector general, a functionary to whom were entrusted almost dictatorial powers in the anticalypso drive. Calypsonians and policemen originate in the same underclass, but the latter, like Corporal Santapee of the calypso opera *Sing De Chorus*, repudiated their origins and persecuted the calypsonians and their *jamette* paramours *sans humanité*.[15]

Nineteen fifty-six promised a new and amicable phase in relations but decades-old jealousy and centuries-old practice are not easily exorcised. The streetwise Sparrow, who, early in his career had fled the forbidden 'Gaza Strip' leaving fellow Grade B hustlers in police custody,[16] simultaneously commiserated with and ridiculed policemen on their misfortune in securing a pay increase recommended by Ulric Lee who had been appointed by cabinet to reorganise the public service:

Them police mad, mad, mad
Ah say they wild here in Trinidad (repeat)
The Government raise on they salary
Still they unhappy
With this raise people know they get
They doh want to pay they debts

Chorus
They use to get a shilling here, collect a shilling there
But all of that stop
If they only say they broke, people say they making joke
They pay gone up
Now the whole Force in misery
No more loans and credit, you see
I hear they planning to lock up Lee
For raising they salary
Anytime they lock up Lee
Is for raising they salary
("Police Get More Pay" 1959)

The calypso charges that policemen practised larceny from the police canteen, and that they customarily abused their uniform to extort 'freeness' at private gatherings, in taxis and the like. Lee's initiative summarily ends their nefarious habits by catapulting them into the ranks of the salaried classes who face the market on its own terms.

Nineteen fifty-six did not reform the force and by 1964 the word 'police' was synonymous with graft protection rackets, arrogance and brutality. Young Killer uses the format of the police interrogation to explain the aversion of the public to the force:

Well, mih wife she want a divorce
If Ah join up the Police Force
She say they getting on bad
And she want the National Guard
Nowadays is big competition
Between Police Force and civilian
Because anything these hooligans do
The police doing them too

Chorus
And don't doubt
Who you think kill the man up Savannah
Is a policeman
Who you think they hold in Manzanilla
Is a policeman
Who stab he wife Diego Martin
Is a policeman
Who accuse poor Cadogan and get away smiling
Is a policeman
("Is a Policeman" 1964)

" . . . poor Cadogan" is Kenneth Cadogan who had been found dead on his bed at the infirmary of the Royal Gaol on Christmas Eve 1962, one day after being transferred there from the St Joseph Police Station where he had been detained following his arrest three days before on a charge of larceny. An inquest into his death was held early in 1963 and several inmates of the cells at St Joseph testified to severe beatings Cadogan had suffered at the hands of Corporal Fitzroy Dasent and others. The coroner, admitting this evidence and the specialist testimony of a state pathologist, ordered the arrest and trial of Dasent for murder. This was reduced to manslaughter by a city court, and even the lesser charge was thrown out after only an hour of legal wrangling. A *Guardian* photographer, unmolested as in past attempts to photograph the accused, managed a shot of a smiling Dasent leaving the courthouse a free man.[17]

"Is a Policeman" explains that Dasent's brutality was merely one of many instances of police wrongdoing, and further, it accuses policemen of judicial murder which was then blamed on hooligans. By way of comparison, Killer referred to the redoubtable Corporal Charlie King, the classic rogue who had met his death in 1937 while intervening spontaneously in the arrest of labour leader T.U. "Buzz" Butler, at Fyzabad at the height of the labour tensions. King, then in mufti, was not a member of the accredited arresting party, but seeing that Butler was about to escape he laid hands on him to the fury of the crowd which turned on the despised lawman and set him ablaze.[18] This allusion argues strongly for a continuity of calypso tradition which one encounters at every turn except, surprisingly, in the calypso considerations of youth violence of the late 1950s and early 1960s.

Killer's calypso was well received and he had an easy passage to the finals of the national competition but, scared by rumours that bets were being made on his surviving until carnival Sunday, he sought assurances from the minister of home affairs.[19] Killer's fear was a real one as Warrior would find out in 1976 when he sang "No, No, Tony May", a calypso similar in intent to "Is a Policeman". At the time of singing, Warrior was a licensed taxi driver plying the north-south route, and to his continuing annoyance a special reserve policeman persisted in molesting him while he was soliciting his passengers. Warrior, a man of fiery temper, ended the provocation by driving his vehicle over the officer's foot. Duly charged, he was acquitted in the High Court, but for several years he had to exercise more than due care and attention and to scrupulously adhere to the Highway Code.[20]

Cypher's "No Police Ent See" (1965) invokes reality of a different order. Developing a seemingly absurd situation, this calypso masks bitter satire at the inefficiency and vindictiveness of the force behind a distancing and modifying humour which prevented Cypher from having to undergo Warrior's tribulations. Cypher's "circle of absurdity"[21] touches reality in its conception of a well-known scenario:

Big cricket match up in the East
Swonton playing against Police
Big, big cricket match up in the East
Swonton playing against Police
A Swonton man hit a lovely four
I clap because I know that is the law
Who tell me to do that
I fell inside of the police trap

Chorus
Mariboutes pelt bottle all over Arima
No police ent see
Superintendent sell gun for two hundred in Caroni
No police ent see
A taxi leave a head in a box quite up Dabadie
No police ent see
But a deaf man say he hear Cypher cuss
Police arresting me

One unpleasant feature of sport in Trinidad and Tobago is that the Police Sports Club, like many others, resents bitterly the embarrassment of defeat, and when engaged in contact sports like soccer, the lawmen tend to be excessive in their tackles, an irregularity often overlooked by civilian match officials. Spectators, cheering on the opposing teams, think it wise to set a judicious distance between themselves and the policemen fans.[22] The popularity of "No Police Ent See" derived as much from the nature of its humour as from its target who could be held up to public ridicule with impunity.

In Cypher's calypso fiction the courthouse was converted from a hall of justice into a den of gamblers staking bets on who would lie the more, Cypher or the police. Then to crown it off, the protagonist of the calypso embarrassed the arresting officer on the witness stand:

> They call upon me exactly nine thirty
> Court say I ent guilty
> This time I have the policeman in trouble
> If you see he mouth it long like a shovel
> I put he on the box, I tie him like twine
> I said why you ent see the Dial ent carrying the right time
> I tie him up just like wax
> They only charge me because I don't pay income tax

THE SOLOMON AFFAIR

Ironically, by 1965 Cypher's imagined circle of absurdity had become a real circle of horror for Solomon, the political master of the police force. Public outrage at the revelations in the Cadogan case had prompted a Commonwealth Commission of Inquiry into the conditions and operations of the police force. Unexpectedly, while testifying before the commission in September 1964, the Secretary of the Police Association, Corporal Oscar Frederick, accused Solomon of removing his reputed stepson, Michael Beausoleuil, from lawful custody on the morning of 28 January, that is to say, several months *before* Cadogan's death.[23] This sparked off national debate: it was claimed that the affair had been public knowledge in January 1962, that is, before independence; that the PNM cabinet was involved in the cover-up and that the Opposition was complicit in its complaisance.[24] Solomon offered to resign and Williams, thankful to be rid of a dangerous rival, accepted this offer with alacrity.[25]

Solomon duly resigned on 14 September [26] and, given the seasonal nature of calypso performances, calypso comment was not expected until January 1965. On 29 September, however, the prodigious composer Sparrow previewed two stanzas of a calypso included on his album due for a mid November release[27] (the first of two albums he would release for 1965). The calypso in question, "Solomon", is the dilemma of the party supporter trapped between allegiance to the party and adherence to the rule of law, and this is reflected musically in the use of the half major/half minor, and thematically in the shifting viewpoint of the commentary.[28]

The calypso departs from the defiance characteristic of Sparrow in celebration or defence of Williams in that the vibrant conviction of those earlier statements is replaced by an unusually defensive opening:

If I had any doubts now they gone completely
I am living in a true democracy
If Sparrow had any doubts now they gone completely
I am living in a true democracy
I am referring to that most regrettable disaster
Through a corporal we lost our acting Prime Minister
He complained to the Commission
And make them kick out poor Solomon

Chorus
Where in the world you could find democracy so
Except in Trinidad and Tobago
If was in America is the corporal that had to go
In the first place a man like he
Couldn't see the Commission of Inquiry
Doh care how he try
They woulda charge him as a spy
And tell the public he lie

Sparrow betrays here his fierce partisanship: he misrepresents the purpose and competence of the commission, thereby making a legitimate and necessary witness appear to be an uninvited and malicious agent provocateur whose testimony made the commission "kick out poor Solomon"; he glosses over Solomon's undeniable guilt and he disregards the dubious ethics of politics which concede resignation for any one caught out in such a situation. By defying the facts which had been splashed across the *Guardian* newspapers for the entire period of the probe and the unexpected political imbroglio, Sparrow presents his own propaganda version of Solomon's enforced retirement ("that most regrettable disaster"). In stanza two, he admits Solomon's guilt but still seeks for him the comforting refuge of an extreme attenuation of the principle that mercy seasons justice in the conflict of interests between upholding one's public duties as minister and one's private responsibilities to one's family:

Oh well, the good things you do you never get credit
But make one mistake, nobody forget it
I agree he was wrong without a doubt
Cancelling the charge, letting the boy out
But the way some of these people criticise him

You would think Solomon shouldn't have human feeling
Just because he in politics
He must leave he step-son like Cadogan in a cell to get kill with licks

Yet Sparrow, caught up as he is in the absurdity of this theatre of the real, does not note that Solomon, while minister with responsibility for the police, had done nothing to protect those who, like Cadogan, found themselves in the clutches of the law. He also forgets that Cadogan died almost a year *after* Solomon had removed Beausoleuil from the cell. Instead he tries to identify a quirk in Solomon's personality that could account for his high-handed action:

Some people say he too bol'-face and outa place
Some ah them vex because they hear he slap the Doctor in he face

DLP supporters had dubbed Solomon "Minister of War" because of his words and actions in the run-up to the general election of 1961,[29] and it is already seen how he reacted in the Carenage affair. Sparrow tries to penetrate the shrouded maze of PNM's internal politics and he speculates about what C.L.R. James had described as "fisticuffs in the Cabinet",[30] the rumoured result of violent disagreement over Williams' championing of his protégé A.N.R. Robinson. But dependence on rumour is not enough consolation for one who is genuinely confused, and although Sparrow temporarily accepts the shelter of a principle endorsed editorially in the *Nation* that the whole affair offered irrefutable proof of the PNM's commitment to democracy and to the rule of law,[31] he still needs to resolve his doubt on a personal plane. Regretfully, he concedes that Solomon had committed political suicide:

It is true our Nation needs strong men like Solomon
But no-one is allowed to take the law in they hand
Drop the charge if you see fit
But it ent what you do, is how you do it
Solomon acted like a lord
Trying to spare the rod
And now he die by the sword

The calypso thus ends by affirming a biblical injunction, but this comes after the singer endorses a Machiavellian principle. From this, one concludes that Sparrow himself had not resolved his own lingering doubts about the nature and exercise of power in a free state.

Then, after several weeks of uncertainty about Solomon's future, Williams announced to a cheering Arima crowd that Solomon owed allegiance only to the PNM and that only the PNM could determine his fate.[32] True to this word, several nights later he informed an equally jubilant Bourne's Road gathering that he was reinstating Solomon in cabinet as Minister of External Affairs, and "who don't like it, get to hell outa here!"[33]

This display of naked power inspired the most powerful and, paradoxically, the most misunderstood calypso of the period, Sparrow's "Get to Hell Out" (1965). Echoes of this calypso remain embedded in the collective folk consciousness as the distillation of authoritarianism, and as a complex of images appropriated in later gems such as Chalkdust's "Reply to the Ministry" (1969); Valentino's "Barking Dogs" (1973); Maestro's "Dread Man" (1977); Crusoe's "I Eric Eustace Williams" (1982); Watchman's "Attack with Full Force" (1991) and David Rudder's "Hoosay" (1991). Yet, the calypso has features which demand closer attention.

First, it was accepted on face value as Sparrow's ultimate endorsement of his hero, and given the belligerent attitude of the *kalinda* batonniers and the bravado of the Midnight Robber masquerader which both Sparrow and Williams shared in addition to their mutual admiration and identification, it seemed safe to conclude that Sparrow had emerged from the shadow of the valley of doubt and was celebrating the triumph of the warrior politician. But it can also be demonstrated that this calypso mocks the towering arrogance of the man who put no limits to his power within the country and who seemed to rule party, parliament and people by unquestionable, unquestioned fiat even though he seemed in principle to accept the legal formalism of parliamentary democracy. This is clear in the opening lines:

> I am going to bring back Solomon
> Who doh like it complain to the Commission
> None of them going to tell me how to run my Country
> I defy any one of you to dictate to me
> I am no dictator
> But when I pass an order
> Mr Speaker, this matter must go no further
> I have nothing more to say
> And it must be done my way
> Come on, come on, meeting done for the day
>
> This land is mine
> I am the boss
> What I say goes
> And who vex los'
> And if I say that Solomon will be Minister of External Affairs
> And you ent like it
> Get to hell outa here

Sparrow had claimed that Solomon's resignation had proved that Williams was no dictator ("Solomon") but the turn of events seemed to have prompted a rethink because the above-cited demonstrated that dictatorship had developed organically within the framework of a constitutional democracy: the Williams persona regards the state as his personal fief which he rules with the authority of a mediaeval suzerain; he recognises constitutional checks and balances as legalistic formulae not as effective limits.

"Williams", as the protagonist is made out to be – he is never named – is more *badjohn* than scholar/politician; he resembles the figure suggested in Blakie's "Doctor Ent Dey", the captain of the steelband who prided himself on his superior linguistic and martial abilities. This in the calypso is borne out in his mastery of the language of the streets:

> Who the hell is you to jump and quarrel
> PNM is mine lock, stock and barrel
> Who give you the privilege to object
> Pay yuh taxes, shut up and have respect
> I am a tower of strength, yes
> I am powerful but modest – unless
> I'm forced to be blunt and ruthless
> So shut up and don't squawk
> This ent no skylark
> When I talk no damn dog bark
>
> My word is law
> So watch yuh case
> If yuh slip yuh slide
> This is my place
> And if I say that Solomon will be Minister of External Affairs
> And you ent like it
> Get to hell outa here

The attitude "Williams" adopts is unequivocal, as unequivocal as the man in whose image and likeness he was created. Sparrow, for once leaving his name out of a calypso on Williams, seems to have been shocked by the arrogance of his erstwhile idol. One would suggest from a close reading of "Solomon" that Sparrow would have settled for a picaresque bending of the rules, not for a Machiavellian disdain of restraint. Henceforth, Sparrow would not sing in support of Williams and the PNM; in point of fact his open criticism dates from 1966 ("Honesty"). He does not mention Williams by name until 1979 ("Wanted Dead or Alive"). Apparently the 'Solomon affair' was too traumatic an unmasking.

SWEET TRINIDAD

Two other songs of 1965, the year of the crossroads as far as the political Calypso is concerned, attest to class and race tensions and so give the lie to the Sniper portrait. Tiger's "Workers' Appeal" registers the anguish of the unemployed by recycling a 1936 Tiger calypso of the same name. In 1936, Tiger had sung:

Anywhere you go you must meet people sad
They search for employment; none can be had
Anywhere you go you must meet people sad
They search for employment; none can be had
They start to drop down dead in the street
Nothing to eat and nowhere to sleep
All kind-hearted employers I appeal to you
Give us some work to do

This remains unchanged as the opening stanza of the 1965 calypso. Other ideas of the 1936 composition have been reworked or rephrased. In 1936 the workers voice their desires in these words:

We are not asking for equality
To rank with the rich in society
To visit their homes in their motor-cars
Or go to their clubs and smoke their cigars
We are asking for a living wage
To exist now and provide for old age

The unemployed of 1965 have the same thoughts expressed in similar words:

We are not asking to smoke your cigars
Or go to your clubs in your motor-cars
All we are asking for is for a living wage
That we can eat something now and save for old age

The one major difference between the two calypsoes is the new protest against automation which creates the distress and disorder consequent upon the inevitable reduction of the labour force:

Every year children are leaving school
Frustrated souls, no work to do
You speaking of economy
Replacing mankind with machinery

The machine don't have no family to mind
He belly don't gripe him at breakfast time

Tiger does not fault the government although he does note that the unemployment crisis affected the graduates of Williams' schools who cannot now be accommodated into his grand design for economic development. Tiger seems to accept social inequality philosophically as a sociological truth but he does not consider that the failure of the modified Lewis strategy[34] meant the failure of the state as a facilitator of employment.

One inescapable conclusion to be drawn from the recycling of the plea of the 1930s is that the only real change in the employment situation is that it had worsened. In five short years it would reach the proportions to nearly unseat the regime.

While "Workers' Appeal" highlights the plight of the underclass, Cristo's "Sweet Trinidad" reveals that the racial tensions which had been submerged under the effusions of independence were fast surfacing. This calypso differs from its many namesakes in that its hauntingly beautiful melody and lament-like chorus suggest not celebration of the real and imagined glories of which the nation usually boasts, but grief for the loss of innocence. It tells a gloomy tale of the corruption of an ideal which had endured and survived Spanish indifference, French occupation and English hauteur only to be perverted by Trinidadian politics. The final stanza articulates an unease felt by many at the latent racial hostility between the numerically dominant groups and the suspicion that independence may not have brought a release from this tension:

In the hands of our Premier
We laid down our future
With good co-operation
We'll succeed as a Nation
But yuh don't know who is yuh brother
You can't tell who is yuh friend
This racialism kind of fever
When will it end
And now we live in torment
And now we live in hate
Though we are independent
I think it come too late
Sweet, sweet Trinidad
Sweet, sweet Trinidad

One needs to evaluate the phenomenal success of "Portrait of Trinidad" against the background of "Sweet Trinidad", "Workers' Appeal", "Get to Hell Out", "Solomon",

"No Police Ent See", "Is a Policeman", "Don't Touch Them", "Doctor Ent Dey" and the numerous calypsoes dealing with urban youth violence. "Portrait of Trinidad" may have earned its acclaim partly because it endorsed a myth that people needed to hold on to in a period of stress, partly because it articulated what many believed; certainly, as Rohlehr observes, it has an air of sincerity.[35]

So effective was this calypso and so powerful the euphoria that greeted it that it won Sniper an automatic Calypso King title in the absence of Sparrow who had again declined to enter the competition, this time out of pique at his third place finish in 1964. One can only fantasise at a Dimanche Gras performance of "Get to Hell Out" if Sparrow, then at the height of his awesome power, had elected to perform it at the competition.

By that cruel fate which sometimes dogs impecunious artistes operating in a commercial context, "Portrait" enjoyed far greater prosperity than its composer, Penman, and its first composer Sniper. Penman commutes between occasional tent-singing and permanent vagrancy, while Sniper, was convicted in 1963 on a minor charge of fraud and was made to serve part of his sentence in 1965, Calypso King status notwithstanding.[36] Sniper did reappear to sing an inspirational "A Way to Success" (1968) but would eventually die in obscurity.

"Portrait of Trinidad" is still very much alive, having survived the meticulous debunking of its cherished premises (Stalin's "New Portrait of Trinidad" 1972). It was rerecorded by Francine and by Baron, and has remained a comfort to a people who retain a yearning for romance. In the wake of the coup bid of 27 July 1990, it was made to serve as a source of inspiration and hope to a bewildered frightened public.

God Bless Our Nation
1966–1970

A period of exciting developments and a test case of differing response to stimuli, of broadening of perspective and developing of style, 1966–70 provides interesting studies in contrast as the calypso reflected widely divergent popular opinions with respect to the state of the nation. Some singers resolutely defended the achievement and myth of the model nation; others described the unpleasant realities of a neocolonial state hamstrung by a satellite economy and menaced by the Cerberus of corruption and race and class discrimination; still others found it possible to do both. Two collections of portraits of Trinidad were therefore on display: the first of these belonged to the genre of nationalism of the independence spirit, while the other, diametrically opposed, exposed the reverse side, the ugly side with which, as Rohlehr writes,[1] Sniper became acquainted after his 1965 success.

Model portraits, clustered around the Penman/Sniper original, claim first attention. Funny's "Sweet Trinidad" (1966), Blakie's "My Sweet Trinidad" (1967), Baker's "God Bless Our Nation" (1967), Duke's "Little Nation" (1967) and Shorty's "Index of a Nation" (1969) are essentially variations on the same theme.

"God Bless Our Nation", in pride of place, fervently endorses the idea of an island paradise inhabited by a uniquely wonderful and understanding people:

> We like a drop of rain in an ocean
> Like a drop in the sea
> But many many nations
> Still got to learn from we
> How we aspire and we achieve
> It's so hard to believe
> Unity that is so unique
> It's fantastic, yes, so to speak

Chorus
It's fantastic, yes it is, the way how we live as one
In integration our Nation is second to none
Here the Negro, the Indian, the Chinese, their children
We jump together in a band
In this wonderland of Calypso
In this wonderland of Steelband
Where I was born
God bless our Nation

(ii) We, we never invent a bomb
Or on the moon never land a man
Our population is not yet a million
But that is no disgrace
For Trinidadians can set the pace
And prove every colour creed and race
In this world could find an equal place

(iii) All I can say is I am so proud
And I'm going to sing it out clear and loud
I'm proud of my people
Each and every one of you
For contributing to humanity
And constituting we always be
Whenever the story is said
How Trinidadians lived what the world thought was dead

Like Sniper, Baker charms with his air of sincerity, but unlike the "Portrait" Baker's calypso contains no hint of discord or dissonance; even the gentle melody reminds one of the nostalgic guitar airs suggesting the bewitching languor of Tennyson's lotus eater paradise[2] or Tom's sentimental recall of the good ole South.[3]

GENERAL ELECTION 1966

As regards Baker's classic, the absence of reference to the leadership is a surprise omission in the wake of a PNM general election victory. One wonders if the election *bacchanal* with its raucous overtones of racism and its undertones of exploitation does not belong in Baker's serene islands. The traditional carnival is there, functioning, as in other calypsoes, as a social leveller, but this glorious 'raceless', 'classless' free-for-all has been purged of its rowdy elements and is presented as a simple bucolic pleasure.

Duke's "Little Nation" (1967) more than compensates for Baker's omission of the political element. Duke had surged to the forefront of the national calypso stage with his "Memories of 1960" (1961) which highlights all the noteworthy events of that memorable year, singling out 22 April when nationalists led by Williams marched through downtown Port of Spain and around the Queen's Park Savannah before handing a petition to the United States Embassy demanding the return of Chaguaramas.[4] For Duke:

> . . . the day of all days to remember
> Was when we march in the rain with our Premier
> One voice, one cry, one cry, one call
> 'Freedom! Independence for one and all

In 1967, faithful to his political allegiance, he sang "Little Nation" which like Sparrow's "Model Nation" after which it is named – Duke, like many a young calypsonian, seems to have idolised Sparrow – is a paean of praise of country and leadership:

> Ah can't find the words to say
> How happy I am today
> Since this little Nation, we
> Have shown our solidarity
> Return again a Government
> The world acclaims as excellent
> No praise for them could be too great
> Thanks could never compensate
>
> Chorus
> So long, yes, long may they reign
> Over our domain
> Never will we complain
> They said and I do believe
> If we could aspire
> Then together we'll achieve
>
> Not too long ago I read
> Where the *Times* of New York said
> Dr Williams is unsurpassed
> A statesman of the highest class
> Another great in truth and fact
> The world acclaim Dr Rudranath
> And these two men have made it clear
> We don't want Communism here

Interestingly, this calypso endorses Capildeo as though he were a member of the PNM team. Duke anticipates those social scientists who hint at conspiracy between

Williams and Capildeo[5] and he perceives the House of Representatives to be properly controlled by these exponents of what Lloyd Best later referred to as "Doctor politics". This leadership principle is, in Duke's calypso, indistinguishable from the natural gifts of which the nation can boast:

> Trinidad and Tobago
> Is the Land of Calypso
> Our chief products are sugar and oil
> With the Pitch Lake where so many toil
> We practise true democracy
> With a very sound economy
> And a group of men who is efficient
> To lead a proper government

Nothing dramatises the celebratory mood of the calypso of 1967, a mood occasioned by the PNM's 1966 general election victory, as Cypher's superb "Last Elections". One of the most popular election commentaries of all time, this composition revels in the 1966 *bacchanal* which brought welcome relief from the tense 1961 campaign so vividly captured in Nap Hepburn's "Mad Scientist" (1962). "Last Elections" satirises the 1966 hustings which had reverted to the accustomed carnival-style street theatre in which personalism, spontaneity and street rhetoric assume greater importance than platform:

> Last election had so much fun
> I am one who sorry it done
> Last election had so much fun
> Cypher is one who sorry it done
> I love to see men turning beast
> Some of them hand trembling like leaf
> On the roadside they testify
> With they manifesto pack up with lie
>
> 'We go take 'way the oilfield from the Yankee
> And divide them up between all ah we
> Tate and Lyle wouldn't have no claim
> We'll take away the factory, also sugar cane
> We'll take the animal and turn to meat
> Horse hoof and cowheel would be very sweet'
> And after all these things have been said
> They stone down the candidate with rotten egg

Specifically targeted here is the manifesto of the socialist Workers' and Farmers' Party (WFP) although Cypher does not deign to dignify them by name. This party, the brainchild of international Marxist ideologue/activist, C.L.R. James, once mentor to Eric Williams, earned particular opprobrium because it was seen as a communist party. Like so many PNM supporters, Cypher is unmindful that the nationalist party of his choice had to be goaded into even a limited programme of nationalisation, and he therefore reduces to farce a serious proposal for the takeover of the commanding heights of the economy.

In like manner, he demolishes the DLP's visionary plan for education and for public transport as a fantasy proceeding from the fevered brain of "this scientist" (Capildeo), the word 'scientist' itself having long acquired the connotation of madness thanks to Williams, Nap Hepburn ("Mad Scientist"), Cristo ("The Mad Professor") and so on. Capildeo is destroyed even before he opens his mouth. The line "With some assistance from me and you" sets up an audience, which had rejected him at the polls, to laugh derisively at the memory of his campaign promises:

> He say that children will be getting education
> From England by television
> Trains cyar make no money in town
> He plan to build a railway underground
> He will be building houses up in the air
> And helicopters will be taking you up there
> And if you fall down like a mouse
> Doh frighten, you'll be falling right down in yuh house

Twenty years later, Leigh Richardson, commenting scathingly on the chaotic public transport which had been aggravated by the introduction of the two-tiered system of secondary school education, favourably remembered Capildeo's far-sighted proposals and he grew bitter at the memory of the pejorative treatment meted out to him by the 'herd'. Capildeo, he recalled, had become the subject of calypso and partisan abuse.[6] In hinting that the calypsonian was the main player in the demolition of Capildeo, Richardson was being unfair to the singers who had simply latched on to Williams' designation of Capildeo which the *Nation* had gleefully publicised.[7] Richardson's selective recall demonstrates the power of the calypso to publicise images but, negatively, it points to a tendency to perceive the calypsonian as the source of much public mischief. Abuse of public figures has been exaggerated and perpetuated in the Calypso but Williams should take the blame for the derogation of Albert Gomes, Butler and Capildeo.

Returning to "Last Elections", one notes how severe Cypher was on Butler, the radical labour leader and politician of the 1930s who had already been reduced by the colonial system:[8]

It have one they calling Bottle
Well that man is real trouble
From the time Bottle mash the platform
Well is laughter the whole crowd gone
And before Bottle say goodnight
He asking the crowd who wey want to fight
Man, hurry up and don't get mih blue
Hear what my government intend to do

He said,
'I am stepping right back to the days of old
I go cut off all the branches off birth control
This present government will ketch they blasted tail
Ah go release all the prisoners from jail (Mano too)
With free food, free clothes, free house, free land
Free land, free man, free 'oom . . . '

The trial of Mano Benjamin, a farmer of Biche in southeast Trinidad, was a sensational happening. Two sisters, Mano's sexually abused victims, swore in open court to the horrifying measures he took to prevent them from having intercourse with any other man. Trinidad of the 1960s was appalled at Mano's sadistic jealousy. It is extremely unlikely that anyone would have wanted Mano out of prison before his sentence was up and Cypher, by making "Bottle" promise to release this character with his unnatural lusts, is doing a tremendous injustice to Butler who was quite a responsible individual.

The highpoint of "Bottle's" campaign promises are the *reductio ad absurdum* of the Trinidadian's love for 'freeness', and Cypher pausedly presents each implausible pipe dream:

Is free food/ free clothes/ free land
Free land/ free man/free 'oom . . .

A universe of the elements of the good life is compressed in that list and especially in the last item which was interrupted by guffaws of derisive laughter. A better hatchet job on Butler could not have been more effective even if done by Williams himself. He had acknowledged Butler's role in raising nationalist consciousness[9] but the exigencies of his own mythologising forced him to diminish Butler and then subject him to the ultimate indignity of having him arrested as a squatter on Labour Day 1966.[10]

Williams is presented favourably in "Last Elections" although the narrator pretends to be unimpressed by his appeal against voting for rum and whisky. "In Princes Town I support Maharaj," he confesses, "He give me a drink, people say Ah bad." It is unlikely that Cypher, one of these proud Arima people (gens de Arima, they call themselves still), would have cast his vote in Princes Town. One suspects that he only used it as a way to *mamaguy* the veteran politician and parliamentarian Stephen Maharaj, the candidate for the WFP who garnered only 530 votes in Princes Town. On the other hand, the triumphant tone of Cypher's imitation of the "short little fellow" who charmed the electorate with his "tone of voice" indicates where his loyalties lay:

> The other Party they call the *macafouchette*
> Only running like *zandolie* that can't find a hole
> (This line is garbled.)
> On the 7th of November the leader and his Party shall all go to Hell.

"Last Elections" helped Cypher to his only Calypso King title and added considerably to his popularity. His "Rhodesia Crisis" (1966) and "If The Priest Could Play" (1967) had made him a crowd favourite.

The PNM's victory, too, had demonstrated that it was still a crowd favourite and reinforced the feeling that it had emerged unscathed from two commissions of inquiry which should have brought the integrity of its leadership into serious question – perhaps in a court of law. The 1965–66 investigations into the operations of the department responsible for the distribution of licences for gas stations had ruffled PNM sensibilities by pointed suggestions of corruption and complicity with corruption,[11] but the calypso of 1967 generally ignored this development. The whole affair was burlesqued in the pro-PNM OYB's calypso drama "One Man Commission of Pitch Oil Inquiry" and it would be three years before the glamorous Gene Miles, star witness at the second inquiry, would be allowed a hearing on a calypso stage (Kitchener's Revue 1970). Even then it is in the nature of Trinidadian ambivalence towards the calypso that Miles' appearance on a calypso stage should be acknowledged as evidence of her degradation, she being white and high born.

A pronounced tendency in 1967 was to count the blessings of the democracy as practised in Trinidad and Tobago. Most would have agreed with Blakie ("My Sweet Trinidad") that:

> We doh have no revolution, no war
> For this we are proud and glad
> We ent have no colour bar
> In Tobago and Trinidad
> No political disorder
> No dictatorship, no hunger
> You could bet yuh hand
> Strangers would die for this happy land

With a white supremacist group seizing power in Rhodesia to the applause of racist South Africa, and with televised images from the troubled South of the United States searing the imagination, it is no wonder that the calypsonian celebrated his model nation and even thanked Williams for it (Cristo's "Mock Democracy" 1966). Obviously, liberty is not the same as equality and fraternity, but the absence of vicious systems of institutionalised discrimination together with the presence of seemingly unlimited opportunities for revelry – if not licence – lulled some calypsonians into overly optimistic expressions of delight, praise and relief.

Nevertheless, a curious picture emerged from under the surface of the intended canvas. Baker's "God Bless Our Nation", Blakie's "My Sweet Trinidad" and Duke's "Little Nation" depict a tranquil, cosmopolitan and freedom-loving people whose happiness is blessed by God and guaranteed by a commitment to the theory and practice of democracy which has ensured the re-election of capable custodians. Yet Duke's "Little Nation" has pledged blind allegiance to a king who has already arrogated to himself powers far beyond those which should obtain in a free state (compare Sparrow's "Get to Hell Out" 1965).

THE REVERSE SIDE OF THE PORTRAIT

While Baker, Duke and Blakie were endorsing the officially approved tourist bro-chure depictions, others were challenging said illusion. New and different focus was given to the problems of unemployment and youth violence which were now being seen as manifestations of the failure of the PNM to deal with the distribution of wealth in the society.

It seems appropriate that open criticism should derive from the new perspective on the wildcat violence. It is even more appropriate that it should be voiced by a young singer with the fitting sobriquet of Leveller, who sought to reduce the "intellectual government" to a position lower than that of the man in the street because the rulers lacked common sense, the commoner's answer to their intellectualism. "How to Stop Delinquency" (1966) establishes a causal link between the restiveness of the youths, their frustration at their marginality and the failure of the planners at the national level to create employment that would channel their energy into constructive rewarding ventures and so alleviate distress and relax tensions in their world. The calypso opens with an overview of a grim situation:

Home-made guns, bombs, gelignite exploding every night
All over Port of Spain
Magistrates and clergymen, probations and policemen
Asking but all in vain

They worse when they come from jail, other deterrents fail
Religion is joke
Make no mistake, man, I have the best plan
Give Tom, Dick and Harry work

His plan, detailed in the chorus, is eminently simple although its practicality is suspect:

Government should sanction birth control
For ten years at least
Just to save the young generation
Some start to turn beast
And employers who say they believe in Trinidad
Make they contribution
Outlaw retrenchment, create more employment
And postpone automation

In contrast to this action plan, the regime can offer only the bread-and-circuses of cosmetic action programmes which the calypso dismisses as "dilly-dallying".

Leveller's tone held the contempt bred of disappointment at the dismal performance of a government of which so much had been expected. Other singers, in an effort to encourage working government in the interests of the commonalty, which both calypsonians and politicians claim to represent, offer advice in varying degrees of friendliness.

Prowler's "Build More Trade Schools" (1969) advocated the expansion of technical-vocational education which already existed in limited form at centres throughout Trinidad and Tobago. Williams' education policy had created additional secondary school places but in the long run was contributing to greater systemic frustration by its failure to guarantee employment for the school leavers who found themselves victims of a system in which patronage was still perceived to matter more than certification[12] and in which, therefore, the unpatronised unqualified stood no chance. "Build More Trade Schools" advised a rethink of the curriculum to ensure a chance for those who could not handle the pressure of major competitive examinations and who had no avenue of employment:

A boy might go to school and pass his GCE
But not everybody would have brain like he
A next one might have three more years to wait
Before he could accomplish a good certificate
So those whose mental capacity is limited
I think they should not be restricted

They try but they couldn't make the grade
Take them from school and send them to learn a trade

Prowler's recommendation, aimed at the creation of an employable or self-employing class of artisans, is a practical step towards resolving an employment crisis which other calypsonians have understood but could not prescribe for.

Sparrow's "Honesty" (1966), however, proposes a novel, though characteristically calypso, solution:

Rich people who doh invest they money
Is crippling the Nation's economy
They can assist things like employment
By simply making a small investment
So whenever a poor man break open a rich man shop
The Government should lock a rich man up
Magistrates always penalising we
But these blasted misers create dishonesty

This calypso, the first of several Sparrow broadsides against a class to which he belongs by virtue of income, strips the mask of virtuous seeming from the self-righteous rich and exposes their modus operandi as a negative agenda for the poor in their quest for happiness and respectability:

. . . if a poor man want to find happiness
He got to learn to be dishonest
Lie like hell, do some tiefing too
And when you get rich nobody honest like you

But Sparrow is as much concerned with the dishonesty of politicians. Taking the lead in attack, as he had once taken the lead in defence, Sparrow satirises and condemns the burgeoning avarice of the once-poor officials who benefited from their appointed positions to capitalise on opportunities before unkind polls return them to obscurity and poverty:

It's good to be honest, I wouldn't deny
But through dishonesty plenty people get by
To cheat and to lie is very very wrong
But that's the way politicians get along
The amount of lies politicians tell
When they dead all of them going to hell
Before elections they talking honesty
But after elections they practising *ratichifeye*

"Honesty" indicates how much the PNM hierarchy was being perceived as having been assimilated into the enemy upper class. By 1966 the evidence of the degeneration of the original PNM purpose was unmistakable, and the mushrooming corruption was highlighted in the probes into the operations of John O' Halloran's Ministry of Industry and Commerce. Nineteen sixty-six was also the year when Williams, at the behest of business interests, torpedoed a finance bill designed by his protégé and Finance Minister, A.N.R. Robinson.[13] It would be several years before a calypso would accuse Williams of collusion with business élites (Chalkdust's "Two Sides of the Shilling" 1971) and many more before connivance with corruption could be laid at his door (Relator's "Take a Rest" 1980), but by 1966 the Sparrow-PNM romance was over, his public statements notwithstanding.[14]

ENTER THE MIGHTY CHALKDUST

After alienating Sparrow, the government needlessly and unwisely antagonised Chalkdust, a singer whose sympathies, one suspects, lay with Williams. Chalkdust had committed the heresy of challenging Williams' definition of the "brain drain", and although in his second year as a professional calypsonian, he had won more minds over to his thesis than, apparently, had Williams. The beginnings of the Chalkdust-Williams 'feud' were quite simple: Williams had criticised emigrating professionals who were fleeing the after-effects of the 1967 devaluation, the first since independence; Chalkdust demonstrated that it was the failure of the PNM regime to make good its promises to artistes and professional people, to honour them properly, to reward them adequately and to provide meaningful work for them, that was precipitating the exodus. Nightly ovations gave the calypsonian the palm over the politician.

On the face of it, Chalkdust's "Brain Drain" (1968) was far less hostile than Leveller's "How to Stop Delinquency" or Sparrow's "Honesty" but was more devastating in its detailing of specific situations. It concerns itself primarily with the PNM's shabby treatment of the athlete and the artiste:

Just because some teachers go away
To improve their status and their pay
Many people calling this thing 'Brain Drain'
But I say they should be shame
They ent see Horace James and Errol John
Teaching drums to foreign sons
They would never see our best footballers
In the States as professionals

Chorus
Police and soldiers went to Expo
And only one true calypsonian go
And when foreign artistes come
They does get lump sum
And calypsonians must sing for rum
And when steelbandsmen teach outsiders
To tune a pan for kisses and favours
All that is what I call Brain Drain

From there the calypso expands naturally to consider the general neglect of cultural forms. It also requests the introduction of a steelband in every school, a revolutionary step attempted by no government despite Prime Minister Manning's designating the steelpan the national instrument in 1992.

Not stopping with what is called 'culture' in Trinidad, the calypso seeks positions for at least three enemies of the PNM. Ignoring the fact that after the Williams-James rift in 1960, the name "C.L.R. James" was like a red flag before the PNM bull,[15] Chalkdust recommended that James be granted tenure in the Department of English at UWI, and this at a time when Caribbean governments were divesting their countries of progressive intellectuals and academics. Chalkdust also requested ministry positions for DLP politicians in spite of their affiliation and in preference to PNM bench warmers. Rational, lucid and invested with the appeal of a good *kaiso*, "Brain Drain" exposed Williams' rhetoric.

The reproach from a junior primary school teacher was not to be borne. The Ministry of Education and Culture advised Chalkdust that his professional singing was in breach of Public Servants Commission Regulation 1966, subparagraphs a) and b) of regulation 65 which retained the right to have public servants seek prior consent from their ministry employers before engaging in income-earning ventures other than their substantive.[16] While making this public – perhaps to embarrass Chalkdust and to ward off those of like mind within the service – the ministry did not offer reason for this nice application of a dead law, and this to someone who was appearing at a tent sponsored by the ministry itself.

It is necessary to go outside of the calypso world to understand why the minister may have made his heavy-handed response to the singer whose immediate supervisor publicly vouched that his singing did not interfere with the performance of his duties.[17] In the mid 1960s, another junior civil servant, Geddes Granger, the guiding spirit of the Pegasus Movement, had filled a vacuum by honouring deserving individuals involved in cultural activities by presenting them with Pegasus Cultural Awards. One of two feature speakers at the inaugural Queen's Hall ceremony was A.N.R. Robinson, demoted from finance minister to external affairs but still deputy prime minister, and among the recipients was C.L.R. James, whose Marxist ideology (never a secret) made him a convenient demon after he and Williams parted ways before independence. James, when apprised of the honour to be bestowed on him, remarked emotionally: "Gentlemen, I am flabbergasted. I am bewildered. I do not know what to say. Don't you realise what you are exposing yourselves to? Don't you know that I am supposed to be a diabolical creature, feared and yet forgotten by my people?"[18]

Pegasus followed this, the first national awards programme in independent Trinidad and Tobago, with a massive street parade in honour of A.H. McShine and Captain A.A. Cipriani. This activity was conducted with the advice and assistance of regular army officers and volunteers, and the salute was taken by Acting Chief Justice Sir Clement Phillips. As James had predicted, Pegasus made the regime unhappy and Granger and others became targets of police surveillance. However, when Pegasus formulated a grand Project Independence which mobilised entire sectors of the national community on a scale which threatened PNM's motive power, Williams riposted heavily. Project Independence was scheduled to be launched in style at the Public Library in downtown Port of Spain by then President of the Senate J. Hamilton Maurice. PNM hastily announced a mass meeting for neighbouring Woodford Square thus forcing a match-off between Williams and Granger from which the latter bowed out. Government then buried Project Independence in commissions and committees leaving Granger embittered and determined to "bring Williams to his knees".

Clearly, therefore, the same government would find a way to deflect – if not eliminate – the Chalkdust threat. He was technically in the wrong and was graciously allowed to continue singing,[19] but it is clear that were it not for his bold defence plus the fact that his absence from the tent would have been questioned, he would have been a victim of subtle state hostility, as was Tiger in 1959.

Chalkdust's calypso answer to this harassment was a double-barrelled salvo: "The Letter" (1969) and "Reply to the Ministry" (1969) which both exemplify the political *picong* with which he would expose the numerous faults and failings of the PNM party and government.

"The Letter" is addressed to Minister of Home Affairs and Personnel, Gerard Montano, who had delivered a sabre rattling speech at the passing-out parade of enlisted men at Teteron, recruiting their assistance in his war against foreign subversives.[20] Chalkdust, apparently, objected to this attempted deployment of national resources on futile McCarthyite witch hunts. Punctiliously faithful to the protocol with which a junior public servant addresses a senior minister, he respectfully redirects Montano's attention:

Dear Mr Minister of Home Affairs
In good faith, please accept my letter

I see you are protecting our dear Nation
From communists and subversion
So you ban Carmichael from our homeland
I'm not saying you are wrong, please understand
But I feel there are, Mr Minister
More dangerous enemies here

Chorus
Like men who join parties to get power
And give their friends big work after
Employers who force our girls on dates
Or else the young girls must leave their place
And restaurants mark up on walls
"No calypso singing at all"
Mr Minister, these men are our enemies
So give Carmichael a ease
Mr Minister, these men are our enemies.

Among the many other internal enemies whose depredations imperil the nation are vicelords, exploitative landlords, drug dealers, quack doctors, anti-trade union employers, racists, corrupt cops, thieves at the hospitals and do-nothing civil servants. "The Letter" ends on a note of elaborate sarcasm:

Happy New year, Sir, please reply to my letter
Sir, it's a must
'cause in you I trust
I beg to remain
    Respectfully yours
        Chalkdust
            [Author's format]

The irony of this deceptively courteous missive is underscored by the calculated arrogance of "Reply to the Ministry", Chalkdust's response to Education Ministry officials who had embarrassed him in public. At first he is careful to mask his defiance making it seem the words of 'friends' among whom are rebellious calypsonians and outspoken enemies of the regime including and especially Gene Miles. These friends expose corruption in high places and they also name the civil servants allowed by the Ministry of Education and Culture to engage in their remunerated cultural pursuits which are even sponsored by the ministry in said practices:

Chalkie . . . What about Miss Mavis John
Chalkie . . . What about Agitation
Martin Albino the steelband man

They sent him New York to teach pan
Chalkie . . . Mr Cyril St Louis
Chalkie . . . He doesn't dance for charity
And how come nobody ent see

These and like examples of sponsored moonlighting infuriate the calypsonian who is already embittered by the self-righteousness of the ministry which publicly called him to account, and so he strips away the mask and confronts the ministry face to face:

Ministers and all building apartment
And, Chalkie, me and you so can't pay they high rent
Some work part-time in the Regiment
Or collecting money as *Guardian* correspondent
But the boat they miss they should first fix
All the *bobol* in the Civil Service
To tackle me they wrong, if they want to keep me down
Tell them to cut out mih tongue

Chalkie . . . The Director of Culture
Chalkie . . . Painting and he selling he picture
Nobody ain't interfere
Hear wha' Blake tell me
Chalkie . . . Sing like you crazy
Chalkie . . . Sing on anybody
And to hell with the Ministry
So Ah following he

Thus is Williams' gage of defiance flung back at him – no one seriously thought that the ministry would tackle Chalkdust on its own volition. Thus did Chalkdust embark on the odyssey which would be his contribution to calypso.

A concluding statement on the two collections of portraits needs to consider the acclaim won by artistes of either school. Leveller was a popular finalist in 1966 but he promptly vanished thereafter, replaced in the calypso constellation by Baker who poet Eric Roach thought represented the "new voice of youth seeking to possess the land which was denied them."[21] Roach's comments seem more valid if made with reference to Chalkdust who started a genre of political *picong* based ironically on the catalogue of the PNM manifesto but employing sophisticated techniques of satire.

Considerations of the passing mood of the times are necessary towards explaining the success of these different singers but they are not sufficient. The 'truth' expressed in the lyrics was not enough to win rave reviews because differing 'truths' were being presented, and all songs based on 'truths' did not find favour nor elicit responsive chords in audiences. What made the difference was the indefinable gut feeling that a particular work rated the accolade '*kaiso*', the appellation reserved for those outstanding compositions/performances which impress audiences at first hearing and continue to do so over time.

"BLACK IS BEAUTIFUL"

By 1969 the coincidence of external and internal developments catalysed a resurgence of black nationalism and prompted a focus on the correlation of race, class and the quality of life. The calypsonian retained a keen awareness of his blackness although this did not form the theme of most calypsoes. Sparrow, commenting on "The Slave" (1963), articulates the emotions which periodically produce calypsoes on issues close to the skin:

> I guess it's been boiling up in me for quite a while. It is tied up with current incidents and some of the recent past like the Little Rock situation, the case of Meredith at Mississippi University and some restaurant signs around town that say 'No Dogs and No Calypsonians'. They remind me of some in New York and in the southern states that stipulate 'No Dogs and No Negroes'.[22]

At the same time Stalin's "United Africa" (1963) and the many other calypsoes on the troubled Congo indicated an interest in African affairs.

The stirrings in the American South form the theme of Cristo's "Mock Democracy" (1966) which provides a (geo)graphic insight into the kind of pressure blacks have to undergo:

> In Alabama they show no mercy
> To people like you and me
> In churches on Sunday during High Mass
> Suddenly you'd hear a big blast
> Men, women and even little children too
> Running helter-skelter, don't know what to do
> Next day when the obituary is read
> Nineteen big people injured, five children dead
>
> For instance, let's take Florida
> And take a peep at what goes on there
> And even in some parts of Britain
> They don't treat you like a human
> They will lynch and torture you in Jacksonville
> Frame and persecute you in Notting Hill

Exercising inhumanity
And still proclaiming to believe in democracy

The growing civil rights movement, personified in Dr Martin Luther King, inspired Sparrow to write "Martin Luther King for President" (1964). The stanzas, sung to an appropriate lament melody, present the plaint of the long-suffering African-American Baptist and his supportive and equally wretched coreligionists:

I was born a Negro in the USA
But because of my colour I'm suffering today
Because of my colour I'm suffering today
The white man preaching democracy
But in truth and in fact it's hypocrisy
In truth and in fact it's hypocrisy

The choruses, however, explode in the ecstatic antiphony of the Baptist faith:

So we want Martin Luther King for President
Tell the story all about
Martin Luther King for President
Tell the North, I will tell the South
Martin Luther King for President
Join together now and shout
Martin Luther King for President
When Kennedy finish without a doubt
Martin Luther King for President

In this way the calypso examines two aspects of Kamau Brathwaite's archetypal (Uncle) Tom figure who is trapped in a vicious and constricting system to which he is nevertheless committed. The rites and rituals of his church serve as a source of spiritual strength, as an affirmation of solidarity with the supportive group, and provide the safety valve for the release of violent self-destructive emotions and tensions. All this Sparrow achieves by means of the juxtaposition of the lament and the "shout".[23]

Then King was shot to death and the world held its breath. Sparrow's "Martin Luther King" (1969) anticipated a mass African American uprising which did materialise although not on the scale anticipated by the singer. Like in his earlier effort on King, Sparrow maximises the dramatic tension inherent in the stanza-chorus cleavage to present contradictory aspects of the King paradigm: the stanzas eulogise King as a pacifist, rejecting the violence preached by H. Rap Brown and Trinidad-born Stokely Carmichael, but the choruses threaten that King's supporters could turn to violent activism to regain their manhood. It has been suggested that when Uncle Tom threatened to become Tom, the authorities who had been monitoring King closely, acted decisively. Sparrow does not discuss this idea but he does capture King in that twilight state between begging for equality and fighting for it, and he does leave King's followers trapped like Brathwaite's leopard withholding the blow they need to strike for their freedom.[24]

King's death was the subject of the calypso which established Stalin on the national calypso stage. "The Immortal Message of Martin Luther King" (1969) comes close to canonising the great African American leader of the early 1960s:

> Never lived by a gun yet he died by one
> This man, Martin Luther King Senior son,
> A gentleman of high capability
> Who never knew the meaning of the word enemy
> But a man who devoted his life to fight
> That all American Negroes might get civil rights.
> His works must be continued although he is dead
> So let us think of the great things that Martin said
>
> Leave your guns at home, don't walk with weapons
> For violence cannot solve the situation
> We want the whites to know and believe whole-heartedly
> We want them as our friends and not as enemy
> For as enemy will bring riot in this land
> And that won't be good for no American.'
> Call him a messiah, a genius or different things
> But I say Martin was a King of all Kings.

By echoing King's words, Stalin captures the spirit of the man in his public character. Stalin has him make soft, courteous answer, the dignified, considered response of a statesman, to a reporter in Mississippi who asked why African Americans should be granted civil rights:

> We build your cities to give your pockets wealth
> Mind your babies and have them in the best of health
> Took part in Olympics, doh care if we die
> Just to keep the Stars and Stripes flying high
> Uphold democracy in and out this land
> From Germany to the foxholes of Vietnam
> All this we do for America so faithful and true
> So tell me why we can't eat in the same place as you

Then, too, Stalin presents King as prophet celebrating the magnificent vision he declared on the famous March to Washington:

Said, 'I have a dream, I have a vision'
And this is what Martin made them to understand
That in his vision this what he see
One day Black and White living so happy
Little Black children and little White children
One day walking the streets of America as friend
From the Black Hills of Dakota to Mississippi
Hand in hand in racial equality

This last is a wonderful example of how the calypsonian creates poetry. This is not to deny the magic of King's oratory because that speech ranks among the most powerful and dramatically intense of an emotional age; Stalin's calypso simply demonstrates literary organisation of a different order. He takes King's choric statement "I have a dream", combines elements of his address with elements of the typical King discourse, and organises them metrically and rhythmically; he also imbues the whole with his own personality. The power of his poetic imagination is evident in the faithful reproduction of the spirit of the message, and even in his concert series in 1991, decades removed from that emotion-charged day in Washington, he was able to recreate the mood of the march.

"The Immortal Message of Martin Luther King" is a lament which never becomes dirge, and which ends on an uplifting note, a note of affirmation that death shall have no dominion, and a conviction that such a great man had not lived in vain:

Now Martin Luther King is dead and gone
But I say that his works must go on
For his business is now left entirely
In the hands of his wife and Reverend Abernathy
These two must fight whole-heartedly
To make Martin's dream a reality
If not the whole then a part at least
Show the world where Black and White could live in peace

So good luck, Mrs King, good luck I say to you
I say every success in anything you do
Though it may take some time but you must keep asking
That they must judge a man by his heart and not his skin
Because Martin once said that Time is nothing
But only how man used Time could Time then be something
So we shall remember the words of your dear husband
That said, 'We shall overcome, we shall overcome!'

King is included by Brynner among the African greats of the modern era. A present day Ibn Battua,[25] Brynner roamed East Africa and returned to Trinidad invigorated by his experiences. "Uhuru Harambee" (1969) visualises ascent of Kilimanjaro which the ancient Egyptians venerated as the birthplace of the race.[26] Departing from the European tradition of descending to a lower or nether world to converse with the shades, Brynner 'ascends' the Mountain of the Moon to encounter the spirits of the illustrious dead:

> I met Marcus Garvey, Malcolm X and Patrice Lumumba
> Nat Turner, Albert Luthuli and Martin Luther King Junior
> They ask 'bout my people
> If we continuing the struggle
> Well I tell them what is the score
> Saying we are stronger now than before

This strength would be glimpsed in the resurgence of race pride which surfaced in responses to developments at home and abroad. As in the 1930s, European aggression in Africa ignited black anger in the West Indies. The *casus belli* of the 1960s was Ian Smith's usurpation of power in the British colony of Rhodesia. Cypher's popular "Rhodesia Crisis" (1966) compares Smith to Hitler and caricatures him, just as Invader's "Hitler's Moustache" had caricatured the Führer, but going beyond mockery, Cypher recalls the antecedents to World War II and warns of a similar conflagration:

> Now I'm going to show you
> Something similar before World War Two
> When Mussolini send planes to Africa
> And drop bombs on Addis Ababa
> Haile Selassie then flew to Britain
> And got no aid from the League of Nations
> So we don't need no glasses to see
> Where this one is heading for World War Three

Zebra's "Rhodesia Calypso Commentary" (1969) also makes the connection between Smith's actions in Rhodesia and the fascist mentality, and he strongly condemns British inactivity in the face of this defiance by a white supremacist group; a paralysis which seems more obscene when contrasted with British haste in its nonwhite protectorate Aden, and colony British Guiana:

> The British Commonwealth is on the verge of breaking up because of your treachery
> And your conniving way of playing blind to Smith and his apartheid policy
> Who else could have seized independence and get away with it
> You would have crushed Ian to death had he been a black Mr Smith
> But just because you figure you might have to shoot down some white people for

some black people
You left the whole of Rhodesia in the arms of a slave master
Old England, you should remember Adolf Hitler
Now the war is over and you done, you don't need us no more
You selling us like fish on a stall for little or nothing at all

Zebra, one of the original Young Brigade singers who emerged with the tent during the war or shortly afterwards, locates the Rhodesia crisis in its proper historical context: Britain had bribed parts of its restive empire into supporting the allied cause with the promise of self-government; now the duplicity of her attitude towards nonwhites is laid bare and could endanger the Commonwealth by which she kept a supervisory control over her former colonies.

Co-temporaneously, and as a result of developments in the United States, new or revived images of self were sweeping through Trinidad and Tobago. Black America is locked into a symbiotic relationship with the Caribbean which provides it with men of ideas who are then returned enlarged to their home islands. The long, hot Afro-American summer of the 1960s ignited the imagination of the Afro-Trinidadian. The assassination of the demagogic Malcolm and the equally persuasive Martin Luther King, the fiery rhetoric of H. Rap Brown and Stokely Carmichael, the militancy of the Black Panthers and the self-sufficiency of the Black Muslims, Muhammad Ali's refusal to make war on the Vietnamese and the clenched black-gloved fists of Tommy Smith and John Carlos at the medals ceremony at the 1968 Olympic Games in Mexico, encouraged the Afro-Trinidadian to adopt the slogans "Power to the People", "Black Power" and "Black is beautiful".

Duke co-opts this last slogan to create his 1969 calypso classic of the same name:

Many, many years it took
Now we've found the natural look
Many, many years it took
For us to find the natural look
Suddenly out of the blue
This thing has struck like something new
Everybody young and old
Going Afro and telling the world

Black is beautiful
Look at the gloss
Black is beautiful
It's the texture of course
Lift yuh head like me
Wear yuh colour with dignity
Black is beautiful

Sing it out loud
Black is beautiful
Say I'm Black and proud
It's high time that we
Get rid of this slave mentality

(ii) We have achieved
What once was just a dream
We have been imitating in the past
Now we have found our very own at last
No more hot comb to press we hair
No more bleach creams to make us fair
Proudly I say without regret
No more inferiority complex

(iv) I hope you don't misunderstood me none
I am not comparing us with anyone
Just simply stating coloured though we are
We must never feel ourselves inferior
The Man above who made the night and day
Has given both their equal parts to play
So if you are on our side
Open your mouth, shout it with pride

It seemed that the unfortunate mockery of Sparrow's "Congo Man" (1965) had been destroyed in this new mood of assertiveness. "Congo Man", a sexual fantasy based on the alleged rape of white nuns in the Belgian Congo, was extremely popular partly because it was a well-written double entendre, partly because its subject was that deep-seated psychosexual condition in which, according to Elridge Cleaver,[27] whites and blacks have trapped themselves. Among the very few who protested "Congo Man" was Gordon Rohlehr who objected to the insensitivity of the thoughtless stereotype.[28]

In the new mood of the late 1960s, black consciousness was the major ideological concern, and given the failure of the PNM intelligentsia to go beyond tepid declarations that the regime had brought betterment for the Afro-Trinidadian, the calypsonian found himself in the role of professor. Composer's "Black Fallacy" (1970) challenged the psycholinguistic base for the insinuation of subtle racism by examining how language is manipulated as the major tool of what one psychologist calls 'mentacide':[29]

Whoever created the English language
Purposely misused their privilege

I say whoever created the English language
They purposely misused their privilege
By using the word 'Black' with a degrading twist
They made words to cause racial prejudice
Words like 'blackbook', 'blackeye', 'black list'
When they know these things don't exist

Chorus
Oh yes, they going on from since in the beginning
Through this language they spreading a false doctrine
Yes, they made up their language in such a way
To belittle this Black colour every day
So that whenever you hear 'Black' you can't feel glad
'Blackball', 'blackbook', 'blackmail', all them things bad
So they brainwashing my people
By always associating black with evil

This trick have so much influence on we
That sometimes you does hear a local family
Saying, 'This hard-head chile more black than he'
Or, 'This soft-hair one have more colour than she'
Or, 'Me ent going no way on a Black Friday
Ah might bounce up a black cat and lose mih way'
Well, this black-name bad-name they instil in we
Is what breeds inferiority

From that there was just one short step to question the status of the Afro-Trinidadian and then to challenge the credentials of the black intellectuals then in power. The PNM launched its counteroffensive against what it thought was an alien hostile ideology. The *Nation* voiced PNM hurt and outrage, the products of its belief in the righteousness of its cause and its feeling that its accomplishments in the interests of the Afro-Trinidadian were being maliciously sabotaged by masters of deceit manipulating misguided youth.[30] Several calypsonians lent their voices to the official line.

Pretender's "A Man Is a Man" (1970) lyricises the essence of the PNM argument which he seemed to have believed as sincerely as he felt that Williams was a black messiah.[31] "A Man Is a Man" continues a line of thought Pretender had begun with his 1943 masterpiece "God Made Us All" which affirmed the then revolutionary idea of the equality of the races. When Williams appeared and testified by his presence that he was more equal than most whites, Pretender agreed and was to remain loyal to this belief. In 1970 he represented the elements of the collective which equated black presence in Whitehall to Black Power, and hence he rejected the principle and demands of the new radicalism in these words:

To tell you, these people must be mad
Bringing this tomfoolery in Trinidad
But any kinda propaganda bound to flop
For in Trinidad is mostly Negroes on top

One year later, Pretender would alter his tune in the face of disturbances which swept the country.

THE WINDS OF CHANGE

By a strange twist, the white governor-general of Canada and an African American couple emerged as the unlikely catalysts of a mass movement in Trinidad and Tobago.

On 26 February 1969, Ronald Michener was prevented from entering the St Augustine campus where he had gone to open Canada Hall, a hall of lodging for male students built with funds provided by the Canadian government. The students who blocked out the governor had intended to line the route to be taken by the dignitaries and to hold up placards indicating their displeasure at the discrimination allegedly suffered by black Caribbean students, who, together with white Canadians, had been charged with arson in Canada. That matter had developed when students at the Sir George Williams University, protesting the alleged racism of a white professor of biology, occupied the computer centre during the course of a 'sit-in'. Authorities attempted to dislodge them and in the ensuing melee the centre caught fire. Ninety-eight students were charged with arson and other offences, but reports reaching the West Indies suggested that the Afro-Caribbean students were singled out for unfair treatment by the Canadian society as a whole.[32]

The Guild of Undergraduates at the St Augustine campus deliberated a course of action to let the visiting Canadian governor understand its displeasure at these happenings. A gentleman's agreement was struck with UWI officials to let the peaceful display of protest placards convey the dismay of local students over the developments in Canada, but the UWI gentlemen, understandably reluctant to embarrass their benefactor, misled the students as to his route. Realising late the parlous deception, the students hastened to Michener's true point of entry and prevented him from setting foot on the campus.[33] Aware that that action had catapulted them into the league of national politics, they allied themselves with the radical trade union movement and on that night was born the organisation later named the National Joint Action Committee (NJAC).[34]

In July of that year, Dr and Mrs Leonard Hanna, holidaying at the Hilton, were refused entry at the Country Club whither they had been taken in search of a game of lawn tennis. The public, many of whom may never have even heard of the Country Club, reacted in shock and horror; the white élites defended their right to exclusivity; the government, predictably, ordered an inquiry.[35]

Sparrow's model nation thus revealed itself as a true mock democracy; a black regime preached "Here every creed and race/Finds an equal place" while guaranteeing that the races and classes remain separate and unequal. Chalkdust's "Massa Day Must Done" (1970) issued a powerful calypso statement which oddly refutes and reflects Williams' "Massa Day Done",[36] a proclamation that the reign of "Massa" was over in Trinidad and Tobago:

We used to boast about our land
Saying we have racial integration
We told the world that our Country
Is an example of love, peace and racial harmony
But all that's now a fake
The Country Club issue made us wide awake
Yet it's a drop of water
In an ocean of discrimination

Chorus
So won't you tell Country Club
Massa Day must done
We want no racialism in our country
No prejudice or colour bar must divide we
This land belongs to everybody
So tell the Portuguese Club to come off our land
To hell with Chung Shan and Chinese Association
This land only has room for Trinidadians
Massa day must done

According to the calypso, discrimination assumed forms many and diverse: preferential treatment accorded Caucasian St Clair youths in private sector employment practices as opposed to the slighting of the African brood of John John; unequal access to bank loans; the selection of Caucasian belles only for the lucrative Jaycee Queen pageant; the continued publication of degrading comic strips like "Tarzan" and "Mandrake"; police partisanship in crime detection; and state blindness to the decadence of party *apparatchik*, the new nonwhite massas. What this all amounts to is that Chalkdust, parodying the title of Williams' fiery address of 1961, is affirming that Williams has failed, and the use of Williams' catalogue style is an ironic underscoring of this failure.

Several weeks later, all the complaints and frustrations expressed in song assumed menacing physical presence on the streets. The disturbance at a calypso show may have been the spark igniting the conflagration; certainly it was the first overt manifestation of violent disapproval with officialdom. That matter began innocuously with a Southern Brigade performance at Woodford Square at a free show sponsored by the Carnival Development Committee (CDC). This show started late – a normal bad practice in Trinidad and Tobago – but was moving along smoothly until a city council official asked Brynner, then in charge of the tent, to wrap up proceedings. Brynner appealed to the crowd which reacted in anger at being denied what they took for natural pleasure. They identified a car as belonging to a CDC official and set it ablaze.[37] Several days later, Black Power demonstrators picketed the Jaycees Queen show, and protest bands appeared at the *Jour Ouvert* celebrations.[38] The Calypso and carnival had thus provided the fora for protest and the Baker dream materialised as nightmare.

The Growling Tiger

The Mighty Sparrow in full flight

The Mighty Cypher

Em7

The Lord Blakie

F7-11

Lord Melody and Lord Kitchener

Dr Williams meeting Baron and Rajah

Lord Superior

The Mighty Prowler

The Mighty Duke

Kitchener and Lord Pretender

4

The Roaring Seventies
1971–1975

THE BACKGROUND

Conspicuously absent from the 1966 calypsoes are any references to the 1965 happenings in the industrial south where Williams had checkmated the formation of a super union. Sugar workers, chafing under the individualistic rule of Bhadase Sagan Maraj, had invited George Weekes, president general of the powerful Oilfields Workers' Trade Union (OWTU), to represent them in industrial matters. Williams, long suspicious of Weekes' growing influence, moved to counter the merger of oil and sugar workers which he saw as a political union of Africans and Indians in opposition to him. Continuing unrest in the labour troubled sugar industry and the timely invocation of the spectre of communism gave Williams the opportunity to declare a state of emergency under cover of which he rushed through parliament the Industrial Stabilisation Act (ISA), a law which among other things outlawed strikes and set conditions for certification of worker representation.[1]

These happenings in the distant south were unremarked in the Calypso, perhaps because of the ideological indoctrination of the society as a whole. The calypsonian may have thought – like others – that Weekes' attempt to politicise labour, taken together with the return of C.L.R. James and the subsequent formation of the WFP with James and Weekes as principals, provided evidence of the communist blueprint, something the free world had been warned against since the early days of the Cold War. The vilification of James and his association with persons named in the long delayed but now conveniently released Report of the Commission of Inquiry into subversive activity in the country, may have persuaded the calypsonian that the nation's only salvation and the only hope for the continuance of the Trinidadian laissez-faire lay in Williams' liberal authoritarianism.

A battle of attrition had long developed in labour. Williams needed a docile labour force for the modified Lewis strategy for economic development that he had adopted since the late 1950s but some unions opposed the procapital stance which represented a radical departure from his earlier prolabour leanings.[2] Williams never sought a trade union base, preferring instead to cultivate leaders and reward them for delivering their followings. Those unionists with their own agenda refused to toe the PNM line and so there followed what the economist Zin Henry calls "an adversarial and a confrontative behavioural pattern" in industrial relations.[3] Battle lines were drawn: the state stood on one side brandishing the ISA as the weapon of right, while on the other side, workers, including many who were otherwise staunch PNMites, waged their colourful campaigns with a cavalier defiance of the antistrike legislation.

In the bus workers strike of 1969, a coalition of militant unionists, radical students and progressive academics, more hostile and determined than the lethargic and ineffectual parliamentary DLP opposition, showed its corporate face in what was their rejection of the ISA. Geddes Granger, formerly of Pegasus and now chairman of NJAC, dispensed with the ISA in the words: "If the workers do not want the ISA they should simply declare a date on which they intend to regard the ISA as repealed. And from then on they should act as though there were no ISA."[4]

Rhetoric of this kind could not dismiss the reality of an antagonist who still controlled the state and the media. Williams declared a fight to the finish:[5] striking leaders and their allies were arrested;[6] hundreds of striking workers were dismissed;[6] *The Nation* attacked "The Lawless Breed";[8] even the few calypsonians who sang on the strike condemned the unionists. An uneasy peace set in.

Then came Thursday 26 February 1970. About 200 NJAC members led by Granger picketed Canadian owned business places in downtown Port of Spain to protest the sentencing of the students in the Sir George Williams University affair. The demonstration had nearly petered out when on an impulse the demonstrators entered the Roman Catholic Cathedral, covered the statue of the Virgin Mary with a cloth and defied the priests who tried to remove them. One participant later described the violation of the cathedral as the rape from which the revolution was conceived.[9] While the nation trembled and tingled, cabinet met in overnight session and, invoking an ancient statute,[10] ordered the arrest of the leaders of the demonstration. Suddenly, the accumulated tensions, frustrations and hostilities smouldering for years and fanned by recent events, burst into flame. By the next week, thousands were massing to hear NJAC's spokesmen Geddes Granger, George Weekes, Clive Nunez and Dave Darbeau and their many allies.

For 55 tense days the nation's streets thundered to the shouts of "Black Power" and "Power to the People" raised by thousands who saw themselves as poor, black and dispossessed. The movement itself was spontaneous and amorphous, and anger was directed as much against whites, local and expatriate, as against the black and Indo-Trinidadian bourgeoisie and bureaucracy and all perceived as enemies of the people. It was race and class consciousness more felt than defined. Despite the obvious anger and passion, the demonstrations were relatively peaceful for although there were incidents of arson and violence and numerous threats, there was remarkably little mayhem as the demonstrators processed with the order of centurions in a carnival band.[11] Fiery demagogue Granger commanded on one occasion, "We shall walk without speaking, without shouting, without smiling. But we shall walk in anger."[12] Thousands obeyed.

The highlight of the street demonstrations was the long march to Caroni, heartland of the Hindu community and of the sugar workers who had consistently rejected Williams' Creole nationalism. This symbolic link-up was intended to be the continuance of the outreach movement of 1937 and 1965. Roman Catholic Archbishop Anthony Pantin offered to join the marchers. He, the first local to occupy the diocesan chair, had seemed sympathetic to NJAC and it is said that his sympathy had spared the cathedral violators harsher retaliation. However, although he was dissuaded from this overt show of support, the lesser clergy was not. Scare tactics failed to abort the march. Rumour ran rife that the invading city blacks would despoil the gentle countryside nymphs, but members of the Society for the Propagation of Indian Culture (SPIC) marched in the first ranks of the 'invaders' and part of their mission on that day was to allay the fears of their rural brethren.[13] For hours the long procession wound its way to Chaguanas welcomed tentatively by residents along the way. At journey's end, speeches were made after which the weary demonstrators made their way home. They had not reached in time to assist the cane cutters as they had planned but the attempt was as good as the deed.

As in 1965, Indo-Trinidadian sugar workers accepted the bona fides of Afro-Trinidadian leaders. A return march to Port of Spain was decided for 21 April, by a fluke of history nearly ten years to the day since PNM's March for Chaguaramas. On the planned day they set out but were stopped three times by armed policemen.[14] Unknown to the workers who started early, a state of emergency had been declared throughout the islands.

Williams had not panicked. He publicly identified with the positives of the movement and he acknowledged the legitimacy of the protest.[15] He accelerated a microprogramme of nationalism which he had hastily initiated in response to the stirrings of the late 1960s[16] and he paid the fines of the students involved in Canada. But he never disclosed his motivations: Did his liberal authoritarianism acknowledge the right of legitimate protest, or did a lingering honesty recognise his indebtedness to the urban underclass whose collective lot had not been significantly ameliorated since 1956? Was he carefully cultivating his image or was he, with a wisdom born of experience, craftily manoeuvring for time while waiting for the marchers to tire? Compared to the crackdowns of 1965 and 1969 and those to be seen later in 1971 and 1975, his forbearance during those dramatic days of March to April 1970 does seem strange; and even when he did act it was, as he claims, in response to the machinations of dissident elements who were bidding to seize power by *coup d'état*.[17] He had a state of emergency declared and 59 NJAC and other leaders arrested. Even so, he made it appear that Clive Spencer, president of the Trinidad and Tobago Labour Congress, had forced his hand.[18]

A mutiny in the regiment threw the government into panic, but Williams kept his nerve,[19] the police stood firm and the coast guard cancelled the mutineers' drive into Port of Spain. Colonel Serrette volunteered to parley with the mutineers,[20] and after a few days of uncertainty with foreign warships lurking in the Gulf of Paria, the mutineers surrendered to their former commander. Elaborate courts martial then followed, presided over by officers from black Commonwealth countries and Singapore, chosen for obvious reasons.

On the political front, then Attorney General Karl Hudson-Phillips drafted a Public Order Bill, the provisions of which were so destructive of individual liberties that the national community, with the significant exception of the Roman Catholic Church,[21] screamed in outrage. The bill was withdrawn only to be reintroduced piecemeal at the next Parliament which the PNM dominated 36–0 thanks to an election boycott initiated by the Union of Revolutionary Organisations. Two defections from the PNM benches – though stage-managed by Williams himself – could not significantly impede the passage of the Firearms Act, the Sedition Act and the sabotage bill which cumulatively achieved the safeguards promised in the Public Order Bill.[22]

Parliamentary opposition rendered nugatory, Williams, believing as ever in a "theory of plots"[23] sought to expose the New Left conspiracy and everywhere struck at the underground movement which supposedly nurtured and sustained undisclosed enemies. Tribunals conducted interrogations of suspects while police units instituted a reign of terror characterised by early morning raids and arbitrary detentions and beatings – up some 3,000 in all between May 1971 and 1975, alleges Dr Martin Sampath,[24] a former PNM hierarch who had his house searched. Greater urgency was forced on the security agencies by the threat of armed insurgency mounted by the National Union of Freedom Fighters (NUFF), a guerrillero movement born out of a combination of youthful idealism and literal acceptance of Maoist and Castroist literature. Their undeniable courage and the spectacular exploits accredited to them[25] invested the guerrilleros with an aura of romance but the better-known leaders succumbed to the elite police flying squad commanded by Randolph Burroughs, other members were arrested and convicted, and the movement died.

In the midst of this activity, Williams suddenly announced that he was retiring. Inevitably, intrigue and power play followed. Hudson-Phillips made a bid for power and, from all accounts, he was within an ace of success when Williams returned. Among the reasons Williams gave for this surprise move was that the unexpected soaring of oil prices in consequence of Middle East politics had made of the local situation "a new ball game".[26] This can be interpreted to mean that it had now become possible for him to resolve, or at least mute, conflicts in society, and to create a kind of model welfare state with himself as benevolent patriarch.

Intransigent labour leaders still disturbed his peace as they had done since he took office. In 1975, the leaders of the OWTU, The All-Trinidad Sugar Estates and Factory Workers' Trade Union (ATSE and FWTU) and the Islandwide Cane Farmers' Trade Union (ICFTU), all veterans of labour and political wars, except for ICFTU strongman, ex-lieutenant Raffique Shah, a veteran of the 1970 mutiny, tried again to politicise the labour movement. All the unions claimed to have genuine industrial problems all of which demanded political resolution: the OWTU was seeking a 147 percent increase for Texaco workers; the ATSE and FWTU insisted upon profit-sharing and worker ownership of the sugar industry; and the ICFTU was demanding recognition as the bargaining body for cane farmers.[27] After many discussions and strategy sessions, they planned a "peaceful religious walk" to Port of Spain purportedly to continue "our prayers for justice, bread and peace".[28] Police Commissioner Tony May, citing Section 118 of the Summary Offences (Amendment) act 1972 which conferred on his office the power to grant permission for public marches,[29] expressly forbade the march, but the leaders, agreeing that March comes before May, were determined to proceed.

On Tuesday, 18 March 1975, thousands of workers in oil and sugar and cane farmers set out from the OWTU's Paramount Building headquarters on Circular Road, San Fernando, after listening to addresses from leaders including the venerable icon Tubal Uriah 'Buzz' Butler, and being blessed by Christian, Hindu and Muslim clerics. On nearby Coffee Street, they were brought to a bloody halt by policemen with tear gas and truncheons. With this, the era of mass militant demonstrations of the early 1970s came to an end.

At the end of 1975, Trinidad and Tobago seemed to have achieved stability and prosperity. Revenue from the sale of petroleum crude made possible mass education, mass development, mass employment, mass consumerism, mass contentment. Overseas, leaders died or were disgraced; monarchies, dictatorships and theocracies were toppled, but in Trinidad and Tobago the 'Pussonal Nonarch'[30] sat securely on his throne and all seemed well with the kingdom.

CALYPSO AND POLITICS 1971–1975

The convulsions which racked the society between 1969 and 1974 heightened the role of the political Calypso, especially in interpreting the puzzling happenings and in defining the many new concepts introduced to the political culture during this period. 'Black Power' needed and received special attention because it upset the well-demarcated relations in the social order and in economic activity. The equilibrium which had obtained in occupational stratification and wealth distribution had been thus understood: "Blacks dominated the security and bureaucratic establishments and the state capitalist sector while Indians, whites, Syrians, and Chinese dominated finance, industry and commerce."[31]

The societal pyramid was far more complex than this. At the apex there were the white descendants of the Spanish criollos, the French Creoles and the British merchant and planter class. They had retreated before the onrush of black nationalism to barricade themselves in banks, business houses, exclusive clubs and prestigious secondary schools; less visible now and forming a mere two percent of the population[32] they nevertheless controlled commercial life and dictated political activity.[33] The caste system which prevailed in business effectively guaranteed their survival.[34] A large heterogeneous middle class of all hues, backgrounds and income activities separated this privileged caste from the majority at the base, but the fluidity of this intermediate group held out hope to the latter. The mass of Indo- and Afro-Trinidadian and Tobagonian labourers at the base of the pyramid sold their labour or set up small businesses of all kinds, and either consumed their earnings or hoarded them for their progeny whose only escape was the social mobility afforded by education and emigration. But Trinidad society was far from being homogeneous, honeycombed as it was by 'tribes'[35] and tribal enclaves,[36] in which race, class and religious differences criss-crossed forming perplexing patterns. To some extent Black Power added to the confusion.

It was one of the duties of the political Calypso to explain to the marginal man at society's base the relationship between himself, Black Power and black visibility in Whitehall. This involved defining new and unfamiliar concepts such as 'neocolonialism' and it also involved giving guidelines for action. The few calypsonians who undertook this monumental task needed to first clarify Black Power for themselves or to rely on a formulated ideological position. The problems implicit in either approach are reflected in the changing positions of individual singers as they wrestled with problems which have always challenged blacks in the diaspora, and also in the differences of opinions among the committed singers.

Even for those who did not delve too deeply, positionlessness became an epistemological impossibility as events ruthlessly vectored singers into one zone of opinion. Humour became political, panegyric almost disappeared and protest blossomed into full-blown militancy.

Although protest occupied centre stage, life went on as did the carnival, and the calypsonian still depended on his stock-in-trade topics to stimulate revelry. The importance of the political or serious singer in this period had a lot to do with the polarisation of street and stage: it seemed that the stage, that is the Dimanche Gras stage, demanded a 'Savannah song' while the street demanded a bouncy tune without meaningful lyrics. Despite their obvious popularity and merit, however, many 'Savannah songs' did not automatically land Dimanche Gras appearances for their composers/ performers. This led to much 'cross song' and yet the political calypsonian remained master of his own stage as is illustrated in the success of Valentino's concert series "Poet and Prophet".

1970 IN CALYPSO

The calypsonian did not anticipate the happenings of 1970. Like most citizens, he was caught unawares by the volume and vehemence of the street demonstrations, because, although he had been indicating that pressures had been building up, he did not envision the power of the alliance being formed by radical unionists, students, academics and the unemployed. The militancy of the one and the rumblings of the other had been perceived as separate and distinct; the social unrest in the east-west corridor, for example, was never connected to the perennial dissatisfaction in labour and the agitation on campus over Rodney's expulsion from Jamaica or the arrests of students in Canada. Nineteen seventy presented the calypsonian with a new vision of reality, a larger vision of the interrelatedness of economics, politics and society.

The immediate calypso reactions to 1970 showed that the singers were concerned about the happenings but were either unwilling or unable to grasp their implications for the future direction of the society. On the whole, they defended the rule of law and the Trinidadian way of life. This conservatism, either innate or the product of conditioned reflex, resulted in noncommittal reportage and a plethora of either narrative or descriptive songs: the calypsoes of 1970 mentioned rather than analysed.

One tendency was to look humorously at the dodges employed by the tomcatting male in order to pursue his amorous escapades. This humouring of the Anansi mentality is part of the larger tendency to smile indulgently at the peculiar foibles of the people as a whole; 1970 simply allowed imagination different rein. While one theorises that escape into comedy keeps the nation sane, one may also conclude that shallowness may well be a by-product of this kind of sanity.

One little-discussed matter was the mutiny at Teteron and the courts martial which followed. This is particularly surprising in light of the tremendous publicity generated by the insurgence and by the first trial. Composer's "Blow the Whole Place Down" recreates the "jokey situation" when Colonel Serrette testified. Serrette, described euphemistically in the calypso as a "brave and bold controversial man", was the first local to command the regiment but *vox populi* had it that he annoyed the politicos by playing squire to the wife of his boss, the minister of home affairs. This hastened his departure[37] and the politicians revenged themselves by abstaining from the customary round of farewells marking his departure. When the mutiny broke out, he volunteered his services and Williams accepted.

"Blow the Whole Place Down" reduces Serrette's days in court to farce. Composer's "Serrette" testifies that his regiment was an assortment of good-time idlers, a perception shared by many in the larger society:

> Look what they done to my regiment
> I can't see where all my teachings went
> Just because I wasn't present
> All I could see now is discontent
> And instead of having a ball
> My men are out there having a brawl
> Bullets kicking up just like a squall
> Man, I rather have no Regiment at all

The main focus of the calypso, however, is the heroic role into which Serrette cast himself:

> You all know that when duty calls
> I cannot falter, I cannot stall
> I am a soldier with plenty gall
> When it comes to me they meet a wall
> They call me back here to pacify
> For they know that I'm a tough guy
> For my Country I'm not afraid to die

This highly entertaining commentary is clearly a satire on Serrette's show of spirit. He was never in any real danger from the mutineers who had requested his services as mediator,[38] and who had wanted him to resume command – it is not certain whether they wished to continue having a ball as the calypso charges. In any event there were disturbingly contradictory statements about Serrette's dealings with the mutineers, and, in point of fact, the restrictions by the court martial against allowing defence attorneys to question him on the matter of an amnesty which the defendants claim that he had promised, was one of the technicalities leading to the quashing of the convictions.[39]

"Blow the Whole Place Down" remains on this evidence the study of a hollow man preening himself for a place in history. If truth be told, many officials claimed similar honours in their self-serving accounts of their roles on those fateful days in April 1970.[40]

This apart, attention focused on the breakdown in the civilian world with the street demonstrations claiming precedence. Duke and Kitchener, who both had earlier endorsed black awareness (Duke's "Black Is Beautiful" 1969; Kitchener's "Africa Is My Home" 1953, "Black Or White" 1953 and "If You're Brown" c. 1959), hid their support for the PNM behind noncommittal description. Duke recycled his greatest hit "Memories of 1960" in his "Memories of 1970" singling out now as then a demonstration of people on the move:

> 1970 gone but Ah sure I'll always remember
> If Ah live 104 like mih great grandfather
> 1970 gone but Ah sure I'll always remember
> If Ah live 104 like mih great grandfather
> In the history of Trinidad
> It was the most eventful we ever had
> But the outstanding day of all
> Was that of the Black Power funeral
>
> Chorus
> Everybody wore red indicating
> Their respect for the dead they were bier-ing
> Man, Ah never see so much crowd
> And everybody singing aloud
> 'Power in the hands of the people now'

While Duke expresses an emotion (". . . this was the saddest day of all"), Kitchener presents an objective report of a Black Power meeting in the manner of those newspaper accounts which carry no byline and thus achieve a kind of anonymity. His "Black Power" reproduces the rhetoric of the meeting in typical road march styling but nowhere does the 'reporter' disclose his emotions or reveal the impression the rhetoric had on him.

Fluke, a simple soul, dismissed unkindly as a simpleton, sang "Black Power", a commentary as inoffensive and as childlike as the man himself:

> In March 1970
> Man from university
> March all over town
> In a silent song
> But when they meet a business place
> Standing face to face
> Then Ah know the silent song
> Had a chorus in town
>
> With they right hand in the air like a tower
> And everybody shouting 'Power, power, power!'
> With they right hand in the air like a tower
> And every man shouting 'Power, power, power!'

This totally unexpected way of expressing things, combined with the sing-song melody and unusual antics, evoked laughter, although Fluke seems to have taken himself seriously. Fluke made "Black Power" become one of the more popular songs of the year, people showing tiredness with the heaviness of politics. In Fluke's mind, 1970 was an extremely simple affair which ended with the intervention of the police:

The police on duty
Move with humanity
They spray a lil gas
And keep watching fas'
But when a fella get the wrong idea
And start to interfere
Is then the police get vex
And make he arrest

With he baton in the air like a tower
He said, 'I arrest you with power, power, power'

One wonders if this calypso was well liked because it was funny or because it bespoke an end to the tension of 1970. It certainly is a simple statement, ignorant of any implication, innocent of any complication.

Another popular song was Cypher's "Black Power" which masks incisive comment behind familiar Cypheresque humour:

A black man hold mih by mih collar
He asking me the meaning of Black Power
A black man hold me by mih collar
He asking me the meaning of Black Power
I told him, 'Well . . . I doh know'
Bam, he hit me a blow
Ah fall down inside a ring
He tell me get up and say something

I told him
'A black man break up a black man store
A next black man ask him what he do that for
Up come a big black police on a big black horse
To find out what the black man make the next black man lorse
He took him to the station, Black Friday was the case
If you see black, black people pack up in the place
The judge and all he was black'
So Ah tell him to get something outa that

Cypher's humour is based on the incongruity of the Clown Prince of Calypso being expected to have a viable opinion on something as serious as Black Power ("asking me, Cypher"), and yet in a situation where 'black' was not synonymous with 'poor' and 'the people' was hard to define, his hypothetical scenario is not as far-fetched as it sounds. In Tobago, for example, it is alleged that the street demonstrations did incalculable harm to the emerging black hotelier class,[41] and in Trinidad there were instances of hostility to the black bourgeoisie. One suggests that Cypher intuitively grasped this problem of race and class confrontation and pointed up the absurdity of intrablack struggle.

Cypher uses his individualistic method of madness to make bold comment on the domestic situation which *vox populi* attributed to Serrette's inglorious retirement:

> He ask me with who consent
> They had the split in the Regiment
> I told him I wasn't there
> Go and ask the Minister of Home Affair
> The answer he give, well, it make me bawl
> He say, 'Minister of Home doh go home at all'

The mere mention of a pubic secret is enough for initiates, and being Cypher he dares thus in safety. After hearing the 'facetious' answers, the assailant realised that it was a case of mistaken identity, as Cypher put it, "is Robinson he taking me for all the time". The very thought is outrageous: even if both were tricked out in the garb of the demonstrators which A.N.R. Robinson was wont to affect, no sane person could mistake one for the other. Cypher may well be using this to criticise Robinson for his adherence to the externals of the movement which threatened the party of which he was still a senior hierarch, and he could also be satirising what he considers chameleon opportunism on the part of the PNM's deputy leader.

After making so many comments on the major political happenings of 1970, Cypher retreats into the mask afforded by farce by defining "Black Power" as a "big, black calypsonian from South", an accurate description of the Mighty Power.

Analytic and evaluative calypsoes were in short supply and, significantly, two of the better won for their composers places in the Dimanche Gras finals. Valentino's "No Revolution" and Chalkdust's "Answer to Black Power" were addresses to Williams, the central figure of 1970. The songs are respectful in tone, restrained in language and eminently serious in outlook; they differ greatly in attitude, however. These dramatic differences make for diametrically opposed approaches to the question of Black Power, and they would determine the direction which either singer would take in later years.

Valentino 'marches' with the NJAC standard-bearers. He did not participate in the demonstrations although the circumstances of his life qualified him as one of the 'people', but he read the newspapers, kept in touch with the situation as it unfolded and admired the spirit of the leaders.[42] Having reflected deeply, he thought it in order to direct a word to Williams:

> They talking 'bout power, Doctor, is you who have power
> Ah know when you act woulda be a horse of a different colour
> You give them a inch, they take a whole yard
> And when you had them under yuh clinch people say you bad
> Well, when I heard you address the Nation
> I knew what was your intention
> But some of the powers you exercise
> Unfortunately I must criticise
>
> We didn't want them trigger-happy police
> We only wanted to demonstrate in peace
> Yet you held my people and charged them for sedition
> We was marching for equality
> Black unity and Black dignity
> Dr Williams, no, we didn't want no revolution

When asked to account for the last line and for the general deference to Williams, Valentino explained that it was "all one big *mamaguy*. The man does come high, so I coming high too."[43] One suspects that there may well be elements of post fact rationalisation in this answer which came after Valentino had been acclaimed "The People's Calypsonian", a title which made him "equal but opposite to the Prime Minister".[44] In 1970, when the calypso was composed, Valentino may still have had that respect for Williams which was ingrained in the collective consciousness, but he was to display true grit in defying the management of the Revue which attempted to censor his song to accommodate the visiting Williams and children. This incident instances the dynamics of the pressures to which the creative soul is subjected in calypsodom. Kitchener, Valentino's calypso 'godfather',[45] had allowed his 'godson' to perform "No Revolution" because it was one of the more popular songs of that season, but Kitchener, the PNM supporter, was averse to offending Williams to his face and he was willing to sacrifice his protégé on the altar of PNM expediency. The attempted shielding of Williams is standard PNM practice. Valentino, although respectful and sober, was making statements which Kitchener thought might have offended Williams.

Stanza three, for example, sets out the rights and duties of the citizen as understood by a man exposed to the oratory of The People's Parliament, as Woodford

Square was popularly called.[46] Valentino, the primary school dropout, threatens Williams, the world-renowned historian, with the judgement of history:

> A citizen should withstand the wrong things in his Country
> Regardless of what happen, that is my ideology
> All we meeting with is oppression and a seta strain
> Trials and tribulations, sorrows and pain
> When we try to shake up the Government
> The result was police ill-treatment
> But justice must be done otherwise History
> Is going to punish you worse than you punish we

Valentino also praised Williams' political enemies, describing Robinson as "a man with love and feeling for the people" and raising a cheer for NJAC and for Geddes Granger who had enlightened the people about the 'raw deal' they had been getting. In explaining "Black Power" as the stirrings of race pride and the movement towards visibility and empowerment, Valentino also laid bare the PNM's failure to transform the society as its supporters had been led to expect:

> You must be aware that Black consciousness is here
> I further declare is time we get an equal share
> Is Black blood, Black sweat and Black tears but is White profits
> Because right through the years is the white man reaping the benefits
> But now we are coming down from the shelves
> And we are getting to know ourselves
> So let us hail Geddes Granger
> For bringing Black people together

Here are the thoughts on political economy that Williams was believed to personify in 1956; now they confront him, the *douennes* of his political actions since then. Kitchener should not have tried to prevent Valentino from singing this to Williams' face because Williams had admitted it for the nation and the world to hear[47] but the loyalty of Kitchener's generation was and is total.

Paradoxically, one singer of Kitchener's generation echoes Williams' public thoughts. Pretender's "Black Power" claims independence for its composer but the ideas therein expressed so closely reflect those voiced in Williams' two radio and television addresses on Black Power – just as Pretender's "A Man is a Man" had versified PNM thought on the appearance of black consciousness – that it is not inconceivable that "Black Power" does likewise. To give him his due, Pretender supports the 'blacks' as he calls the demonstrators, "after examining all the facts" and "after weighing all the evidence". He admits that PNM's education policy has not delivered the qualitative change in the standard of living for Afro-Trinidadians and has not secured its stated goal of securing employment for them. "They *mamaguying* the coloured population!" he exclaims, carefully losing Williams in the anonymous "They", but he does not prescribe either a change of regime or of leader. He may well be the first calypsonian to pose in song the question which would resonate throughout the early 1970s ". . . who you go put if you move 'way he?"

Other serious commentary on 1970 seems to have accepted Williams' prime ministership as a given, something to be reformed, redirected but not removed. Chalkdust's "Answer to Black Power" seems as much concerned with shoring up Williams as with securing better conditions for the Black Power demonstrators. Stanza two criticises Williams' ineffectual efforts to plug cracks in a collapsing macroeconomy and proposes a revolutionary political economy which can realise Black Power for both the regime and the disaffected masses:

> You giving the unemployed every year
> Jobs to mend the streets here and there
> But that wouldn't solve the situation
> You only sowing the seeds of revolution
> You got to create more opportunity for all black men in society
> With the emphasis
> On helping them to form their own small business
>
> Doctor, the answer to solve Black Power
> Is to tax the rich some more
> And build houses for the blind, the lame, the poor
> Houses for everyone we must ensure
> Vital areas like sugar and oil
> Must be run by sons of our soil
> Why must the small white minority
> Control us economically
> Make sure that our Black majority
> Fill up every hole, nook and cranny
> That's the answer for Black Power

Williams' urban Afro-Trinidadian supporters can be forgiven for expecting this kind of programme from the PNM in 1956 and beyond. The fact that their children joined mass movements against Williams, the hope of the fifties made flesh and living – though not among them – meant that messianic prophecy had not been fulfilled.

One notes that Chalkdust, like Pretender, is concerned with the ineffectuality of Williams' education programmes. Like Prowler in "Build More Trade Schools", Chalkdust sees technical and vocational education as the practical alternative to the Oxbridge-oriented academics which Williams encouraged to the detriment of the underclass as a whole. Chalkdust recommends compulsory skills training for those who show no inclination towards book work. The sentences "Force them to learn a skill" and "Compel them, Doctor, to join the army", attest to Chalkdust's endorsement of Williams' authoritarianism and to the existence of similar tendencies in himself. One schoolmaster advises another on the best way to handle recalcitrant or refractory children: compel them in their own best interests and when they come of age and experience they will be forever grateful.

In many ways "Answer to Black Power" reads like a memorandum to the prime minister; its comprehensive programme indicates a viable course of action intended to rescue the floundering Father of the Nation. This is the only construct that can accommodate the advice to have ministers declare their assets on a yearly basis, a suggestion that has nothing to do with the demonstrators and everything to do with the public image of the regime and of its leader. It seems clear that "Answer to Black Power" is by way of being timely, friendly advice; even the *mamaguy* "In my opinion, Doc, you did you best" seems to harbour no malice. One may suggest that Chalkdust demonstrates in this song an affection and caring for Williams which would later underlie even his most trenchant criticism.

Chalkdust's vigorous programme and the sincerity with which he presents it contrast with the servility and myopia of Lester's appeal to Williams to allow the Carnival to continue:

> You are a man of great intelligence
> Forgive them, Sir, for their ignorance
> Everything is now in your hand
> It is you who cool the unrest situation
> Tourists could now come from oversea
> Things are right back to normality
> Hoping your answer will be yes
> Carnival '71 will be our best
>
> Oh Lord, Doc, I'm begging you please
> Oh Lord, Doc, I'm down on my knees
> I know we under the State of Emergency
> Doc, please don't do that to we
> Doc, you and me will be no pal at all
> If you stop our Carnival

Lester's calypso ignores the future of the society and concerns itself with the continuity or interruption of the carnival, an issue which interested Stalin ("No Politics in Carnival"), Pretender ("Don't Stop Carnival") and others. Carnival is serious business for the calypsonian because it is at this time that he generates steady income at home and he profits from the general liquidity afforded by the tourist and returnee dollar.

One of the things effected by 1970 was the highlighting of levels of seriousness and levity in the society, and the demonstration that seriousness for some was comedy for others. Chalkdust's "Answer to Black Power" and Valentino's "No Revolution" take for granted that the demonstrators were serious. Stalin's "What Consciousness?" scoffs at the idea of a new awareness among young Afro-Trinidadian males who persist in their traditional derogatory remarks to women and their taunts when rightly ignored; similarly, the women show the same preconsciousness and preoccupation with hair straightening and other artificial processes which bespeak an obsession with Eurocentric notions of beauty. Paradoxically, his "Freedom Day" on the same recording expresses the certainty that the African American will one day celebrate a genuine Liberation Day. Prince Valiant's "Don't Spoil this Country" captures the 'kicks' mentality of those who personified the "put on a dashiki and come" attitude:[48]

Twenty thousand, twenty thousand strong
Mama, Port of Spain burning down
Twenty thousand, twenty thousand strong
Mama, Port of Spain burning down
I and all join the band
Shout for power, raise mih hand
Ah thought was a joke, Ah thought was fun
Until Ah see police and machine gun

Valiant's protagonist bears close resemblance to many persons still living.

An important calypso cycle revolved around the need for national reconstruction. Sparrow's "Lend a Hand" urges the citizenry to nonpartisan effort:

Now is the time to rebuild
Make up your mind to climb the hill
It's reconstruction time in Trinidad
So put your shoulders to the wheel, mih lad
Move on, don't stop
'til you reach the top

You put a hand and I put a hand
And we will see
In no time at all for big and for small
Prosperity

There's no other way to do it
Show your patriotic spirit
Unity somehow
If Trinidad ever needed you it's now

(ii) Trinidadians one and all
Hear my plea, answer my call
The peace and happiness we had before
Was lost with everybody fighting war
Let's hope that done
So move on . . . upwards

(iii) Forget political policy, political ties
And rebuild your Country before the good name dies
If everyone will learn to play their part
That is enough to make a useful start
Soon we'll have had
A better Trinidad

Stalin nearly 'broke down the tent', that is, he brought the house down, with his "National Reconstruction" which echoes the title of Williams' nationwide radio and television broadcast of 30 June 1970.[49] This calypso presents the mooted reasons for the 'jam session' as a basket of options originating in the many popular theories about the street demonstrations. Premises include the intention to change the system, the idea that the demonstrators were seeking post-carnival thrills, dissatisfaction with the gains made by "them settlers" at the expense of locals, and the politicisation of the Afro-Trinidadian along the lines of African American militancy. Stalin shrewdly abstains from choice just as he refrains from defining his own position. His response is to be found in the common multiple, the general conviction that the nation needs to be rebuilt after careful, serious investigation of 1970:

If we going to rebuild our Nation
We must first think about what break it down
We just can't put it back on the same old foundation
For to put it back on the same foundation
Will sooner or later mean another destruction
And we just can't afford another February Revolution
We also need mental reconstruction
Financial, educational reconstruction
For our Country is a ship,
We don't want it to sink

BLACK POWER AND THE CALYPSONIAN

The leaders of the February Revolution taught the Afro-Trinidadian that he belonged to the wretched of the earth, a universal class of dispossessed neocolonials in Asia, Africa and in the Americas, but the leadership fragmented over the precise ideological nature of this perception and the correct strategy to be employed in obtaining redress and in constructing the revolutionary society. From its inception, NJAC had been a plural organisation comprising groups and individuals of widely divergent philosophies and agenda. Ideological differences sharpened by the clash of personalities led to a parting of ways: the National Youth Council's members returned to the adult PNM nest; some individuals rallied around the banner of Pan-Africanism and others opted for one or other of the several variations of Marxism-Leninism. The cultural nationalists retained the name NJAC while their more 'scientific' brethren became the National Movement for True Independence and so on. The calypsonian instinctively avoided the neo- and proto-Marxist groupings and answered the call of the blood. This led to the development of a genre of Pan-Africanist calypsoes too numerous to be listed here. It must be said here, too, that while NJAC was synonymous with black consciousness, many singers operating out of a black consciousness perspective did not necessarily belong to or endorse NJAC.

NJAC had inherited from Granger the spirit which had energised Pegasus. This movement had honoured the calypsonians and had spearheaded efforts to have Brynner released from a debtors' prison in Jamaica where national mourning for the late Prime Minister Donald Sangster had wrecked his concert plans and embarrassed him financially.[50] Months after its formation in 1969, NJAC organised its first Black Traditions in Art featuring musician Andre Tanker. Black Traditions in Art ran during the 1970s and 1980s before merging with the annual awards ceremony, which has become more formal and pretty much a middle class affair. Applying its organisational skill and marketing expertise to the business of calypso performing, NJAC has sponsored shows like the Young Kings, the Calypso Queen, the Calypso Pioneers (for singers between the ages of four and eight) and the Calypso Jewels (for those above the age of eight). These have gone a long way towards rewarding and inspiring the artistes and enriching the calypso scene.

Along the way, however, NJAC has thwarted the calypsonian. Stalin, the first calypsonian to be honoured and featured (this was at the second Black Traditions in 1969), explains why his relationship with NJAC cooled in the 1970s:

> All along I always have a nice relationship, still have a nice relationship with NJAC, but then again, like Ah say, you know, we still remain two separate bodies. eg Once we start to 'Yes' and 'yes' it comes a domination, and the moment I keep eg saying 'Yes' and you keep going on this, none of we ent nothing. It have points eg where, like Ah say, although

I depend on singing kaiso to live, I have more important things in my lyrics, when I go on top there to deliver it, than making money. So although is not a money thing with NJAC, it have a time when you got eg to stop.[51]

Valentino, whose connection with NJAC dates from 1971, experienced a like disillusionment. During his years of association, he appeared at their many happenings and his lead-off song was invariably "Liberation" (1973):

Now just because I represent my people
Who really dint come out for war
Yuh know Ah get caught up in a struggle
I might have to go to jail or even die for
But then we all have to go one day or the other
We dint come here to live forever
Although they take away my people's liberties
And they make certain laws
But they could put me where they put them detainees
But I will die for a worthy cause

I go to jail
To balance the scale
That justice should prevail,
We are not for sale
I am willing to die for my brother man
In the fight for the Black man's liberation

Now I know that right now in this country
That my life ain't worth fifty cents
'cause some SLR bullet may find me
And put me clean out of existence
You have authority to use your trigger
And you are getting away with murder
But like yuh blind, Mr Policeman,
This is a family affair like if yuh didn't know
Check out yuh mind try and understand
Is your Black people yuh treating so

But if I see the Man
I'll do the best I can
To make him understand
For Afro-Indian
It could be Coast Guard, Regiment or policeman
I go die for Black people's liberation

Valentino insists that he is the I-narrator in his calypso, but a literal assessment of "Liberation" suggests that the I-narrator personified the top NJAC leadership which had survived imprisonment in 1970 and 1971-72 and had undergone unrelenting police harassment between 1972 and 1974. Filled with admiration for these men, Valentino fuses the "I" (himself) with "them detainees" creating the inspiringly complete figure, the prophet of politics and poetry.

Within the decade, however, the Valentino-NJAC relationship foundered. "The People's Calypsonian" was acquiring the restrictive connotation of the NJAC calypsonian as NJAC's people fell by the wayside, and even he expressed disenchantment at the stasis of the movement and the degeneration of purpose and revolutionary spirit among the masses and leaders alike:

Afro-Trinidadian, you are getting me mad
What is your mission in Trinidad
Did your sense of direction leave you completely
Or did vanity take thy vision from thee
Yet you have eyes but cannot see
So you just moving around awkwardly
Blindfolded by doctrines and philosophies
And a fear that is caused by a man's strategies

I can forward facts, my people, to prove
Since 1970 we made a move
Where we going
And since then on we still on one spot
My people, are we moving or not
Where we going, where we going
Is it a fact or you change your mind
What is the reason for lagging behind
Where we going, where we going
For your own welfare I ask you sincere
My people where do we go from here
("Where We going" 1977)

Stanza two contains references to "a flock of lost sheep", and to blind Israelites who cannot expect a Moses. This is very much at variance with the optimistic lines from "Third World":

I see Black shepherd leading some sheep
And as I meditate and mih thoughts run very deep
Leading the demonstrations with the shouts of 'Power!'
Was Geddes Granger

And he told me
'Ethiopia will rise again
And in the Third World, the African will reign.'

Chorus four of "Where We Going" poses the critical question:

I don't mind meeting you inside Woodford Square
But tell me without fear: From Woodford Square to where?

"Every Brother Is Not a Brother" (1978) records Valentino's disillusionment with the movement for which he was poet and prophet:

Through observation I notice
The Brotherhood is losing its interest
Is only when some folks need a favour
Their approach when rapping is 'Brother'
But I'm aware of these wolves in sheep's clothing
The way they come to you when they want something
But this brother say you could take a walk
And blow away with your brother talk

You clench your fist, you shout 'Power'
But I doh ever judge no book by the cover
Because when is time for us to come together
You will never ever see the flag-waver
The struggle get harder and harder
Every brother is not a brother

A few "just, righteous and faithful" individuals – not necessarily identified as NJAC leaders – escape his condemnation.

Impatient at the dissipation of revolutionary fervour among the people and disenchanted with the leadership, Valentino retreated to the peace of his chalice and the nirvana of Rastafarianism.

While Valentino's romanticism led to disenchantment and early desertion of the cause, others more practical, soldiered on. Maestro stressed the imperatives of Black Power with a broadening vision informed by a maturing perspective of the many elements involved. His first major song "Black Identity" (1973) presses for the reclamation of ancestral names as the first step in the quest for retrieval of psychological identity:

Presently almost everybody
Talking about Black Identity

But if you check out the majority
They only using these words falsely
Because the first thing that is a shame
African people with European name
That is the first step we have to take
To correct a pre-historic mistake

If you hear Seecharan, Ramklehawan, Lalchan, Balchan
Well bet yuh life that is an East Indian man
Jose, Juan, Gonzalez, Manuel, Sancho, Pablo
Yuh sure them fellas from Mexico
So why my name couldn't be Njaca
Lumumba, Makeba or Kenyatta
If we use these names then we sure to be
On the stairway to true Black Identity

A name encapsulates an identity, the calypso explains, and the continuing use of European names contributes to 'slave-time traditions' and to the disappearance of African greatness:

Now some people walk 'round in dashiki
Some preach Asante, some Swahili
While others think a bracelet of silver
Creates reflections of Africa
But when they dead go and look on they tombstone
Is Patterson, Atson, Jackson, Calhearn
That is counterfeit identity
These people must be lost in world history

Reclaiming one's name has immense practical significance if one has achieved greatness which can inspire others but which can easily be denied the race because of the achiever's European name. Loss of name and identity puts the Afro-Trinidadian at a disadvantage in a competitive society where others have retained their names, language and so their sense of identity and destiny.

A very interesting feature about this calypso is the fact that Maestro has spun into it elements of the impish humour which many calypsonians seem to share. This does not detract from the seriousness of the calypso and may in fact add the close personal touch which Trinidadians seem to relish. To cite two examples, Maestro advises Chalkdust to change his name to "Pygmybus", a dig at Chalkie's diminutive stature, not that Maestro was any taller, and he recommends that George Weekes rename himself "Wakamba" ("Workamba"), a thinly veiled criticism of Weekes tendency to call strikes (Maestro was an oil worker). These references and similar ones in other serious songs prevent the calypso from becoming too sermonising and make its lessons an enjoyable exercise.

Returning to the message of "Black Identity" one notes that although Maestro condemns the retention of European names, he himself never thought to change his, neither did he associate with the NJAC leaders who had changed theirs.[52] Perhaps it was that Maestro felt that he as an individual did not have an identity problem. Other calypsoes seem to bear this out because he moved beyond the issue of naming to encompass the practicality of creating black economic power.

"The Poor Man", the second in the tandem which landed him a berth in the 1973 Dimanche Gras finals (his first), addresses the question of dubious poverty as 'understood' by the spendthrift African worker and the ideologue who equates 'black' with 'poor'. In this song, Maestro exposes the sophistry of the cant which is used as a basis for race and class antagonisms:

> I tired I can't take no more
> With we the people who say we poor
> I really want so much to believe
> Who it is we really want to deceive
> All around me I see growing industry
> Creating many job opportunity
> So mucha money passing through we hand
> And still we saying things hard in the Land
>
> The poor man
> The prettiest Banlon jersey you could ever see
> Is on a poor man like me
> The poor man
> You might think he is a top-notch the way how he drinking Scotch
> With an expensive gold watch
> He say he poor
> He won't save a cent and pay house rent
> Tell him wear khaki he get violent
> With a terylene suit looking so refined
> This time he jockey shorts rag up like Parmassar[53] mind

Firsthand observation has provided Maestro with examples of Afro-Trinidadian prodigality. From his vantage point of working at the Texaco oil refinery, Pointe-à-Pierre, easily boasting the best-remunerated positions in Trinidad and Tobago, he was able to observe how well-paid oil workers squandered their salaries:

> I know fellas who work Texaco
> Forty years and resign with they pocket low

Some of them ent have a chick nor a child
But only work and get pay and spend money wild
And these are the men who complain 'bout price
When they business was nice they didn't take advice
Some of them house falling down flat on the ground
But they driving round town in new-brand Toyota Crown

The poor man
Is Clarks for fifty dollars, rings on all he fingers
And a Raeburn peepers
The poor man
Went to work with crimplene pants, ent missing a dance
Won't give restaurant food a chance
Is *whe whe, whappie*, wine women and song
And if he get a stroke and lie down
He wife take a next man, he bawling hard
And bold-face enough to cuss she and say she bad

The extravagance of the Afro-Trinidadian worker has created a class of enemy millionaires ("By the sweat of your brow their fortunes are made") who hold him in contempt ("All they give you is a almanac Christmas time"). All that remains is for the 'poor man' to deliver himself into enemy hands ("Let Barclays and Royal be your friend"): having squandered the present, the calypso suggests sarcastically, the 'poor man' might as well mortgage the future.

Clearly, Maestro is coming to grips with the complex race/class paradigm, although he does oversimplify its complexities somewhat. Free of Marxian or cultural nationalist blinkers, he sees the black worker as an individual responsible for his own actions. To Maestro, the 'poor man's' faults lie not in his stars but in himself.

Given this perceptive appraisal, one is surprised that the following year "To Sir with Love" presents the impoverishment of the Afro-Trinidadian as a function of Williams' attitude towards him. The calypso opens with a condemnation of Williams for favouring tribal enemies at the expense of his faithful supporters:

Mister, mister, is me yuh Black brother
Pressure, pressure, indeed inward hunger
The people who oppose you endlessly, they get plenty
But you ent care 'bout we
With the 28 percent I vote
Now yuh turn round and stroke a yoke on mih throat
90 percent of the daily buyers
Are of African descent

But when we buyers confront employers
We get ole talk and not employment
The only time they want the knotty-head fella
Is when I come over they counter to spend my dollar
No, Bossman, no, I ent talking race
Ah just tracing what taking place in the place

One notes that the chorus, and stanza two, detour into private sector employment (mal)practices which were a cause of complaint in 1970 and have ever remained so. Clearly these are not in Williams' domain, but many thought that he should insist upon equality of treatment for all, and especially the Afro-Trinidadian who was underrepresented in this sector.

Stanza three, on the other hand, reveals that Afro-Trinidadians were upset because Williams had done nothing towards assuring them access to bank loans. Compare Chalkdust's "Massa Day Must Done", and to cap that he has dropped on their unsuspecting heads a tax on luxury goods. This now makes it impossible for those who canvassed the country to ensure the PNM victory, to improve on their "broken down old car". While the faithful fuss and fight with their fickle transport, Williams, who as prime minister is naturally exempt from paying the luxury tax, is chauffeured around in a "big black Austin Princess", the official limousine.

Stanza four gets to the heart of the real quarrel with Williams:

Very slowly
Yuh killing we softly
So crude, no food
Outright ingratitude
We give you a fighting chance for 18 years
And all we get in return is blood, sweat and tears
Now everywhere your rivals have shares
And under your reign became millionaires

You watch as advantage is being taken
On your supporters in the land
We keep supporting and getting nothing
While millions going from hand to hand
Tired, retired old timers going from job to job
Young strong teenagers on corners hustling for bobs
I do not rap to trap anyone
Ah just singing a song on what really going on

If one were to interpret this last stanza-chorus in the language of the nineties, one would say that Maestro is aggrieved that Williams has levelled the Afro-Trinidadian players on the playing field, leaving the others standing tall.

"Portrait in Black" (1976), a little-known calypso, ignores Williams, probably as a lost cause, and addresses his constituency, continuing the tendency begun in "The Poor Man" to involve the people in the business of managing their future. "Portrait in Black" is a study in sombre tones of a colourful people who disport themselves, unaware of the dark shadows closing in on them:

> Papa, Mama, Black son, Black daughter
> Brother, sister, right on together
> Everybody else have something
> Only we still scrunting
> Is high time we learn we shouldn't throw stone
> The fault is we own
>
> Too mucha fete, too much Blackorama
> Too much emphasis on clothes
> And when we sweat we ent know a banker
> We giving we own self blows
> Look around and see what is happening
> Everybody selling, we alone buying
> This ain't no racial attack
> Ah come out to paint a portrait in black

Despite the exclusiveness of his target audience, Maestro denies 'preaching race' here as he does in "To Sir with Love". His calypsoes do not seek to despoil others nor do they advocate their overthrow; they simply call upon the Afro-Trinidadian to appraise his situation and act accordingly. This kind of appeal was a standard of the 1970s and one is quite amused by the exaggerated response to Cro Cro's "Rise African Rise" (1992) and "Allyuh Look for That" (1996). One can remark as well the absence of humour in this song. As the situation deteriorates, the singer's vision blackens and his normally impish humour disappears in the desperation of his appeal. "Portrait in Black" is quite a humourless song unlike "Black Identity" or "The Poor Man".

One is struck by the fact that on the eve of a general election, Maestro deems it advisable to warn about the threat to the last bastion of Afro-Trinidadian power:

> While we down here making argument
> Other people want to control Parliament

"Yuh Fooling" (1977), written in the wake of the 1976 PNM triumph at the polls, continues the urgent appeal for the Afro-Trinidadian to redeem himself by his own effort:

Mr Voter, Mr Voter
The government cyar take you off the shelf
If we doh make efforts to help weself
You must remember our behaviour making one race inferior
And all others superior
If yuh think we go just sit down and bawl
And the Government go get food for all
Yuh fooling, yuh fooling
Some sit down, they expecting miracle
You ent see all we getting is pool table
Yuh fooling, Brotherman, yuh fooling
Educate your children at any cost
Win back the land yuh fore-parents lost
Leave colour TV
For folks with plenty money
Is we alone wasting
Brotherman, I say we wasting

Clearly Maestro discerns that the election victory of the party favoured by the Afro-Trinidadian promised no ready amelioration of his lot, and so he prescribes a clear simple plan of action. Maestro further proposes that the Afro-Trinidadian begin immediately with the resources at hand. One can add that he was recommending his own private values because, although delinquent as a school child, he had worked diligently towards becoming a skilled craftsman, and he worked hard on his market garden. In these ways he embodied the peasant values of industry and thrift he was endorsing in song.[54]

There is a movement in the song away from the present and towards the future:

Mr Joker, Mr Worker
Well at least yuh children deserve a chance
It ent fair to leave young lives in balance
This you got to know little boys will grow
To be men of tomorrow
Simple interest you must show
But if you think the fact that your Party win
Go ease the rising cost of living
You fooling, Brotherman, you fooling
We shall overcome we keep saying
But while the grass growing the horse starving
Yuh fooling, Brotherman, yuh fooling
We ain't co-operating we much too proud
So we getting pressure from every crowd

If we doh take heed
We eat the bread the Devil knead
Is we alone wasting
I say, Brotherman, we fooling

Reviewing Maestro's calypso 1973–77 one's attention is drawn to two images. "Black Identity", begun in hope, had promised that if the Afro-Trinidadian adopted ancestral names he would place himself on "the stairway to true Black identity"; "Yuh Fooling", concluded in despair (Maestro died in a vehicular mishap in August 1977), comments grimly "with a heavy load/We going backward down the road". These two measure the distance lost by the Afro-Trinidadian, from being close to taking a positive step upwards into identity and power ("stairway" further suggests the difficulty of upward movement) to the easy slide back into slavery.

Unfortunately, Maestro's recording choices (partly explained in the posthumously published autobiographical "Brimstone" 1977) may have resulted in the underexposure of "Portrait in Black" and "Yuh Fooling", neither of which appear on the three albums and two singles published between 1976 and 1977. Maestro had opened the 1976 tent season with "Portrait in Black" but despite winning several encores he opted for the recorded "Fiery" and "Boom Bam", two popular fast songs which earned him a place in the finals. Having placed last there (this is cause for major shame in calypsodom), he reverted to the slow-fast formula and so he selected the unrecorded "Yuh Fooling" to partner the up-tempo "Savage" for his 1977 assault on the national title. "Portrait in Black" and "Yuh Fooling" thus remained 'tent calypsoes', a truly dismal fate in an oil-rich economy. One meagre consolation is that, given the ineffectualness of the political Calypso, their message may not have wrought much change in the attitude and behaviour of Afro-Trinidadian listeners.

While Maestro moves away from consideration of the psychological ("Black Identity") to those of the physical ("Yuh Fooling"), Chalkdust moves in the other direction, that is, from considering the physical welfare of his people ("Answer to Black Power") to reflecting on their psychical welfare ("They Ent African at All"). At first, in a statement of ideology reflecting that of Williams in 1962,[55] he had opposed the frenzied search for roots in distant continents and the formation of allegiances to 'Mothers' other than Mother Trinidad. "We Is We" (1972) stresses the cultural patterns evolved here over many generations, and is critical of those who seek ancestral frames of reference alien to this common experience:

The young people colour-crazy
Wearing fat-head and dashiki
They want to know more 'bout India
Some want to go back Africa

But I want them to start thinking
And stop this damn race-searching
For although we are of black pigment
Yet culturally we are different

Because they have no *roti* over in India
They don't know 'bout curry and *kuchela*
They do not sell oysters by the Croisée
Or dance our kind of Hosay
And Africans cannot beat steelband
Most of them never see a pan
Only you the Trinidadian
Know about *obeahman*
So that is right here you go find yuh identity

In another chorus he defines the Trinidadian in terms of shared cultural practices:

And when you go 'way from this Country
Well, once they know you are a Trini
They will say, 'Sing a kaiso for me
Beat a pan, make a pelau or *roti*'

The political representative of this cosmopolitanism may well be the roti-loving Afro-plaited Black Power advocate who draws Maestro's ironic comment in "Mr Trinidad" (1974).

In 1972, Chalkdust is several years away from declaring in song "I am a Trinidad-born African" ("They Ent African at All" 1984), but he nonetheless proclaims himself a Black Power advocate ("Who Next" 1972), and in an interview later that year, he confirms adherence to a Black Power more moderate than the NJAC version.[56] Chalkdust's Black Power accommodates the Roman Catholic Church which, in his opinion, is not hostile to the masses. Years later, even though a member of NJAC, then entrenched in its Africanist phase, he still considered himself a "Black Power Catholic" and defended his calypso singing in "When the Roll Is Called up Yonder" (1984). This may be taken to mean that the Afro-Caribbean experience has many complexities and that these must be considered in any new dispensation.

As time went by, however, Chalkdust's appreciation of the African past and present underwent significant change. Politically, it took the form of endorsement of NJAC. "Say Thanks to Daaga" (1979), which offers a belated tribute and apology to the NJAC leader at a time when Stalin and Valentino were distancing themselves, is a manifesto in song partly intended to herald NJAC's entry into conventional politics. Chalkdust tries to convince the electorate that the Afro-Trinidadian's modest post-

1970 successes (whether these be elevation to bank manager or ownership of a huckstering enterprise) are due to Daaga, as Granger renamed himself in the 1970s. Williams is strictly denied any credit in this version of history, something he should not have too many problems with, having himself a similarly selective view of the past. Culturally, Chalkdust tries to bolster a sagging collective consciousness. "Stay Up" (1973) posits new positives for the black family and for the race in general, while "Black Inventors" (*c.* 1979) records the many achievements of Africans of antiquity and of the modern era, many of the latter "lost in world history", as Maestro would say, because of their European names.

"They Ent African at All" is the crowning achievement of Chalkdust's new insight into the soul of black folks insofar as it intends to strengthen pride in the resilience and pervasiveness of the African spirit while accepting that many are ignorant of their glorious heritage. The calypso begins properly with the family:

I see Black women running from they race
They own Black children they can't face
They don't know their roots has a glorious bloom
Blessed be the fruit of their womb
They does be acting as though they shame of their history
They does be proud of other people's own
They does be glad to disclose their baby's ancestry
Putting their child up on a false throne . . . not their own
Or hear them boast to they friends and they neighbour
My baby's nose from he Spanish grandfather
Which is why the eyes so pretty and he have such thick eyebrow

He dimple from mih husband side who great grandmother was Irish
And watch how the eyes pretty and wide because my mother mixed with British
And watch at me, I am Carib and Portugee
But the baby black down to the eyeball
They ent see Africa at all
The baby black like a voodoo doll
They ent see Africa at all

Mothers are the living transmitters of culture but the Afro-Trinidadian mother grasps at the most tenuous connections with Europe and Asia while ignoring the obvious evidence of Africa. This refusal to accept the African presence in things familiar instances and inculcates mentacide.

"They Ent African at All" testifies to Chalkdust's development in other ways. In 1972 "We Is We" had criticised "colour-crazy" youths for their interest in ancestral homelands. In 1984, he demonstrates a familiarity with the African origin of things like musical instruments which shows that he had embarked on a search for roots in order to explain the present and to enlighten the future. Also, one notes that he eschews masking, the trademark of his political pieces, and he strives for musicality. "They Ent African at All" is more artistic and musical than the prosaic and workmanlike "Black Inventions" or "White Man's Plan" (1985) which are mere versifications of scholarly work.

In this context, it should be noted that the impact of NJAC thought on the calypso has been made through its publications and those sold by NJAC members. Duke's "Teach the Children" (1976) and Chalkdust's "Black Inventions" and "White Man's Plan" all show the influence of NJAC's *Black Truth Bulletin* series, the numerous publications of Josef Ben Jochanan, Chancellor Williams' *Destruction of Black Civilization* and other works; Valentino's image of the "bloody river" in "Stay Up Zimbabwe" (1979) derives from Ngubane's *Ushaba: The Hurtle to Blood River*. But Stalin's "Burn Dem" (written in 1979), the fiery statement which ignited the 1987 calypso stage, shows no influence of NJAC education programmes. "Burn Dem" is an expression of the visceral, an exultant prophecy of eternal damnation for the many enemies, past and present, of the African race. Among the villains are those Englishmen heroes of primary school texts: Drake, the swashbuckling pirate, Morgan, the brutal buccaneer and Raleigh, the intrepid explorer, rather than the far less glamorous Hawkinses, father William and son John, whose pioneering efforts resulted in the middle passage. The reason for this is that Drake, Morgan and Raleigh are featured in the *Cutteridge Readers* which were standard texts until the 1980s. One wonders if Stalin's reverting to those primers could be interpreted as the submergence of the NJAC education programmes or simply a means of reaching a larger public which had chosen not to indulge in educational reading beyond the mandatory sessions in school yards.

To conclude, a survey of the calypso of this period reveals that Black Power meant different things to different calypsonians; even those who sang consistently on the theme needed to change their focus as they came to terms with the many facets of this complex reality. NJAC could never command their loyalties permanently and as this organisation worked its way back to Pegasus, many calypsonians saw it principally as an enabling institution. The commitment to Africa is there still as one can see from the many calypsoes on South Africa, for example, but the urgency with which calypsonians analysed the situation of the Afro-Trinidadian at home has lessened considerably.

THE LEADERSHIP CONUNDRUM

The events of 1970 directed attention to the national political directorate as nothing had done until that time. Bomber had surprisingly raised the question of Williams' death ("Political Wonder" 1970) but he was more concerned with the manner of his passing and the permanent memory he would leave than with the question of succession. Pretender in "Black Power" (1971) could not envision a Williams-less nation and he put forward the question that would dominate the 1970s: "Who you go put if you move 'way he?" It was unthinkable that Afro-Trinidadian calypsonians voicing the majoritarian views of an urban Afro-Trinidadian constituency would endorse a leader outside of the PNM. Valentino was a voice in the wilderness praising Robinson and Granger ("No Revolution" 1971; "Third World" 1972). In 1971 Blakie reached the finals of the Calypso King Competition singing "Message to Granger" and "Don't Damn the Bridge You Cross", the second a sharp reproach to Robinson. When he performed at the PNM Rally, Expression '71, the crowd was unsure of how to react to the mention of Granger, whose crusading mission was ideologically in tune with their own aspirations; and whom, more importantly, they did not regard as a candidate for Whitehall. The mention of Robinson, however, brought boos[57] which left no doubt that they were hostile to their heir-presumptive become presumptuous. During the early 1970s the calypsonian would reproach and upbraid Williams but he could never imagine life without him. *Tapia* explained the Williams mystique in terms of his mastery of speech games: "The nation at heart still loves and reveres him, because he is still the best guntalker, picong-slinger, opposition crusher of all."[58]

This is what Cypher had termed his 'tone of voice' ("Last Elections" 1967).

Chalkdust pounded away at him, however, hinting that he was dictatorial, vindictive and corrupt ("Two Sides of the Shilling" 1971), insane ("Somebody Mad" 1973) and egotistical in his choice of incompetent sycophants whose mediocrity would ensure his genius greater luminosity ("Bring Him In" 1973). But it seems that Chalkdust was wary of the man who had struck down so many – not all necessarily good men and true – but people of some standing in party and community. This is the message of "Goat Mouth Doc" (1972) which lists the victims of the man whose capacity for breaking people seems to have an almost supernatural force. The fear that that same force could be easily unleashed against a mere school teacher surfaces in "Let the Jackass Sing" (1974) which is supposedly Williams' answer to "Somebody Mad".[59] The line "If I pounce on him *crapaud* smoke he pipe" is evidence that Chalkdust is aware that beneath Williams' imperturbable exterior there lurks a frightening will and power which prove fatal to those who oppose him.

Some opinion had it, however, that Chalkdust was in no danger and that the immunity he enjoyed was proof of a special relationship: to wit, Chalkdust performed regularly at the PNM Buy Local Competition and he claimed friendship with high-ranking PNMites who leaked to him the confidential discussions on his 'application' and so inspired "Bring Him In". Also, if Chalkdust is to be believed, he and Williams often conversed "as one academic to another" and it is probably during one of these sessions of intellectual camaraderie that Williams confided, "Chalkie, no one captures my spirit like you."[60] Whatever the truth, Chalkdust catalogues the errors and failings of the PNM with an untiring zeal although with a singular lack of bitterness, and it can be noted that he never advocated a successor to Williams save for the lone endorsement of Daaga ("Say Thanks to Daaga" 1979).

What he did do was to discredit Williams' political enemies and rivals within the PNM. "Two Sides of the Shilling" (1971) satirises the dissensions which culminated in the resignation of heir-apparent A.N.R. Robinson. Chalkdust assumed the role of investigative reporter bringing to a bemused public the 'truth' behind the surprising moves, but his technique of having either protagonist expose the other's faults, results in serious damage to the credibility of both. The end result of their condemnation was a draw, the calypso equivalent of the 1971 no vote campaign which left Williams in total control of the apparatus of state. "Williams" delivers the Parthian shot:

> You waiting on election time
> But Ah going to open up your behind
> I will pound you like a nail
> And even if I fail
> Chokolingo go take your tail

Patrick Chokolingo, the fearless editor of the *Bomb* and dean of Trinidad's yellow press, presented himself as hostile to Williams but he showed himself even more hostile to Williams' enemies. In other words, there is little to choose from between Chalkdust and Chokolingo in terms of their handling of the Williams factor in national politics.

Chalkdust's "Ah Fraid Karl" (1972) effectively destroyed any ambitions Hudson-Phillips may have had of becoming prime minister. It impresses horrifying images on the collective psyche which was prepared for them. One observer sums up the fears that Hudson-Phillips aroused in the minds of many:

> Karl has become one of the most dangerous persons in Trinidad and Tobago today, the Beria of the PNM. He most fully shares Williams' Afro-Saxon contempt for the people sufficiently to use the law and power of Parliament to create monsters and abortions like the Public Order Bill, the Defence Amendment Act, the Firearms Act, the Immigration Act. He is to law what Hitler's experimental doctors were to medicine.[61]

All the fears about right-wing dictatorship were crystallised in "Ah Fraid Karl":

> Like mih friends them doh like me
> They want them to jail Chalkie
> The kinds of thing they want me to sing 'bout
> This Government go jail my snout

They want me to sing and say
Move the Labasse from Beetham Highway
And have the whole stench instil
Right inside the centre of Whitehall

But not me
Ah fraid Karl, Ah fraid Karl
Ah fraid he jail me like he jail Rex La Salle
They want me to sing when Bhadase died
Kamal Mohammed sat down and cried
But Ah fraid, Ah fraid
They say a young Minister was found
In a hotel with a call-girl in town
But I ent singing 'bout that
Ah fraid the Sedition Act

"Ah Fraid Karl" is essentially the typical Chalkdust catalogue of PNM misdemeanours presented as a list of unspeakable secrets guarded over by the sinister Karl Hudson-Phillips. The most interesting feature is the development of the Karl image over the four choruses.

At first he is the dreaded attorney general whose vindictive personality abuses the majesty of the law for private vengeance. One story making the rounds is that while Hudson-Phillips was negotiating with the mutineers at Teteron, he had been humiliated by the soldiery.[62] Another story puts said humiliation at an earlier date when LaSalle commanded at the main gate and Hudson-Phillips arrogantly violated standard military procedure of halting to be identified. (Chalkdust also includes this 'incident' in "Clear Your Name" 1974).

The second image of Hudson-Phillips is that of the "new black baron of Maraval" which makes "Karl" to be a feudatory ruling his fief with the authority and rigor of a mediaeval seigneur. The power of life and death may or may not be suggested here but certainly the divinely sanctioned baron is of a more dangerous order than the constitutional law officer. Thirdly, Chalkdust claims that Karl "eating like curry barb wire and dhal". Dishes made with dhal, the Indian delicacy, enjoy universal popularity in Trinidad but Chalkdust suggests that beneath his suave urbanity Hudson-Phillips is an excruciatingly painful imposition on the nation's innards, a kind of delicious death, as it were. Finally, Hudson-Phillips is described as the "Better Village dress designer from Maraval". When the logic of the calypso should have dictated the most telling, the ultimate image of terror, one is greeted with the curiously deflatory image. Hudson-Phillips did enjoy some distinction as a dress designer[63] but in Trinidad and Tobago such is considered beneath the dignity of the macho man. Chalkdust may well be suggesting that under the steely exterior Hudson-Phillips may be less than he seems.

The foregoing is a prelude to Williams' resignation in September 1973 and his return in December 1973. Political analysts are divided on the issue.[64] Some opine that the whole affair was a mean trick designed to flush out the opposition within the party into the open where they could be shot down; others are convinced that Williams was serious but changed his mind for reasons undisclosed. He did admit that the astronomical increase in oil prices won by OPEC against the background of the Israeli-Arab war made of the local scene a different ball game. "If the Sheik could play, who is me," he jested in conscious parody of the Cypher classic "If the Priest Could Play" (1967). While this was good enough for his followers, it does not reveal how far his decision to return was a combination of other factors including the obstinacy of the Women's League, the prayers and pleas of the Inter Religious Organisation, his own aversion to relinquishing power and his fear of Karl Hudson-Phillips.

In any event, the calypsonian laughed the whole incident to scorn. To him there was no doubt that the affair was a charade and he seemed as little impressed as was the general public. After the crisis of 1970, Williams had threatened to lay himself down "like a bridge over troubled waters" in a calypso parody of the Simon-Garfunkel pop song. The 1962 Independence King, Brynner, showing no resentment that Williams' reluctance to spend a paltry $4,000 had left him languishing in a debtors' prison in Jamaica,[65] begged the prime minister to reconsider that action ("Heaven Help Us All"). In 1974, however, most loyal PNM calypsonians were ominously silent. Cypher's "Don't Go Doctor" is a detached satire on the reactions of the people at the Convention Centre, Chaguaramas, when the last act was played out.

On the other hand, the leaders of the Regal Calypso Tent, perhaps competing for mastery, covered the story in detail. Duke ventures the mild reproach of "Trinihard":

Doc, Ah beg you in '66
And Ah warn you in '72
You paid me no mind
Like you didn't believe is true
Now things have gone out of proportion
And man gone up in the hill
Like is hungry people you want to kill

Is beef gone up
Dasheen bush gone up
Chicken leg gone up
Now the Country reach starvation
That's the time you looking to split
What a captain that you deserting a sinking ship

Composer and Superior, who both made it to the national finals, contrive interview situations to have the Williams persona reveal what the calypsonians thought were his motivations. Composer's "Williams" was brutally frank:

They playing with me
Yuh think it easy
Like a *mapepire*
Ah come back indefinitely
Ah pretend to resign they had to beg and coax
But now Ah ready to give them rope
And Ah go show all of them how politics works
Is different strokes for different folks

He boasted that

My pretence to resign was a seta smoke
So Ah could ketch them under mih yoke
So Ah could get rida the rest of them blokes
("Different Strokes")

Composer refers to a story, carried in the *Bomb*, to the effect that Williams had been warned that his deputy, A.N.R. Robinson, was contemplating treachery. According to this story, Williams pretended to leave the country but timed his return perfectly to surprise Robinson leafing through his papers. Obvious nonsense, this story was nevertheless widely believed and the fact that Robinson later sued the tabloid successfully[66] was generally ignored. One wonders why a serious calypsonian such as Composer dredged up such a rumour but he was perhaps trying to satirise the intellectual prime minister by having him 'creolise' himself along the lines defined by popular imagination.

The Superior creation was an atypical "Williams" who admits to error. "I have made mistakes, maybe quite a few," he confesses. "They must remember I'm only human too." When quizzed about the reason for using "such a creole tact", that is, a low dodge favoured by commoners but a ploy inconsistent with the education and position of a prime minister, "Williams" replied:

I have many problems within my Party
Don't talk about problems in the whole Country
I have to settle this bacchanal
Party groups don't want Kamal
And, as you know, the Country 'fraid Karl
("Why I Left, Why I Returned" 1974)

While Duke reproached and Composer and Superior scoffed, Chalkdust was ambivalent. One of his two calypsoes, "The Silent Song" purports to be the acceptance speech Hudson-Phillips would have delivered were it not for Williams' return. Instead, the convention heard a diatribe of wrongs that the aspiring leader had had to endure:

> Mr Chairman, you know why my nomination causing so much confusion
> You see, I hold secrets like sand for this man
> Look, he even put them soldier boys against me
> Many times I cried to save the Party
> Now he too busy for me

Hudson-Phillips had fronted for Williams in 1970 and the popular belief that Williams was not party to the Public Order Bill defies reason. In 1973, Hudson-Phillips received his comeuppance for overrating his role in the Williams realpolitik.

"Clear Your Name", which suggests that Chalkdust may have taken Williams' resignation seriously, requests that the prime minister scotch the many rumours about his private and public lives. The direct address, unusual in Chalkdust's message to Williams, hints at genuine concern for the man and the politician:

> In the near future our young children will study you in class
> They would want to know if you were a giant or simply a jackass
> I do hope, Doctor, they would find you a man of integrity
> But to hold a place in our history, Doc answer me truthfully

Chalkdust reminds Williams that great men have been undone by the revelation of unsavoury secrets about their past and so, with an extravagant deference, the very satire of which is undermined by its exaggeration, he pleads:

> I bid you, kind Sir, as a great intellectual
> Let your life be an open book to be seen and read by all

The final chorus is a typical Chalkdust mixture:

> Why did you not attend your mother's funeral?
> Did you return just to spite Karl?
> Where did Kamal get money to build Mohammedville?
> Did you leave your son, Allistair, one dollar in your will?

One cannot help thinking that while Chalkdust was in love with *picong* for its own sake and for the purpose of unsettling its target, the calypso betrays a deep personal interest in Williams: the strong elements of *picong* obscure but do not obliterate his fascination for his inscrutable hero.

Chalkdust qualified for the final with this extremely popular calypso but a member of the judging panel warned him of a conspiracy to disqualify it on Dimanche Gras night.[67] The informer judge did not say if the conspiracy originated in the CDC, the logical cradle for that kind of sabotage, but Chalkdust, eager as always to win a calypso crown, replaced it with "Deaf People" which did not impress as perhaps he thought it might.

Over at the Revue, Maestro was endearing himself to patrons and establishing for himself a niche in posterity with "Mr Trinidadian", one of two calypsoes played every August in tribute to this meteor of song who perished on 31 August 1977. "Mr Trinidadian" which contains all the stylistic and thematic elements of Maestro's political calypso, examines the paralysis which afflicts the citizenry when the matter of national leadership is tabled. It begins with that address to the people which had begun to replace the address to Williams:

> Mr Trinidad, tell me what scene you on
> Do you just like political confusion
> You criticising the way you live
> Yet you cyar produce an alternative
> You say you against the power structure
> You ent like the Opposition either
> But take care you jump out the hot water
> And end up in the centre of the fire
>
> 'cause you refuse to vote in election
> But then you ent want revolution
> You strongly against Communism
> You walk out on colonialism
> You say Eric Williams have to go
> But who to replace him you ent know
> So to make a long story short from in front
> Trinidadians really ent know what they want

Despite the wry humour at the end of each chorus, this is a bleak calypso, but the despair and anger which pervade it are so controlled and presented so reasonably that the Trinidadian does not feel the lash of reproach; so far from being offended was he that he could chorus "*Kaiso!*" at the end of each telling statement. Thus "Mr Trinidadian" suffered the fate of the ineffectual good calypso: fans acknowledge and acclaim its sensitivity but do not feel impelled to any action if even compelled to re-evaluate their attitudes. As an examination of stasis "Mr Trinidadian" remains just that because the calypsonian, preoccupied with analysis, offers no answer to the burning question: "Who we go put?" It must be said in defence of Maestro, however, that he probably did not recommend any successor to Williams for the reason that the public really did not want any.

Maestro was encored on a nightly basis to the point that he had to beg fans to let him rest. He had fallen victim to the snowball effect of his amazing composing talent in that the additional stanzas he had written to give the audience something new to stimulate their craving for good calypso led to their increased demands. In this way, a four-stanza calypso took root as a seven-stanza classic. Normally, all of this would have been lost or, if recorded by radio stations, consigned to bins in libraries, as seems to be the case with recordings of live calypso performances. Fortunately, Harold "Rocky" McCollin, author of Nap Hepburn's pro-PNM political pieces, but a patriot blessed with a purist's love for *kaiso*, taped a live performance at the Princes building, home base of the Revue Tent, and he later recorded seven stanzas and choruses complete with audience noises. This he marketed on a 12-inch disc, one of music technology's latest developments.

A second Maestro calypso (preserved on the same disc) signals that some Afro-Trinidadians considered Williams a traitor to his race. The title of the calypso itself is a cruel parody of the E.R. Brathwaite novel, *To Sir with Love*, which deals with the unstinting efforts of an immigrant West Indian teacher to educate and socialise tough adolescents in a depressed area of London. Maestro is saying that unlike the protagonist of that novel, the founder of the University of Woodford Square had callously betrayed his students who have always demonstrated great love for him. The calypso begins with an admission of hunger:

Mister, mister, is me yuh Black brother
Pressure, pressure, indeed inward hunger

"Inward Hunger" is the title of Williams' political autobiography which traces how a youth born with an inward hunger for greatness realises his destiny in the land of his birth. Maestro observes that the price at which Williams assuages his symbolic hunger is a growing physical pain in his supporters/students from whom he has long been alienated. Maestro expresses the frustration and bitterness of the cheated supporter as the violence of betrayal muted and translated into bitter humour, the inalienable prerogative of the powerless:

We take we broken-down old car and we campaign for you
You say who could buy car could pay purchase tax too
And while you talking this foolishness
You driving round in a big black Austin Princess

Williams, observes Dr Winston Mahabir, is not the first Afro-Saxon; he is just the greatest. After estranging himself from his Caribbean Commission employers he reluctantly surrendered the Buick and the posh Chancellor Hill house he had used in their employ.[68] In a remarkably short time the Buick had been replaced by "a big black Austin Princess" thanks to the drivers of the "broken-down old cars" who canvassed the entire country.

While Williams' shenanigan did not cost him his calypsonian friends – their silence may have indicated embarrassment rather than alienation – it contributed to the diminution of his image in the Calypso. Earlier that year 1973, he had committed the faux pas of having Shorty's "The Art of Love Making" banned from the televised broadcast of the Dimanche Gras show and had set in process the moves which resulted in Shorty's being charged with indecency.[69] In 1974 Shorty's "PM Sex Probe" countercharged that Williams' problem with his graphically didactic calypso was that "it hurt him where he most lacking". Melody's lovemaking Doctor of the late 1950s was now a spent force. Prince's "Come as You Are Party" (1974) and Squibby's "Streakers" (1975) further strip Williams of his customary jacket and tie and present him as the Trinidadian emperor in a new costume of nudity. Relator's "Deaf Panmen" (1974) reduces him to a deaf steelband leader and the surviving PNM aspirants – if that they are – to a cacophony of unhearing panmen who ultimately find fulfilment in 'turdity'.[70]

What is most important in the development of the political calypso is that the combination of inaccessibility, noncaring and now gamesmanship may have convinced the calypsonian that he needed to address the public directly, leaving Williams out of the new dispensation. This acquired enough momentum to become a style of political discourse and from it derives that irreverence for all politicians and for local politics itself. So this would remain until the mid 1980s.

NUFF IN THE CALYPSO

Despite David Millette's excellent monograph,[71] little is known about the National Union of Freedom Fighters (NUFF) save that they espoused violent overthrow of the status quo and that their leaders included secondary school graduates and the scions of the educated black middle class. Bracketed by police and press fusillades amid the inhospitable hills, NUFF's leaders lacked opportunity to log their organisation's history, and their untimely deaths denied them occasion to refute or confirm the deeds attributed to them by a befriending romantic imagination and hostile propaganda.

The calypsoes on NUFF need to be examined because they illustrate the spectrum effect against the background of the larger political crisis. Duke's "Trinihard", concerned with reproaching Williams, makes casual and passing reference to NUFF.

His offhand " . . . man gone up in the hills" implies that NUFF had nothing to do with the burning questions of national leadership and the state of the nation. Maestro, on the other hand, focuses on the guerrilleros as necessary actors in the leadership dilemma and he comments bitterly on society's ambivalence in what was a life-or-death struggle for those who tried to fight their way out of the political quagmire:

> My friend, if you don't want democracy
> The opposite is guerrilla activity
> If you don't want democratic improvement
> Well then you have to want a revolutionist government
> And yet when Guy Harewood went in the hills
> With Jennifer Jones you let them get kill
> All you doing is grinning and skylarking
> You come like the ass in the lion skin
> ("Mr Trinidadian" 1974)

Three years later, he blames the alienation of the youths on Williams' failure to keep faith with their parents. "Them who put him up they/Children going astray" is his caustic comment ("Dread Man" 1977).

Cypher turns the matter of the guerrilla movement into morbid comedy ("The Guerrilla" 1974) but others see in the fate of the guerrilleros a possible end for the protest calypsonian. Valentino's "Victim of Society" (1974), echoing the slogan "Liberty or the cemetery", seeks to achieve that kind of psychological identification with the hunted fighters that he had attempted with NJAC's leaders in "Liberation" and perhaps for the same reasons:

> I am a victim of society here in Trinidad
> People pressurising me, people treating me so bad
> Some of them want me to starve and dead
> Like they doh want me to earn a bread
> But these bastards, my friend, they could kill me dead
> But they just cannot tief this head
>
> Because I am what I man am supposed to be
> As free as a bird a fish in the sea
> My worth, my wealth, is not material
> And my values are real spiritual
> And my motto reads very clearly
> Liberty or the cemetery

If the guerrilleros are fighting for their manhood, then he, doing the same on a calypso stage, is one with them.

Stalin's "Nothing Ent Strange" (1975) explores the possibility of the singer/narrator being eliminated by the system:

Leh we say that when you read your marning newspaper
The headlines say that they hold Stalin for guerrilla
Ah know plenty people may want to shout
But, Brotherman, what is there to shout about
I am living an a yes-man society
Where all the no-men become the enemy
And if you decide to hold tight to your 'no'
The system have so much different ways of getting you to go

Nothing, nothing, nothing ent strange
In the life of a man out for change
Once you doh want people talk for you
And won't do the things that they want you to
Your life ent safe whether night or day
Because any number could play
Nothing, nothing, nothing ent strange
In the life of a man out for change

The system have a vicious way of operating
It's like a vulture when it about to attack its victim
Once you say they wrong and feeling you right
It can attack you like a thief in the night
One day you are a hero, next day a traitor
One day you're wealthy, next day a pauper
And just play you smart and too intelligent
You could die in Mayaro in some freak accident[72]

Operating out of the internationalist perspective from which he sometimes explains the local situation, he wraps himself in the mantle of the timeless hero-martyr of the universal black struggle:

Now I know all 'bout this system and its working
But for a better life for my people I keep fighting
I cannot be destroyed and I'll tell you why
Tell me how many times can a man die
Ah die on the shores of Africa
The Klu Klux Klan lynch me in Alabama
Ah die in '37 striking with Uriah
So charging me for guerrilla you playing with fire

Most surprising of the NUFF calypsoes was Kitchener's "Jerico" (1974) which presents the guerrillero as the mythic hero of a counterculture opposed to the one which Kitchener normally endorses. He fuses the exploits of the NUFF hero and those of Jerico, a noted bandit who once haunted the Lopinot area of East Trinidad. The Jerico persona is invested with the qualities of a cult hero who avenges rather than mourns the death of his associates:

> They kill mih little sister
> By the name of young Beverly
> They plan and they ambush her
> They destroy her mercilessly
> Jerico ent sleeping
> Ah say Ah taking night to make day
> Any time you miss a policeman
> Jerry snatch him away

Kitchener could not bring himself to condemn or even criticise Williams for the deaths of the NUFF youths, and so the narrator of Jericho blames the agents of the shootings rather than those under whose orders they were acting:

> Ah hear they looking in town
> Leaving houses in such a state
> They ransacking all around
> Searching doctors and magistrates
> Them people so wicked
> They even searching the PNM
> But if they search Jerico
> Ah sorry for them

It is unlikely that the police would have dared search the homes of prominent citizens on their own initiative. The Jerico persona chooses to accept the 'wickedness' of the police because this is the limit of freedom allowed by his creator.

Commentor's "Thousands More" (1977) treats the death of Beverly Jones as the inspiration for the continuance of the struggle:

> (i) We will always remember how brave Beverly
> Took up arms against the puppet army
> Their bullets pierced her body
> But she destroyed their lies
> That said that we
> Are too cowardly
> So let them think they conquer we
> It have a thousand more just like she

(ii) Thousands more to come
The struggle ent done
Thousands more, thousands more
Fighters for liberation

Duke, in uncharacteristic criticism of the ruling regime, prophesies that the final solution to the NUFF problem will be accountable here or in the hereafter. "Someone Will Have to Pay" (1980) honours the slain militants:

Guy Harewood, wherever your soul may be
We'll always think of you respectfully
Guerrilla or freedom fighter
Your name we'll always remember
For your death I say
Someone will have to pay

Valentino's "De Roaring Seventies" (1986) presents the NUFF soldiers as victims of a system which needed to hypercorrect itself after promoting independence of thought:

A lot of men lived fast and died very young
In this most historic decade
When Randy B used to come to town
With his Flying Squad on parade
The emphasis was on education
And when them young folks get too bright
The same institutions
Turn and put out they light

It is the supreme irony of Williams' life and career that he never resolved the dilemma of public education. He marketed academics as a saving commodity but he never wanted those whose education he encouraged and facilitated to object to his philosophy and/or oppose his policy. Professor Gordon Lewis, the esteemed social scientist, sums it up perfectly when he observes that Williams could not suffer fools gladly but he could not suffer equals gladly either.[73]

TUESDAY 18 MARCH 1975

When police stopped the mass march by workers and farmers into Port of Spain an era came to an end. All the circumstances surrounding that 'Bloody Tuesday' are critical to the history of organised labour yet they have been virtually ignored in the Calypso. Probable cause for this omission may be that the calypsonians saw in the affair the hand of known communists and they reacted predictably. One is also inclined to the belief that urbancentric singers saw it as something happening 'down south' and therefore of little interest to them or to their audiences.

Be that as it may, Maestro, a pipe fitter at Texaco Inc., Pointe-à-Pierre, who had seemed unsympathetic to George Weekes' style of unionism (compare "Black Identity") produced "Some Came Running" (1976), an important documentary on Bloody Tuesday. His style employed the techniques of the newsreel: action and interviews are presented in a lively four-minute sequence complete with background voices, vocals and music. A brief explanatory sketch sets the stage:

> The United Labour Force ask for permission
> To hold a demonstration
> A religious procession
> Some came a-praying, some came saying
> The Police Commissioner had strong objection
> He say that demonstration
> Is too much provocation
> Some came a-funning, some came running

The chanting voices which fill the spaces between the segments create the impression that the choral activity is meant to be a constant commentary on the state of mind of the assembling marchers. Then the cameras pick up one of the marchers describing the main activity:

> We take on we own account
> And assemble at Paramount
> I couldn't believe it come to pass
> You know they throw tear gas in the grass

The full-voiced chorus is heard as the marchers chant to the rhythmic shuffle of feet:

> We marching
> We come out for bread
> We marching
> We ent 'fraid to dead
> If you see the crowd
> How they cheering loud
> But the big protest
> Turn to one *commesse*

Stanza three is the camera eye at work roving through the streets of San Fernando:

San Fernando was just like on Carnival Day
Then Panday told Tony May
'There'll be trouble along the way'
Some came a-hailing, some came wailing
Some journalists get licks – at least so they say
They join in the *la couree*
And get caught up in the fray
Some came a-swinging, some came singing
A lady with big belly
Say how the Police kick she
But then up comes another guy
And tell Chokolingo she lie:

The story ends in the surrender of runaway ICFTU leader, Raffique Shah, whom, for some reason, Maestro considers the leader of the protest action, although he was obviously a junior partner in the alliance in terms of his experience of industrial action and of the importance of his union. Maestro had targeted him in "Mr Trinidadian" and it may be that the singer never forgave the former soldier for his leading role in the mutiny. At any rate, he seems amused at his running feat:

When talk about runner, Comrade Shah is a runner
He pass two truck and a car
And a 350 Yamaha
Some came a-screeching, some came preaching
He run from Royal Road to Marabella
When he reach Guaracara
He jump over the river

Shah eluded a police manhunt for a few days before surrendering, cravenly, according to the calypso.

This style of protesting proving to be ineffectual, the unionists formed the United Labour Front (ULF) – the political party many suspected them of planning all along. They captured only those traditional opposition seats, and Shah, Maestro's singularly uncharismatic leader, became the Leader of the Opposition. He elected to sit opposite to Williams who studiously ignored him.[74] Maestro's suspicions of ex-Lieutenant Raffique Shah seemed well founded.

THE NEW PORTRAIT OF TRINIDAD

The turbulence of the early 1970s necessitated the repainting of the portrait of Trinidad. Stalin's "New Portrait of Trinidad" (1972) erases the features of the Sniper/Penman original by meticulously painting in the new reality over the old cherished fantasies:

Now, people clap their hands, people felt so glad
When Sniper paint the portrait of Trinidad
But look around today, your eyes may get sore
What Sniper say we have, it down here no more
When a man say we not what we used to be
Doh care how much it hurt but we must agree
From '65 to now we are no more great
Our Country has vastly deteriorate

No more are our students ranked among the best
No more are our scholars passing every test
But dropping out of school every day in this island
No money to continue their education
Our Pitch Lake is the finest the world has seen
Yet roads here are the worst in the Caribbean
Don't hang down yuh head, Brother, don't feel sad
I'm only painting a new portrait of Trinidad

In this manner, the clinical demolition of the images proceeds but always accompanied by the apologetic disclaimer which several protest singers use either formulistically and/or as a means of distancing themselves from unpredictable crowd response.

In concluding, however, Stalin restates a commitment to the original dream:

By Sniper's portrait of this Country
Let your kids know how Trinbago used to be
It is their Land too so you let them know
That you want here to come back just like long ago
And if you 'fraid to say then tell them I say
In this task let no obstacle stand in their way
The struggle may be long, yes, it may be hard
But let's restore the old portrait of Trinidad

Despite Stalin's pious resolve, one must point out that the ideal he seeks to recreate never existed outside the imagination or the patriotic calypso.

After 1970, people were made to confront ugly realities and the enormity of their presence as the calypsonians took a long close look at hitherto untouchable social institutions including the judiciary (Smiley's "The Law for One Is the Law for All" 1974), the Law Society (Chalkdust's "Who Next?" 1972), the church (Stalin's "Now Is the Time" 1974 and "The Ole Talk" 1974) and other invisible groups (Smiley's "The Chinee Man" 1974). Slow sounds of plaint filled the air. Smiley employed a slow, traditional minor for which he has been dubbed "The King of the minor", a title bestowed, one suspects, to give him some respectability and reputation in calypsodom. Composer makes appropriate use of the minor in "Workers' Lament" (1971) which incorporates the dirge like chorus of voices to fix attention on the wage slave who subsists in the closed circle of existence of need-toil-survival-toil which is his lot, his patrimony and his legacy.

Valentino presents his protest in a mixture of rebellion and blues enhanced by the use of the 'blue note' of African American music. Rohlehr describes the effect of the blues in this way: "The feeling of being cycles old in both suffering and survival, constitutes the peculiar tonality of the Blues; which can convey a sense of ageless woe and wandering gloom, counterpointed by a strength of affirmation even to the point of dry or tragic laughter."[75]

In Valentino, the poet-and-prophet role exists uneasily with an incipient misanthropy. This ambivalence is present in the songs he performed in 1972. "Third World" has him prophesying the resurgence of Ethiopia and the pre-eminence of the African in the new world order but "Life Is a Stage" has him in despair over the play acting indulged in by the Trinidadian. Again in 1973 the ambivalence manifests itself dramatically. "Mad Mad World" has Valentino trying to reason out the actions of people and coming to the conclusion that he is the only sane person in a totally mad world. "Liberation", the other side of the 45rpm on which "Mad Mad World" appears, is a statement of commitment to struggle. It is as if the record features the two opposite sides of the calypsonian.

Despite the fragmented consciousness Valentino retains clear insights into his society. "Barking Dogs" (1973), a statement which reverses the model nation image of 1965, likens the advance of Trinidad's men of the 1970s ("beggars", "preachers", "thieves", and "junkies") to the nursery rhyme procession which is signalled by the barking of the dogs. The unceasing clamour of Valentino's 'dogs' is a ruckus that heralds the arrival in succession of the varied types, all costumed in the rags and tags of necessity or the velvet gowns of status and masque. The calypso opens with an unambiguous identification of singer with song and with an undisguised declaration of intent:

> Now, this word is me and I am this word
> So let my voice be heard
> Fix your hearing-aid and hear what I say
> Wipe your glasses and see things my way
> The sound that you hear is an angry one
> And I'm sure if you see things clear you'll see that all happiness is gone
> And then the dogs, the dogs are barking too long
> It is a sign, a sign that something is wrong

Here is a statement that the 1970s have wrought a new dispensation. No longer can Williams still dissenting voices with the words, "When I talk no damn dog bark." That Jupiter like authority has been blown away in the trade winds of the 1970s.

Other singers testify to the new dispensation, some pointing to the danger of the erosions of individual freedoms. Kitchener's "No Freedom" (1973) objects to the internment of Weekes, Granger and others in 1971. Kitchener had had no difficulty in coming to terms with their detention in 1970 because it seemed clear that they had been inciting action which did lead to violence and political instability. In 1971, however, they could hardly be accused of such agitation. To Kitchener, Williams' actions invited comparison with the mock democracies of Rhodesia, Alabama and South Africa, but Kitchener, although disturbed, does not rebel, and he limits himself to a mild up-tempo protest which carefully avoids direct mention of Williams:

> Well, long time in the 50s
> You could hear them say
> 'This colonial ruling is a blight
> And must go away'
> But since we independent
> What they do for we
> Introduce the IRA
> And the State of Emergency
>
> Oh what a country
> Oh what an awful sin
> How come they
> People just so without a hearing
> Where is your freedom
> Somebody put a hand
> Oh God, the vengeance of Moko
> Will surely fall on this Land

Kitchener bewails the situation created by the passing of the Sedition Act ("If you only squawk/They snatch you up like a chicken hawk"). This fear had been voiced by others including Sparrow ("Sedition" 1973) and it seemed to be very much in Chalkdust's thoughts ("Who Next?" 1972). This last calypso was as much a criticism of the Law Society, the injured party, as of the politicians who could manipulate any institution to suppress dissent. After the tension over Shorty's being arrested in 1973 for indecency fizzled out, it was said that the real target was Chalkdust,[76] a view endorsed by Shorty himself ("The PM's Sex Probe" 1974).

Perhaps the most significant development after 1970 is that calypsonians stopped viewing madness as a condition which could evoke superior laughter from the (seeming) sane; it became a metaphor for the state of the nation itself. It is a long list of calypsoes which extends into 1996: Valentino's "Mad Cure" (1972) and "Mad Mad World"(1973); Chalkdust's "Somebody Mad", "Port of Spain Gone Insane" (1986) and "Chalkdust Gone Mad" (1986); Maestro's "Tomorrow" (1976); Terror's "Madness" (1978); Sparrow's "Yuh Mad" (1980) and "Capitalism Gone Mad" (1983) and David Rudder's "Madness" (1987) and "Tales from a Strange Land" (1996).

"DIS PLACE NICE"

In the early 1970s, Trinidad was shaken by inflation imported from the metropole. Sparrow's "Ah Digging Horrors" (1975) describes the uncertainty in the quality of life produced by this imported scourge and by the breakdown in essential services:

> Cost of living strangling everybody
> No food in mih house to mind mih family
> It's a free-for-all here I am afraid
> I believe we need psychiatric aid
> Unscrupulous employers and unscrupulous workers
> Couldn't care less
> This place in a mess
>
> Ah digging horrors
> Ah digging the blues
> Anytime Ah choose to peruse the daily news
> Ah digging horrors because
> All Ah reading 'bout is guerrillas
> More laws and wars

Other stanzas detail the headline horrors which Sparrow piles against the ruins of his model nation until he exclaims in frustration, "Ah cyar take no more!" The idea of madness dominant ("I believe we need psychiatric aid") and of madness let loose ("Nurses aiding mad people in escaping") corresponds to a preoccupation with madness which has been mentioned before.

What is most interesting about this calypso is the year of its release. By 1975 Trinidad and Tobago had begun to wallow in the revenues from the oil boom and it can safely be suggested that the year marked the end of the era of mass public protest. Despite this, however, the quality of life had not improved; in point of fact, the influx of money only served to highlight the ugly in society. Nineteen seventy-five was also the year of Valentino's "Dis Place Nice".

This immortal calypso deplores the giddying effect of the oil boom on the unthinking, and it attacks them for their foolish belief that the little wealth percolating down to them is evidence that "Trinidad is nice, Trinidad is a paradise." This myth had been shattered in 1970 but with the influx of petroleum prosperity seemed to have regained its ancient currency. Valentino begins his calypso with subtle mockery:

> Yuh talk 'bout a place where the people have carefree living
> It is such a place of fun-loving, spreeing and feteing
> It's the Land where people
> Doh care if Ash Wednesday fall on Good Friday
> Man, they love to struggle
> In this happy go-lucky way
> Is Blackorama, feteorama
> And just now is masorama
>
> So the foreigner come for Carnival
> And he telling heself after he had a ball
> Trinidad is nice, Trinidad is a paradise
> Mr Foreigner, in La Trinitee
> The people have a Carnival mentality
> Trinidad is nice, Trinidad is a paradise
> They are not serious, very few conscious
> So I cannot agree with my own chorus
> Trinidad is nice, Trinidad is a paradise
> But Ah hear mih Brother talking revolution day
> Fire on the way

Valentino's people, lost in their masquerade, do not have the wit to note that the collusion of Williams and the multinationals spells the return of monarchy (". . . mih chorus singing 'God Save the King'") and of slavery ("Like the slave master want to bring back the whip"). As the song develops so too does the singer's despair until the mockery of the first stanza becomes a cry of anguish:

> They don't know their worth like they have no sense of value
> They don't know their rights even that they cannot argue
> You mean three-quarters of a million people
> Cannot get up and do something 'bout the struggle

One wonders, too, how far Valentino believes in imminent or even distant revolution as he keeps promising at the end of each chorus. The last hope of revolution for the 1970s had faded, the fire extinguished by gushing oil wells, the fighters brought to earth by Randolph Burrough's Flying Squad. Revolution had died except in the minds and hearts of a diminishing number of believers, and as a message in the Calypso it would grow less urgent although protest would remain.

Henceforth, the dream of a man-made millennium would give way to the fears that the society would be consumed in a holocaust sent by a vengeful God annoyed beyond measure by his people's adoration of Mammon.

"Dis Place Nice" was acclaimed as one of Valentino's greatest hits and when he celebrated his first concert series, "Poet and Prophet", it was the finale performance. But 1975, the year of this concert series, was also Valentino's worst year in terms of competition success.[77] After the successful run of "Poet and Prophet", Valentino fell dinosaur-like to the changing times and the fickle tides of popularity. Nothing else demonstrates this than that after 1975 a new cycle had begun.

"I, Eric Eustace Williams"
1976–1981

The petroleum prosperity of the early 1970s impacted on the political Calypso in ways that were separate yet related as are the diverse societal influences on the Calypso. First, it diminished the grounds for protest by making available to the general public lucre which financed a spiralling consumerism based on long-coveted American models. Secondly, the chief target of protest disappeared into the role of corporation sole from which fastness Williams disbursed revenues with an eye to his political image. This remote-control manipulation encouraged the growth of a cumbersome bureaucracy and unwieldy state sector, administered ineptly by officials profiting from a lack of supervision in an age when accountability was waived with the flourish that money was no problem. In consequence, the citizenry, conscious of squandermania yet unwilling to essay the dialectics of embattled neosocialist states such as Jamaica and Guyana, accepted fatalistically that Williams the provider was their destiny and consoled themselves in the *carpe diem* philosophy of escapism through the twin anodynes of drugs and fete. Invitations to 'breakdown' parties blossomed from lampposts and walls hiding the harsher graffiti of earlier years, and everywhere the fete seemed the order of the day.

It was natural that the calypsonian should seek to profit from the fast expanding entertainment industry and, fortuitously, he had arrived at a new 'partyish' sound called 'soca'. Like so much else in the Calypso, the origins of soca are still being debated but one feels that the role of Lord Shorty deserves to be recognised and honoured in its creation.

Born into the largely Indo-Trinidadian community of Lengua, South Trinidad, Shorty first used his familiarity with the melodies of India for subtle mockery ("East Indian Singers" 1966; "Indrani" 1973) but *The Love Man* featured the *dolak* on most selections as Shorty sought rhythmic variation. Accused of trying to "Indianise" the music, he took the expression played by the *dolak* and put it on the drum set and thus arrived at the sound first heard on *Endless Vibrations*. 'Sokah', so spelt to reflect East Indian influences,[1] was the creation for which Shorty takes credit. For reasons unknown he does not mention his role in the creation of soca, which is calypso mixed with soul, and yet he has written far more soca than sokah, and is better remembered for his soca songs than for his sokah, except perhaps for the controversial "Om Shanti". In point of fact what first caught the ears of the youths was "Endless Vibrations" (1975) which is clearly an admixture of calypso and soul. Even Shorty's definition songs "Sweet Music" and "Soca: The Soul of Calypso" incorporate strong elements of soul music. It was soca rather than sokah that attracted Maestro, Merchant, Rose and Kitchener, who all lacked Shorty's training in East Indian music.

While this book cannot pause to discuss the development of sokah or soca, it must mention that what is now accepted as soca is the result of continuous experimentation by many calypsonians and musicians; the necessary consequence of their diverse backgrounds and the survivalist need to co-opt passing musical fancies on the international pop scene. For a short time during the late 1970s, controversy raged as traditionalists fulminated against the levity of soca lyrics and the adulteration of the 'true' calypso beat. The dancing public, however, declared in favour of soca, and radio disc jockeys tuned in to the new sound. The better-known radio DJs were much in demand at parties, and they used the airwaves to advertise themselves and the songs they favoured. It has been said that a system of payola flourished at the radio stations.[2]

The dominance of 'soca spasms' was interpreted by some as a sign that protest as a major communicative element in the Calypso was in decline, yet this was demonstrably untrue. For one thing, the inequitable distribution of wealth plus the excesses of the ruling regime remained as permanent grounds for dissent, while at the same time political *picong* and protest, developed to a high degree in the earlier period, underwent greater sophistication in the use of language and music as singers adapted their tone and tune to express their own developing aesthetic and vision as well as to meet the demands of disaffected or dancing audiences.

New scope was added by the puritanical reaction against prevailing hedonist tendencies, and one significant measure of this Trinidad-style Reformation was the appropriation of the language, symbolism, ideology and music that are associated with Rastafarianism. The adherence of Trinidadians and Tobagonians to the Jamaican culture elicited from the local public a mixture of derision and approbation which was reflected in the calypso.[3] Several singers caricatured the local cultists as the personifications of negativity, hypocrisy and mindless imitation, but others recognised in Rastafarianism and its musical dimension 'roots rock reggae', an ideological base for opposition to and escape from a moribund society lost in a frantic *danse macabre*. The political expression of this belief was a reaffirmation of Pan-African nationalism although, paradoxically, several espousing the universal kinship of blacks failed to see themselves as keepers for their Caribbean brothers.

On a less admirable level, Rastafarianism provided the facile justification for the endorsement of the 'weed' subculture with which several calypsonians had become involved earlier in the decade.

In connection with the religious aspect of Rastafarianism, one may remark upon the introduction of a dimension of morality as applied to politics. It has been observed that in the 1940s the sudden invasion of American servicemen, lavishly furnished with American dollars, had reinforced the naturally anarchic tendencies of the society.[4] Atilla, dismayed by the disruptive American influence, confessed ruefully:

> . . . they helped us financially
> But they played hell with our morality
> ("No Nationality" *c.* 1946)

In like manner, the latter-day infusions of wealth generated a gross and pervasive materialism. There developed in the Calypso a natural reaction to this, based to some extent on the involuntary austerity of the Rasta, the puritanism of the Revivalist Christian sects as well as the lingering memory of village simplicity, and the dubious influence of a peculiar Trinidadian morality which simultaneously condemns and condones sexual irresponsibility and public thievery.

Another feature of this period was the admission that censorship existed and that the state was using its agencies to deny the voices of alternative traditions and viewpoints exposure in conventional nontent media. Protest singers have always complained of this practice, and in 1975 proof was furnished in the published list of banned calypsoes.[5] The published list seems to have been a shortened version of the longer rolls of the proscribed because it covered the sexual, the obscene, the libellous but never mentioned the political songs which seemed never to get air time. Efforts to sanitise and to muzzle the Calypso were mocked by major controversies centring on songs which, being innocent of subversive, obscene, drug endorsing or violence glorifying sentiment easily escaped official sanction.

Those calypsonians who thought themselves victims of censorship sought to create alternatives to the tent, to the Calypso Monarch Competition and to those fora which were perceived as agents or instruments of repression. Accordingly, they set up the People's Kaiso Court to promote meaningful calypso which, they claimed, was being lost in the tent and in the party. Equally important was the need to change the operational procedure of the traditional tent with the primary aim of giving greater exposure to singers and of eliminating the abuse and exploitation of young singers by management and by influential veterans. The court also hoped to exorcise the ghost of seasonality and to return the Calypso to its prestigious place in the hearts of Trinidadians.[6] The failure of the court and the transformation of its successor, the Kingdom of the Wizards, into a conventional tent meant that the singers of protest had perforce to operate in an orthodox setting and therefore to devise suitable strategies for survival.

The rapid development of mass communication technology which made stereo players and cassette players cheaper, plus the availability of money which made them accessible, was a mixed blessing because while the protest singer could now invest in his own recording label, so too could the singers of 'soca spasms'. Faced with such threats to his survival, the protest singer added dimensions of poetry and music to his song thus adding to the political Calypso of this period emphasis on the style and music of the age.

GENERAL ELECTION 1976

One consequence of the imbroglio of the earlier period was the almost universal deprecation of politics and of politicians, as evidenced in the pre-election calypso commentary. Blakie denounced the PNM as the source of all the evils in the system:

> Too long we leave them there too long
> Now they going wrong, they weak but playing strong
> I won't be deceitful as to say
> They did some good things but in their own way
> But with the good things they did for us we still loss
> You will be shocked when you check back how much it cost
>
> I say any government, they could be past excellent
> They may be the best thing in the world
> They could come from a convent and always sharing present
> And giving paupers their weight in gold
> But any time you leave them in power
> For twenty years, sweet bound to turn sour
> I ent taking sides, I ent talking tough
> Ah just saying twenty years is enough
> ("Twenty Years Too Long" 1976)

Despite his unsteady record for commentary and the harsh laugh which undermines the seriousness of his message, Blakie's calypso was so popular that the administration of the state owned CDC tent where he was singing tried to censor it in the hope of precluding Williams' well-known anger. These 'censors' only brought upon themselves Blakie's righteous anger as he defended himself and his freedom as an artiste:

If I was against the Government I would be a guerrilla in the hills. But I am a calypsonian, and until freedom of speech is restricted I feel that a calypsonian, like any other artiste, should be allowed to deal with any topic within the bounds of the law, without victimisation or discrimination.[7]

Ironically, as any citizen with a constitutional problem of this nature, he threatened to approach Williams for justice.

At the Regal, Chalkdust used his prestige to institutionalise satire at the electoral circus. Reviving calypso drama, he scripted a skit of impersonations of the leaders of the major political parties, each presenting his manifesto and campaign strategy in one stanza sung to a traditional *sans humanité* melody. Chalkdust thus presented the election as a theatre of personalities, and he communicated images of politics and of politicians that the public had already approved. For instance, Vernon Jamadar, leader of the Social Democratic Labour Party (SDLP), a splinter from the DLP, is given what might be considered an Afro-centred perspective of Indo-Trinidadian politicking:

Allyuh Indians come and vote for me
I don't have a racial party
But if my party flop
The negroes will then be on top
If I win, every Indian man
Will get access of sugar land
We go plant cane everywhere
Including Woodford Square

A.N.R. Robinson, leader of the Democratic Action Congress (DAC), is given short shrift in what is oddly reminiscent of the cruel satire of presentation of Cypher's "Last Election" of 1967 and anticipatory of Sparrow's "We Like It So" of 1982:

I am the only man in North and South
Who knows the PNM inside out
When I was a top boy in the Party
For the dirty work, they selected me
But when DAC comes into power
I bringing down all the girls from Miramar
To have them on show up at Piarco
For when the Cuban troops come and go

Chalkdust was particularly severe on Lloyd Best and James Millette, whom he derides as "them two Moko Jumbie", thus likening the two UWI academics to the towering but ineffectual figures of an earlier carnival; Millette, too, had been the coeditor of the publication *Moko*. On the other hand, Williams is presented as the omnivorous "Jaws" from the movie of the same name:

I accustom fighting wars
That is why they call me 'Jaws'
I eating from kingfish to salmon
In this general election

Even more hard hitting was the postelection skit with its quota of whining apologies, self-pitying excuses for failure and querulous recriminations. Chalkdust reproduces the Bestian idiolect, the amalgam of academic terminology, sporting phrases and local slang, as the Tapia leader explains his surprise defeat in his home town. The punch line is a vicious dig at Best's white wife, he being perceived as black conscious:

So the next time when we voting
Yuh boy will be friending
With a nice, sweet black-hen chicken

"Millette" bemoans the switch from his eastern base to Fyzabad where he had spent part of his childhood:

The ULF boys made it hard
Move me from town and send me Fyzabad
And the people down dey tell me
I am a doctor, like he
And two man-rat cyar represent we

Other election commentary reveals instructive attitudes to the PNM and to the new phase. Kitchener drowns his doubts of "No Freedom" in "PNM March" which captures the secure feeling of PNM invincibility in the use of the *kalinda* mode with its elements of ritualised boasting:

We go beat them this election
It is not as easy as they say
It go take a stronger opposition
To beat the PNM party today
The Doctor say
PNM
He here to stay
PNM
So take it cool

PNM
We here to rule
PNM

Chalkdust's prize winning "Shango Vision" visualises the degradation to which the PNM and satellites would have been reduced in the wake of a ULF victory. The scatological "Big boys would be toileting/If Raffique Shah did win" summarises succinctly the images of enfeeblement, helplessness and madness which he uses to describe the possible future of the PNM in defeat. The reverse is the violence, vengeance and brutality that the erstwhile victims would visit on the fallen.

It is hard to dispel the suspicion that Chalkdust welcomed the PNM victory, and two incidents, both played out at Skinner Park, San Fernando, surface from deep memory to confirm this. In August 1975, to conclude the pre-election skit, "Williams" (played by Chalkdust, naturally?) embraced "Daaga" (played by Valentino, naturally). One can only surmise that by this unexpected gesture, Chalkdust was trying to bring about a united Afro-Trinidadian front through the wish fulfilment of sympathetic magic. In 1977 when he sang "Shango Vision", NJAC members, who had stood all evening stolidly listening on, suddenly capered for joy and their jubilation seemed incomprehensible outside the suspicion that NJAC was delighted over the PNM victory.

No such triumph informs Maestro's "Yuh Fooling" for he regards the PNM victory with deepest gloom reckoning that it could have no positive influence on the floundering Afro-Trinidadian. Forgetting that he had alerted the Afro-Trinidadian to the dangers of losing political power ("Portrait in Black"), he pours cold water over the victory celebrations:

If you think the fact that your Party win
Could ease the rising cost of living
Yuh fooling, Brotherman, yuh fooling
and again:
If you think the fact that you cast one vote
The rich would sink and the poor would float
Yuh fooling, Brotherman, yuh fooling

The calypso also dismisses Williams' strategy of declaring his assets in an attempt to demonstrate his integrity:

I hear threats and frets to declare assets
You could bet no one declare nothing yet
Open allyuh eye
And stop taking *mamaguy*[8]

Similarly, the much mooted Integrity Commission becomes a colossal exercise in deception:

> We getting six for nine that's how it looks
> And we sending crooks out to capture crooks
> With a heavy load
> We going backward down the road

The image of the "heavy load" and the idea of "going backward down the road" suggest a return to the well-remembered portage roles of slavery.

"POLITICAL MALFUNCTION"

The election did not change the government and therefore did not change the attitude of the protest calypsonian. Maestro's "Tomorrow" (1976) employs two pithy phrases, "Hypocrites in politics" and "Political malfunction", to categorise the men and their operations, and the truth of his perception is borne out by subsequent developments especially related to the flourishing of corruption.

The political hierarchs, accused many times of peculation, profiteering from inside information and the like, flaunted wealth which was popularly thought to be ill-gotten. A hue and cry was raised and an embarrassed government ordered then Attorney General Selwyn Richardson to spearhead an anticorruption drive. To no one's surprise, this exercise was sabotaged and it ended not in the bang of judges' gavels in sentencing wrongdoers but in the attorney general's whimper as he conceded defeat.

Explainer, unimpressed by Richardson's efforts which had yielded a few minor culprits, explains to the minister the mechanics of implementing an anticorruption drive:

> You wasting too much of precious time, Mr Selwyn
> As far as I see is fool you fooling
> Lock up all the big boys at the top
> Who have this Country corrupt
> That's the only way to end corruption
> Is to jail all them big rat in the nation
> ("Selwyn" 1977)

This advice is driven home again:

> If you want your job to be set
> What you have to do is to start off with Cabinet

and again:

If the PM tief
Is to lock up he backside too

It is only fair to report that Richardson did wish to "start off with Cabinet". Selwyn Ryan, the prominent political scientist who was partial to Williams and the PNM, writes of an incident in which Richardson explained away his refusal to take up Williams' dinner invitation. According to Ryan's account, the attorney general explained to the prime minister that he could not sit to table with John O'Halloran who was his prime suspect. Interestingly, the rest of Ryan's statement includes quotes from O'Halloran's son and mistress to the effect that this worthy chose to be 'fall guy' for an unnamed person who could only have been Williams himself.[9] Also, while he was attorney general, Karl Hudson-Phillips had written to Williams about imprudent behavior on the part of two ministers, one of whom was Errol Mahibir, widely thought to be an intimate of Williams.[10] Williams made a most remarkable declaration at the 1980 PNM Convention. According to veteran reporter, Raoul Pantin, who covered the convention, Williams addressed charges of corruption in the matter of the 1979 DC-9 scandal by quoting the British hero of the Indian wars, General Robert Clive, who when brought before a Royal Commission to answer charges of corruption, declared, "Gentlemen, I stand amazed at my own moderation." Williams also cited American General Lafayette, who when accused by his neighbours of living off ill-gotten gains, said simply, "If I had stolen less the people would have thought I was a fool."[11]

It is up to us to make of this what we will.

Returning to the calypso under consideration, we note that an air of condescension pervades Explainer's address as he reduces the cabinet minister to a callow youth unversed in the wicked ways of the world. This lack of respect is mirrored in other calypso references to cabinet ministers and technocrats, and one may conclude that in the mind of calypsonians the only man of substance worthy of respect or respectful reproach was Williams.

While Explainer limits himself to guardedly general accusations ("If the PM tief"), Chalkdust, characteristically, lays specific charges, although carefully not against the cabinet:

Give the police involved in Garib case
One hundred dollars apiece, we got money to waste
We have bread, go and buy a boat for ten million
Don't care if the damn boat cyar run

In the Police Canteen money missing
Right in the Red House them clerks tiefing

Goods coming through the Port disappearing
Leh we give the Cement boss twenty thousand a month
Because we have bread so we can't let him scrunt
And the Cement Board get 'way
'cause the Police them say,
'Leave them. Money ent no problem'
("Money Ent No Problem" 1978)

A typical Chalkdust statement, the incidents so briefly alluded to are the celebrated murder of a well-known Couva restauranteur and the acquittal of those accused thereof; the purchase of a river boat to ply the Trinidad-Tobago route (some say, to ferry Tobago voters away from A.N.R. Robinson's Democratic Action Congress); traditional charges of theft from the police canteen; theft at the Red House and at the docks; the inordinately high salaries paid to officials at the cement plant. The answer to all these is a parody of Williams' welcoming words to returning Olympic sprint gold medallist, Hasely Crawford, " . . . money is not a problem."[12]

Secure in their privileged positions, politicians and technocrats spent lavishly. By this time, of course, the leading government politicians had long been assimilated into the business class and their entrenchment solidified class differences which were accentuated and perpetuated by the inequitable distribution of wealth. This occasioned a renewed focus on the condition of the poor.

Maestro attacks the smug and sleek dispensers of the theories of divinely appointed poverty in "Not Call Them Name" (1977), a soca-reggae song which employs the language, structure and music of reggae as the most fitting medium and context for the protest of the Rastafarian persona, the archetypal protest figure of the late 1970s. Maestro's narrator, the 'rude bwoy'-turned-Rasta of the Tosh-Marley song "Get up, Stand Up", rejects the definition of a poor but humble sufferer narcotised and rendered innocuous by biblical prophecy:

'Peace on Earth, goodwill to men'
They say they want to be my friend
Pulpits of hypocrisy, culprits of democracy
And want me to be and isn't true
And verily I say unto you

Not call them name
But them ent got no shame
Not call them name
But them ent got no shame, no shame

Saying, 'Listen, listen well
A hungry man nah go in Hell'

While I right on honestly
Them dey fighting currency
And want me to be in poverty
That goodness and mercy will follow me

Taking cue and pattern from the reggae-rockers singers, Maestro adds a coda to his soca-reggae:

Some people live in bungalow
While other people crying in the ghetto

Some keep on having
While some again keep on starving

'Live peacefully,' they telling me
How could a man be peaceful and hungry
No shame

While Maestro condemns the church ("Pulpits of hypocrisy") for neutralising the anger of the poor at their degraded condition, Relator's "Colour Television" (1976) chastises state officials for widening the gulf between classes by introducing colour television which effectively puts blinkers on those who most need to see clearly:

Some people might say that Relator strange
And I'm not in full agreement with change
But I say that changes must be discreet
To the level of the average man in the street
But colour TV shaping as a farce
To suit the middle and upper class
Believe it or not we back to square one
With this question of class and colour question

"Colour Television" has that looseness of approach in that it elevates the private want for a luxury item into a major governmental shortcoming. Mass demand for colour sets overheats the economy in that it promotes conspicuous consumption and accelerates the export of foreign exchange, but to blame the demand for colour sets on a government already fairly burdened with its own multiple sins is overelaboration. Stanza four continues the attack:

The present position ent looking good
Concerning this aspect of nationhood
I think our concept and policy

Is irrelevant to any Third World country
'cause the advent of colour television
Doesn't develop any young nation
A move like that in truth and in fact
Is one step forward and two steps back

What probably disturbed the calypsonian was the state's abdication of its responsibility because this is what acquiescing to the influx of Western televiewing really amounts to. This is a legitimate grievance, not the fact that many citizens now feel wealthy enough to be able to acquire colour sets.

Stalin's "Piece of the Action" (1976) voices the poor man's demands for his share of the national cake:

Oil drilling, money making
Mr Divider, here is a warning
Mih blood in this Country
Mih sweat in this Country
So when you sharing yuh oil-bread
Ah say remember me
This ent no Black Power talk
This ent no revolution
Ah say Mr Divider, listen to me
This is man talking to man

Once a oil dollar making here
Black Stalin want a share
Piece of the action, Ah tell you, piece of the action
Ah say, remember that I have family too
Who want food and clothes just like you
Piece of the action, Ah say, piece of the action
If the Country scrunting, that ent nothing
But once oil-bread sharing
Run something

Born and raised in poverty in and around Mucurapo Street, the home to derelicts, prostitutes and vagrants in San Fernando, Stalin was well acquainted with neglect and want,[13] and his continued education in that street of iniquity and misery gave him the perspective on the issue of indigence in the midst of affluence and free spending. Also, Stalin seems to be haunted by the fate of Butler, the forgotten legend, who had been arrested on Labour Day 1966 for squatting at Fyzabad, the cradle of the 1937 labour riots which had brought him fame and following. Butler had been ostracised by the rich and powerful OWTU for nearly

20 years before Weekes secured for him much needed benefits including a house,[14] thus making comfortable the last days of the man whose militancy had made possible a class of well-remunerated oil workers and unionists. Williams, who had once acknowledged Butler's contribution to nationalism,[15] did not extend to him the pension offer made to the widow of Atilla,[16] and for several years 'The Father of Labour' existed in a state of penury, abandoned by the OWTU and by the nationalist movement which grew out of his agitation. His arrest on Labour Day 1966 is the ultimate in tragedy and farce. This is the terrible fate that Stalin envisages for others and this is the fate that he rejects for himself:

> Call this a warning, say Ah threatening
> Say Ah quarrelling but send me something
> Ah tired asking, Ah tired crying
> Mr Divider, like the switch ent working
> So much old people I see
> Begging under them streets in town
> And them was people who sacrifice
> For this Country when they was young
>
> Not so
> Fix up my little piece of dough
> Before oil finish and the Yankees go
> Piece of the action, we want piece of the action
> You can't trap me like you trap Butler
> Work me when Ah young then leave me to suffer
> Piece of the action, we want piece of the action
> Stalin old and begging
> Is one thing he ent seeing
> Is six feet first I going
> So run something

HOUSES VERSUS HORSES

The crisis in housing catalysed anti-PNMism as nothing else could with the possible exception of corruption. During the years of plenty, land prices soared and the real estate business boomed, but the homeless, augmented by the unchecked numbers of illegal immigrants, posed serious problems for national planners. The government could not keep up with the demand for housing, and its constitutional inability to admit failure to resolve a problem, the magnitude of which it really could not imagine, made it seem unwilling to handle the crisis. The policy of demolishing squatters' shacks created resentment even among those who had their own homes, and calypsonians, regardless of their material circumstances, joined the ranks of those speaking out for the homeless.

Sparrow, reputedly a millionaire, who had triumphed over a childhood of poverty and a brief stint in a reform institution, took up the cudgels on behalf of the homeless but perhaps more in support of Hudson-Phillips who, seeking a comeback after the 1973 debacle, had involved himself in the National Land Tenants and Ratepayers' Association (NLTRA):

> Talking 'bout the housing situation
> Terrible nightmare for everyone
> Endless trouble
> For young couples
> Pure frustration
> Created by this artificial inflation
> The cost of land so high it could drive
> You mad
> If you think you could get through and don't connive
> You mad
> If you think on your salary you'll survive
> You mad
> When things improve if you think you'll be alive
> You mad
> Things that are duty-free
> Costing you more money
> Consumer protection is so bad
> It could drive you mad

His final stanza endorses the NLTRA plan for housing, a plan which goes far beyond the PNM's policy of building "a few two-room flat" and organising a housing lottery to distribute them:

> National Land Tenants Association
> Want government to acquire land
> From those who possess
> Idle lands in excess
> Subsidise the poor
> Sell to poor people who couldn't buy otherwise
>
> So you think faith in the system has been revived
> You mad
> You say proposals like that can't take a nose-dive
> You mad
> Yes, you think at last the people have won the strife

You mad
Opposition to that Bill would never be rife
You mad
But political wars
Have citizens outdoors
To compromise for them is too hard
So we going mad

Unlike Sparrow, for whom the housing situation was a political quarrel picked up to demonstrate solidarity with the very wealthy land owner Karl Hudson-Phillips, Merchant knew the squatter's plight at first hand. The graduate of a reform institution, Merchant suffered the personal trauma of having his shack demolished at a time when he thought to enter upon a new and, for him, unfamiliar phase of respectability. "Who Squatting?" (1980) articulates his rage and helplessness at being frustrated by agents of the law in his attempt to live within the law:

John tired begging for lodging
So on a empty spot nearby he start building
Just a simple one-room, the man in nobody way
Is a wife and four children he have to support each day
The man only want to survive
And keep his family alive
But you come and break down he house and tell him he squatting
It's a crude and uncivilised thing you doing

Mr Government
You looking for argument
Who squatting
I or Joe Sabga
Who squatting
I or Abdullah
Who squatting
I or Kirpalani
Answer Ah want you to tell me

"Who Squatting?" reverses the accepted idea of squatting by stripping the phoney mask of legitimacy from the parvenu hustlers in the business community who are squatters in the sense that they have no permanent stake in the land beyond a leech-like fastening on the nation's lifeblood.

Merchant creates a distance between himself and his experience by interposing a fictional "John", but the story is that he broke down while performing the song for the visiting CDC judges as he attempted to impress them with his best material. Stanza four dismisses "John" and leaves Merchant face to face with his pain:

Ah vex each time Ah remember the John John fire
Folks had to live in the Community Centre
It's ridiculous the way how you treat poor people
And if they talk too hard you say they causing trouble
We know yuh want we to go
But, Jeezanages, not so
To come and break down mih house four o' clock in the morning
Even Ayatollah wouldn't do such a thing

Ayatollah Ruollah Khomeini was perceived as the ultimate in dread. The former client of the USA and their approved replacement for a former protégé, the Shah of Iran, Khoemeini had inflamed American anger by holding hostage their diplomats in Iran, and so American media set about discrediting this fundamentalist leader. As usually happens, Trinidad and Tobago swallowed the American propaganda. Merchant, having experienced the reality of Williams' callousness, thinks that Williams' antisquatting policy is beyond any evil Khoemeini is reportedly guilty of.

Explainer ("Dread" 1979) clearly agrees. He empathises with the Rastas who were then being subjected to much hostility and abuse while "dread, dread baldhead" did as they pleased. In a special stanza created for his Dimanche Gras presentation he condemns the antisquatter policy:

Poor people can't buy houses in this Country
So they decide to squat on State lands
Eric send the Police and the Army
With weapons to break the houses down
So much families homeless
About the kids they couldn't care regardless
Oh what a barbaric act
Tell me, which Rasta ever do that

The housing crisis forms part of the context which one must understand in order to appreciate the widespread dissatisfaction with Williams' economic and fiscal policies. A bone of contention was his loans portfolio. Stalin's "Piece of the Action" challenges the loans Williams seemed ready to disburse:

News went around
We getting oil-dough
All yuh friends coming
They want borrow
Some armed with blue-print for big industry
Some want the loan for airline industry

But Ah warning Mr Divider, listen, me ent making joke
Ah say this Good Samaritan business with me this time wouldn't work

Give your people decent homes
Before you start posting 'way loans
Piece of the action, we want piece of the action
Remember the first needy is me
Then you could fix up everybody
Piece of the action, we want piece of the action
15 million spending to keep LIAT flying
And TTAS diving
So run something

The "friends" referred to are the leaders of the Caricom states whom Williams baled out with timely loans, which John Public believed were really gifts because they would never be repaid. It is interesting to observe how the Trinidadian nativist returns to type in blaming his Caricom "brother" for cheating him out of his "piece of the action". Explainer's "Caribbean Intigration [sic] " had celebrated the brotherhood of all Afro-Caribbeans with the choric line "Once yuh Black you is my Brotherman", yet his "Charity Begins at Home" taxes Williams with "posting 'way loan/And forgetting charity begins at home." One suspects that the proper use to which some of the lendees put their loans may have rankled in Trinidadian breasts. Chalkdust, for example, describes how his national pride suffered when:

. . . them Barbadian say Tom Adams
Outsmart Eric Williams
And get a whole airport scotch-free
And when I go Barbados and find
Them airport nicer than mine
And Barbadians laughing at me
("National Pride" 1982)

Stalin did modify the position taken in "Piece of the Action" in his "Plan Your Future" (1980) in which he acknowledges Trinidad's debt to the islands whose citizens had slaved in the embryonic oil industry but he still cautions a more prudent loan portfolio lest one lend money to ingrates:

'cause if you lending Manley money
And he bad-talking yuh in front yuh eye
Then wha' Manley go do yuh
When the oil wells run dry

Michael Manley, then Prime Minister of Jamaica, had made unfavourable comments about Trinidad's lack of planning,[17] comments bitterly resented by Trinidadians who share a natural dislike for being criticised by others. Most Trinidadians would have agreed privately that Manley's assessment of Trinidad was accurate but this does not prevent them from feeling that Manley was "dam' farse" and that as a debtor he should have adopted a more respectful and ingratiating attitude to his creditors.

Swallow, Calypso King of Antigua, offers a rational and sensible view of the matter of loans:

> When them nations get in a jam they run to Trinidad
> 'Eric, help we out, boy things bad'
> And with open heart and hands Eric like a real father
> So sympathetic and kind lending them the petro-dollar
> Better to borrow than to tief this I must agree
> But it's rather embarrassing when you down financially
> Some does borrow and borrow and doh give back
> This is a piece of viciousness I find it slack
> Trinidad like a big brother round the Caribbean
> She does lend money like rain
> From Jamaica right down to Guyana
> Making use of the oil dollar
> Trinidad, our big brother
> Oh yes, is the Caribbean Godfather.

Swallow, while complimenting Trinidad's generosity, does caution Williams that he has to see about Trinidad first. Trinidad's calypsonians seem to think that Trinidad has enough problems, for example, housing, which should take care of all the money Williams felt free to give to others.

One is intrigued by the fact that Williams' loans to Caricom states generated so much hostility. Rosina Wiltshire-Brodber calculates that a total of $420.81 million was loaned to the Caricom partners,[18] an infinitesimal sum compared to the revenues squandered by the Trinidad and Tobago government during the period of petro-prosperity. Billions were consumed in unwise 'government to government' arrangements with foreigners,[19] a foolish practice which did draw some criticism (Contender's "We Smart" 1982; Cardinal's "Productivity" 1983) but which did not evoke the bitterness aroused by the half billion given to Caricom. A united Caribbean, always a fragile institution, was threatened by a kind gesture on the part of a prime minister with good intentions.

While the government was implementing draconian policy against squatters, it undertook to finance the construction of a Central Racing Complex at Caroni to facilitate thoroughbred racing, the luxurious sport of kings. Even in terms of business, this venture, touted as a loan to the Racing Authority, did not make sense[20] and the injudicious timing and crass insensitivity of the act were as bitter as gall. An acrimonious debate ("houses versus horses") was joined between those in favour of the complex which had already exceeded its original budget by 100 percent and those who thought that government would do better to spend money on housing. The calypsonian joined the latter and voiced his protest in strident song.

The idea of 'horse worship' triggered off in Delamo's mind the grim prophecy of Revelations, and he assumed the role and language of the austere Old Testament prophets in chastising those responsible:

> Last night while I was trying to rest mih head
> A vision appeared to me as I was lying on mih bed
> Four riders, each on a different horse
> They say they going down Caroni, they want to check out the new race course
> Ministers, President
> Kneel down worshipping this horse as if it was the Day of Judgement
> Though He was present, they ignored the Son of Man
> Because like to worship this horse was their religion
> So Ah turn and Ah ask what this all signify
> And to me everything was revealed by the Most High
>
> I see a horse laughing kee-kee-kee
> He say he have connection in a big political party
> Guess which party was what the horse say
> But then Ah notice he tail was a *balisier*
> ("Apocalypse" 1981)

Then President of the Republic, Ellis Clarke, was, and is, an avid racing fan, as was John O'Halloran, the flamboyant patron of illegal cockfighting, and it was believed that the influence of these principals was responsible for the cabinet decision re the complex, Williams demonstrating no particular liking for racing and harbouring a decided aversion to gambling, a most necessary feature of that sport.

Stanza three is even more vehement in its condemnation of the PNM politicians behind the decision to favour horses at the expense of humans:

> Behold a second horse, like unto the first
> But this one was red signifying that things really getting worse
> A ex-Minister involved in the Tri-Star racket
> But when you see him racing day he dressed up in tie and jacket
> And a certain Minister who used to work Texaco

Building a big palace, where he get the money nobody know
And the rider of the horse had a sword in he hand
Forever handing out disrespect to the poor man

I see a horse laughing kee-kee-kee
Boasting that he sure he have a better house than me
He say from the beginning the horse come before the buggy
So build a home for the horse and leave the people in boxboard shanty

The "houses versus horses" debate acquires greater urgency with the vacillation of the government in the matter of providing low-cost housing. It had instituted a lottery system to award as yet unbuilt housing units to lucky winners but the failure of the Malabar Housing Project[21] and the leisurely approach to other schemes meant the lottery, like the government itself, was becoming a national joke. Delamo, not at all amused, urges the electorate to "Vote out these horsemen next election."

As far as the calypso of this period goes, politicians were an unwanted, iniquitous breed: Explainer reduces all parliamentarians to comedians and junkies ("In Parliament They Kicksin'" 1978); Funny relegates PNM hierarchs to the world of the scatological ("Ah Soul Man" 1981); Penguin demonises them ("Look the Devil They"); and Crusoe ("Wet Yuh House" 1980) and Sparrow ("Wanted Dead or Alive" 1980) threaten them with the ultimate sanction, removal from office. Nineteen seventy-nine, the year when "The rule of the tyrants decline," to quote "Wanted Dead or Alive", was held up as a warning. Looking at changes of regime in Haiti, Uganda, Nicaragua, Iran, Pakistan and Grenada, Sparrow remarks that:

Eric Williams taking a back seat to avoid bacchanal
But everybody know he 'fraid Karl

drawing first upon Williams' widely publicised intention to take a back seat,[22] and secondly upon the Chalkdust classic "Ah Fraid Karl". Delamo, however, does not envision retirement or electoral defeat for Williams and the PNM; there is a more foreboding prediction in the final stanza of "Apocalypse":

Woe unto you, leaders of my Land
For aiding and abetting the sin of covetousness in this island
And for lending out my money to build facilities for horse
When you breaking down my humble shack with your
Regiment and Police force
But, behold, what the prophecy say
That this fourth horse, he was a mangy grey
And the rider of this horse was like unto no man
Because the jockey on the horse was a skeleton

So allyuh be careful allyuh don't end up like that unfortunate jockey
Because he Racing Complex is the Lapeyrouse Cemetery

A BALANCE OF BLAME

In all fairness, it must be noted that the calypsonian recognised that the public was
partly responsible for the political situation. Stalin's "Breakdown Party" (1980) describes the facets of political malfunction: degeneration of national will; clientelism
gone mad; the flight or demoralisation of the scholarship class; and rampant consumerism. Williams is the lead player ("Mr Divider start the habit") but citizens have
enjoyed their roles:

Man in town walking
Big stereo playing
Twelve o'clock in the day rockers listening
Woman in town shopping
Big radio playing
Three o'clock in the day story telling
Brother, man waking up early
Boarding he BeeWee
And going and shop in Miami
So much for car they charging
Everybody bawling
But, Brother, look Ah see it still selling

Rajah's "Is We" (1979) accuses the citizen of destroying any chance of developing
a sense of community:

They give we a Centre
Well-furnished and equipped, Brother
Before you could say, 'Rajah'
Well look, we tief 'way the furniture
And if you hear we complaining
'There's no chair for sitting'
Everybody giving comment
And we cussing the Government

When is we
Who throw rubbish on the street
Is we
Who does litter up we beach
Is we
Who does tief the rubbish bin

To put drinks to cold for when we feteing
Ah tell yuh, yes is we
Who does do all these things
Is we
Who does cause we own sufferings
Is we
Who does fuss and complain
But I say, it is we to blame

After Williams' "Meet the People" tours of 1963–64, the government, heeding the submission by locals, built and furnished community centres in several localities for the cultivation of domestic arts and for the development of cultural pursuits. In a short space of time, the centres were systematically looted leaving only open spaces for interested parties to rehearse for the prime minister's Better Village Competition which had come about as a result of the "Meet the People" tours. In this way citizens undermined a serious attempt on the part of the state to foster a sense of community. Given this, their continued carping against the government is hard to understand. Rajah grants that by 1978 the government had lost its sense of mission but a rapine minded, fete oriented public needs to understand its responsibility for the predicament faced by the entire nation.

Short Pants refutes Rajah's contentions in "Is I" (1979) by advocating a Thoreau like attitude towards taxation:

I ent paying tax in this Country
If they vex send police for me
I done sit down and I study
The tax-man can't get my money
Donkey years now I paying
And hear what the tax-man doing
He collecting but hear the big shock
Is I have to do he wuk
Is I
Does find the Labasse
No dump-truck does pass to empty my trash
Is I
Does boil the water
WASA doh have no purifier
Is I
Does light the flambeau
It doh have no light up by me, you know
I doing all these thing and more
What the hell I paying tax for

He excuses the picaresque illegal activities of the small man in the light of the state's negligence in providing necessary infrastructure:

Is I
Who join the racket
I had to borrow to buy onion black market
Is I
Beg for guava please
I had to make jam, I couldn't get cheese
Is I
Who went to Barbados
I smuggle in ten pounds of potatoes
I just couldn't take no more
What the hell I paying tax for

A close look at the calypsoes of the period indicates that while the calypsonians credit the citizen with some blameworthiness, they tax the government with greater responsibility for deteriorating national purpose. Barring diehard PNM supporters like Kitchener and Bomber, this seemed a general view on the eve of the 1981 general election.

ON THE EVE OF GENERAL ELECTION 1981

In calypsodom, the approach of the general election generated satire of an extremely sophisticated kind. Penguin's "Doggie Look a Bone" (1981) cries shame on the politicians for their cynical exploitation of voter gullibility:

Ah shame for them politician
Like old puppy they does treat we
When time to run for election
All this dog treatment does done
And what make the thing a joke
Like this trick does always work
They would treat the puppy beat the puppy
Then they come to coax

'Doggie, look a bone
Doggie, doggie look a bone, look a bone
Doggie, doggie, look a bone, look a bone
After election
All the bone done
So come and touch it

Don't look so shock
Don't just watch it
Doggie, suck'

(ii) All through the years
We shedding tears
They too busy
They can't see we
Time to depend on we vote so then
Just so we and them come friend
Stopping to say howdy do
Shaking hands with me and you
They will hug yuh granny
Kiss yuh baby
Wipe he dribble too

(iii) Is now they care
They start to share
Plenty favour
Their behaviour
They so concern
Is time they learn
Years now people getting burn
So they run to one and all
Begging big and begging small
'Doggie, look a back pay
Look a highway
Look a hospital'

(iv) In little track behind God back
See them reaching
Hear them preaching
'We quite aware
Of problems here
Have faith deliverance near
We go clean yuh dirty drain
We go build a water main
Life will be so happy
If you only
Vote for we again'

Doggie look a bone
Doggie, doggie look a bone, look a bone

In Penguin's mind, the voter is also to be blamed for letting himself be reduced to that level ("Doggie, look a backpay/Look a highway/Look a hospital"). Penguin awaits the hustings with mixed emotions: he is amused by the hustling ("They would hug yuh granny/Kiss yuh baby/Wipe the dribble too") but under this laughter there is deep sadness. The inevitable success of the barefaced strategy and the tragedy that the electorate is content with its dog like status fill him with the despair of being trapped.

Stalin's "Vampire Year", on the other hand, counsels that withdrawal is the only escape from the politicians. In order to convey his impressions of their machinations he utilises not the familiar and comparatively harmless *soucouyant* but the diabolical killer vampire transferred from European demonology to Hollywood fantasy, thence to Trinidad and Tobago:

'76 was the Year of the Woman
They give the whole of '79 to the children
But Brotherman, Black Stalin say beware
'81 in Trinidad is vampire year
Trini vampire pack up with class
Is every five years they does pass
With crucifix and cross they could make the grade
Is only chalice and loud smoke they fraid

So keep the chalice smoking, vampire passing
Big vampire, small vampire, party vampire, maestro vampire
So keep the chalice smoking, vampire passing
They passing with whisky, holding a party, giving way money, just to suck we
So keep the chalice smoking, vampire passing

(ii) Vampire with PhD, DC and AC
Vampire from in the university
Vampire with dashiki, shirt and tie
Vampire telling you they doh lie
Just a little bit of blood won't do
They taking some sweat and some tears too
And from the time you join up you in pain
You seeing them the next five years again

So keep the chalice smoking, vampire passing
Coalition vampire, maestro vampire, humble vampire, lick-up vampire
So keep the chalice smoking, vampire passing
Close up your front door, close up your back door, hang up your stale bread, turn round your bed-head
Keep the chalice smoking, vampire passing

(iii) Vampire like bees passing through ghetto
When they looking for blood, Oh Lord! they know where to go
With banners and placards ever more
Every minute of the day knocking at your door
But they making sure before they pass
They taking all we chillum and grass
And a hour so before they come
They servant forward with whisky and rum

Keep the chalice smoking, vampire passing
Coalition vampire, maestro vampire, humble vampire, weird vampire
Keep the chalice smoking, vampire passing
They saying how they care 'bout welfare, see them with they mout' cock
begging for a suck
Keep the chalice smoking, vampire passing.

The smoking chalice of marijuana is the only safeguard against the vampires, and the Rasta user is thus insulated; not so the nonsmoking Christian who can be seduced by alcohol and by the seeming religiosity of the vampires. Stalin accepts as a given the complicity of the church in the political process and observes that church and state are deathly afraid of the dread other. It is this fear, the calypso alleges, that has policemen sweeping the blocks of the weed smokers before the advent of the politicians.

"Vampire Year" voices concern for the labouring class, the Boxers of Trinidad and Tobago. Stalin never belonged to a trade union since he never worked in industry or in the public service, but residing in the industrial capital, San Fernando, and being familiar with workers – his brother worked at Texaco, Pointe-à-Pierre – he felt obliged to direct lethal barbs at the 'vampires' on behalf of his friends and of those who, in the normal way of Trinidadians, sublimate nodding acquaintance with the brother into friendship with the calypsonian:

The best kinda blood for Trini vampire
They say is when they suck the blood of Labour
So from the time they come you sure to hear them say
'A A, We come out to give Labour a play'
But them driving round in big Cadillac
Chauffeur-driven with them at the back
And the only play that Labour getting
Is the man behind the steering wheel driving

Labour in the 'vampire' scheme of things is afforded only as much play as is allowed by the steering wheel on the limousines owned by representatives in government and in the trade unions.

"Vampire Year" makes derogatory reference to NJAC ("Vampire with dashiki") which had entered conventional politics at the insistence of the people as their spokesmen avouched. Valentino and Stalin had recorded sharp criticism (Valentino's "Where We Going" 1977 and "Every Brother Is Not a Brother" 1978; Stalin's "The Same Old Thing" and "More Times" 1979), but "Vampire Year" commits the ultimate indignity of lumping NJAC with the mainstream politicians, implying that entry into vampire castle constitutes automatic assimilation.

There was a decided absence of calypso support for the Organisation of National Reconstruction (ONR), and one hazards the guess that the calypsonians were frightened away by the perception that the ONR was a 'bourgeois' party and that its leader, Karl Hudson-Phillips, was a man to be feared. Sparrow campaigned in song ("Karl Say") but this was hardly enough to undo the permanent damage of Chalkdust's "Ah Fraid Karl" (1972). Commentor, recalling that Hudson-Phillips had drafted the Public Order bill, reinterpreted the acronym ONR to read "Organised Nazi Rule", while the Network Riddum Band demanded that ONR desist from playing its "Squatters' Chant" at its meetings. Network's Brother Resistance publicly disavowed any association with the ONR: "We came about as a result of hard work and sacrifice. We accepted no help from anyone and we are not about to get tied up in this 'vampire politics'."[23]

Resistance, a Stalin protégé,[24] is indignant that a wealthy middle class movement like the ONR should mendaciously latch on to the struggle of the squatters. It was indeed strange, but essentially of the nature of politics, that Hudson-Phillips, a wealthy city landholder, should associate himself with land tenancy and rate paying. Resistance's statement shows that the poor were not fooled by this show of caring.

The results of the election show that, at this stage at least, the calypso was of uncertain value in determining voter behaviour. No one can say conclusively how far the voter would have been won over to one party or other; no one can say how far he would have been alienated by Stalin's nihilism or paralysed by Penguin's dilemma. The National Alliance, based on the old DLP and the newer ULF and DAC, won traditional opposition seats without any help from the calypsonian; NJAC does not seem to have profited from the singing support of 1981 Calypso Monarch, Chalkdust; and it is unclear how far Sparrow popularised the cause of the ONR. The PNM won the election but Kitchener and Bomber, who both sang at their meetings, do not publicly claim credit for this victory. What psephologists and political scientists are agreed upon is that the surprise death of Eric Williams was the decisive element.

THE PASSING OF DR ERIC WILLIAMS

Eric Williams passed away on 25 March 1981, succumbing to "circulatory failure and collapse because of diabetic coma in turn secondary to diabetes mellitus".[25]

After occupying the highest elected post for 25 unbroken years and dominating politics and public life during that period, Williams had retained the mystique attached to him in 1956, and the visions and voices from that early period were still very much alive. He had come in for some rough treatment in song, but the newer images of an ageing, deaf, blind incompetent could not erase those etched in his glory days, and so the calypsoes of the later years of his life reflect a duality best examined in terms of contrasting views, and moreso in terms of the changed attitudes on the part of several significant commentators.

One can begin with two calypsonians not noted for political commentary, Rose and Shorty. Rose, who in Calypso played the *bacchante* and sexually irrepressible female, registers her thanks to Williams ("I Thank Thee" 1978) for the kindly words of encouragement which initiated her professional career.[26] After Williams died, her "Balance Wheel" (1982) encouraged voters to respect the memory of the stability he provided ("Eric was the balance wheel"), and in some mystical way she transfers this quality magically to his successor ("Chambers is the balance wheel").

Shorty, "The Love Man" in song as in life, took the opposing view. He had abstained from political comment claiming that his public did not expect such from him,[27] but when Williams objected to "The Art of Love Making" (1973) and initiated the moves leading to Shorty's being arrested for indecency, the calypsonian retaliated by unmanning the politician ("The PM Sex Probe" 1974). According to this calypso, a female who besought Shorty to induct her into the pleasures of *ars amandi*, commented:

> How the PM could object
> I have a feeling this thing touch him
> Where he most lacking

Shorty followed this in "Oh Trinidad" (1976) which employs suitable sexual imagery in the appeal to Mother Trinidad to give up her doddering lover:

> Too much of one thing good for nothing
> Dig it, dig it
> If you have a hernia that can't get better
> Cut it, cut it
> If yuh man old and falling on he face
> Get a younger fella to take he place
> Put him out
> He ent care 'bout you
> Put him out
> That's the thing to do
> Put him out

The gross image of Williams as an incurable hernia is uniquely Shortyesque. It did not attract much attention because "Oh Trinidad" was a 'silent song', one which languished unheard while the public was taken with the incredibly beautiful "Sweet Music", Shorty's self-declaration as avant-garde composer, which was charming everyone with its ornate orchestration. It would have come as a shock to many that "The Love Man" had chosen to descant on politics while in the midst of musical experimentation.

Two protest singers whose attitude to Williams had changed over time are Stalin and Maestro. Stalin, who had voiced a pro-Williams view in "Leave the Doctor Alone" (1968), a calypso he overlooked in his candid discussions with a somewhat credulous biographer,[28] treats Williams with a distant respect in his "Piece of the Action". Although this calypso seeks to level Williams to the position where he can be made to listen to sense, it contains the many features of the traditional address to Williams, namely a respectful nickname, the appeal to him as prime mover, the insistence on being heard, the disclaimer of malicious intent, the disavowal of ulterior motive, and the veiled threat/warning. Despite the 'man talking to man' formulation, however, Stalin does not see himself as equal to Williams. He treats Attorney General Selwyn Richardson with offhand familiarity ("Plan Your Future" 1980), but this is out of the question where Williams is concerned. "Breakdown Party" (1980) is evidence of Stalin's inability to accept that he and Williams are equal but opposite. Although he was incensed at Williams' stinging criticism of his theory of Caribbean Unity,[29] and was countering by showing up Williams' inability to govern, Stalin still retained enough of that guarded respect to refer to him as "Mr Divider".

In Maestro, the change in attitude towards Williams takes the form of a movement away from jest to rejection. During the 1960s he sang in "Great Inventors":

Marquis de Vaubaun invented the income tax
A lot of stupid Trinidadians feel Eric Williams invented that

One takes the liberty of presuming that this implied if not support for Williams at least understanding of his position. This wry jest became bitter reproach in "To Sir with Love" (1974) and grim rejection in "Dread Man" (1977). In this last song, Maestro uses "dread" in the sense of causing fear and anxiety:

Dreaming of a dread man
Dread man on an island
Where bigger brother squander
While smaller brother hunger
Dread man mash the small man down
They used to love the ground he walk on

They voting
But now they groaning

Is this a dream
Is this a cruel vision
A cruel scheme
Maybe hallucination
I see a war
That's going on forever
I see the poor
As the eternal loser
Don't want no dictator
We don't want no dictator
No Mister
We doh want no dictator
No Sah

Plenty money making
Plenty belly aching
Them bring Self Loading Rifle
To hassle who give trouble
Promises the man doh keep
Some people saying
'Baa Baa black sheep'

The calypso employs stark contrast, a technique Maestro was already mastering; it is as if he is suggesting that the Williams regime can best be defined and explained in terms of antagonistic extremes, extremes which Williams cannot reconcile and may even be doing his best to promote.

The special Sparrow – Williams and Chalkdust – Williams relationships demand attention because of the dominant personalities of the singers and because they, better than most, illustrate complex attitudes towards the politician. Sparrow had championed Williams from the outset but profound disillusionment with the naked face of authority had inspired the brilliant and subtle "Get to Hell Out". He later endorsed his friend and lawyer, Hudson-Phillips, a one-time Williams 'face-man' and, paradoxically, someone credited with less finesse than his former boss. Between these political choosings there falls the curious remark: "I love Dr Williams like god and a half."[30]

Whether this is a confession from the heart or a mere public relations gambit of the kind Sparrow was wont to make, it is impossible to determine.[31] In 1980 when Sparrow was celebrating his sparkling silver anniversary of professional calypso performing, Williams returned the compliment. John Donaldson, minister of national security, reportedly come from visiting Williams, who rarely left his official residence, declared that the prime minister wanted it known publicly that:

> On his first most difficult assignment, he turned to Sparrow for inspiration and he came up with 'The Yankees gone and somebody take over now'.
> The government's taxation system was sold to the nation by Sparrow's calypso 'Pay As You Earn'.
> During one of his most difficult moments, Sparrow came to his rescue with 'Leave the Damn doctor',
> When the Federation came apart, Sparrow expressed the views of us all with, of course, 'Federation'.[32]

While Williams was admitting things which he should have entered in *Inward Hunger*, one wonders at the timing of his disclosure. It was rather late in the day to be giving Sparrow the credit rightly due him, and one wonders if all this was not an attempt to woo the singer away from his new allegiance to the ONR and back to the PNM fold. It certainly explains to some extent the contradiction of Sparrow's singing "Karl Say" in the tent and several weeks later embracing the PNM founder at the party's Silver Anniversary Convention at Chagville, Williams' last hurrah as it turned out. By this token, the famous photograph of Sparrow embracing a somewhat unresponsive Williams may have been evidence of a *rapprochement* in the making; one cannot rule out the possibility that it may also have been mere *mamaguy*.

Despite this, one suspects that Sparrow loved Williams. It has been suggested that "One Day" (sung in 1987 by Sparrow's protégé, Natasha Wilson) was originally meant to be Sparrow's public confession. Certainly the ideas correspond perfectly to the stages of the Sparrow–Williams relationship: the selfless affection and loyalty; the horror when Beauty revealed itself as Beast; the humiliation; and finally "One Day", blues become ballad, retrospectively reproachful rather than prospectively revengeful.

Chalkdust, who had been a secondary school student when Williams irrupted on the national stage, was as fascinated by Williams as was Sparrow. He is by far the most prolific calypsonian on the subject of Williams, but while his opposition is taken for granted one wonders if his obsession with Williams, as evidenced in the volume of political *picong* as opposed to outright hostility, his impersonations of Williams in his two 1976 election skits, his calypso tribute in 1981, and several comments made in and out of calypso, may not in fact testify to a love-hate relationship on his part. "Eric Williams Loves Me" (1979) is a frank admission of his obsession:

> I does often wonder who is Eric's hero
> I does sit and ponder whom does this man follow

I does stay so and think what it is makes him tick
To make him do the things he does in public
For instance, why doesn't he attend a Caricom meeting
And why in Parliament he does not say a thing
I've read books in History, Politics of all kind
Yet his reasons I cannot find

Because when a man could crash George the Fifth Park just so
Then rebuild it at Mucurapo
Whom does he follow
Karl Marx ent say so
And tell me, what kinda theory
Could make a MP resign promptly
Once he leave his Party
Well that short man does have me thinking
But now Ah size him up by concluding
Is just calypso he want Chalkie sing
Ah read all kinda book in History
No leader ever have three deputy
You ent see is Calypso they want Chalkie sing

Reading between the lines, one gets the distinct impression that Chalkdust is actuated by the need for Williams' attention; in other words, *Chalkdust* loves Williams. His apologia presented in the brochure sold at his calypso tribute to Williams supports this contention:

> I disliked some of the policies that seemed to ignore lessons of history with respect to destructive effects of Capitalism and Imperialism and its accompanying racism and degradation of black people, yet I admire him for his beliefs and practices of non-discrimination on grounds of race, colour or beliefs.
> While I dislike him for trying to solve all problems by historical documentation and use, and while I abhor him for taking lots of borrowed ideas historically developed and used by others and replanting them wholesale in our society, I am proud to have been a schoolboy in Eric Williams's heyday for it was his application to study, and his love of the academic disciplines that fired my thinking process and helped me to arrive at the decision that I too shall become a historian.[33]

Chalkdust says elsewhere[34] that Williams complimented him on a reference to A.N.R. Robinson in "Two Sides of the Shilling", an admission which, if true, would make Williams a somewhat dense person, which he never quite managed to become. It also contradicts the newspaper report that Williams had viewed impassively Chalkdust's performance of this calypso.[35] Also, Chalkdust confides, improbably, that Williams needed his historical knowledge. In June 1989, by way of explaining away a conference with Prime Minister A.N.R. Robinson, whom he had satirised in the crown winning "Chauffeur Wanted", Chalkdust admitted: "He wanted to discuss some cultural issues relating to our nation, and I suppose he was simply tapping my resources as historian. I used to have similar meetings with deceased Prime Minister Eric Williams also."[36]

It does seem unlikely that Williams would need to tap Chalkdust's "resources as historian"; it seems more likely that he was using him as a source for other information or was hoping to overwhelm him psychologically as he did and tried to do with others.[37]

With respect to other singers, 1980 illustrates perfectly the ambivalence of calypso response to Williams. Charmaine McCarthy, National Junior Calypso Monarch, objected to the pejorative treatment of "this great leader of mine":

> I vex with all my countrymen
> Each and every one of them
> But 'specially with my teachers
> And all other educators
> Who teach me about Marcus Garvey
> Amin and Mahatma Gandhi
> Nothing did we hear
> About the great man who living here
> The only time we know about him
> Is when people criticise him
>
> Saying twenty five years ruling is a long long time
> But this great leader of mine
> Hold on to the reins of power
> My Country's political leader
> A real native son of the soil
> A man through the years has toiled
> More than any other man
> To build up this great Nation an unequal contribution
> So why no praises for Dr Williams
> ("Son of the Soil" 1980)

While the junior monarch considers Williams' 25-year tenure to be a great achievement, her senior counterpart, Relator, charged that Williams' extended stay in office was responsible for all the country's problems:

> No lights no telephone and no water
> We in the middle of a big power failure

I'm sorry but the breakdown is governmental
Is because of fatigue physical and mental
Is useless that we continue to blame
A horse that is tired and almost lame
If Government can't cope nowadays
The Nation should send them for holidays

Now this is not an overthrow
I ent saying that we must kick them out just so
So please don't jump to any hasty conclusion
And cause any confusion
Because they exhausted from working too long
So before they suffer from a nervous breakdown
As a loving Nation we should all suggest
That Dr Williams and the PNM take a rest

In 1961, Sparrow's "Present Government" had blamed hostile trade unions for the breakdown in essential services. Now in 1980 Relator suggests that the "power failure" is the ebbing away of the remarkable energy that had sustained Williams for decades. Relator therefore recommends:

A nice rest for the Doc
Before the poor man fall down on the wuk
("Take a Rest" 1980)

As fate would have it, Relator's words – and Delamo's warning of "Apocalypse" – turned out to be prophetic.

Strangely undignified scenes attended the state ceremonies marking the death of the 'superman' as Crazy refers to him ("No Face, No Vote" 1982). Excitable crowds, suddenly reacting to the rumours that Williams was not dead and that the closed casket was empty, demanded to see his face or they would withhold their vote in the general election constitutionally due later that year. Several officials and Williams' daughter, Erica Williams-Connell, once the light of his life but estranged since late 1973,[38] pleaded with the masses who then subsided into a sullen silence when they realised that their demand would not be countenanced.

The passing of the titan was remarked in the Calypso although the singers most taken with him in life found nothing to say about him in death, and the duty of penning the necessary calypso obituaries and eulogies was undertaken by lesser figures. The Original DeFosto proffered the genuine tribute of the ardent PNM supporter:

His vibration was one in a million
Just like the power of the rising sun

He was the right and truly Honourable
A philosopher, author, premier, teacher, the Nation's Father
He put aside luxury which was of no importance to him
He was the people's majority, a simple man, a simple king

The time had come for him to go
Shed no tears, don't prop sorrow
An illustrious master, that's who he was
A true born Saviour sent from above
It was written and so well done
His number was called, his time had come
Together we aspire, together we achieve
Parts of his thoughts, parts of his beliefs

Crusoe and Penguin resurrected Williams' ghost to have that powerful spirit deliver his own funeral oration. Crusoe's tribute "I Eric Eustace Williams" echoes the arrogance of Sparrow's "Get to Hell Out":

Opposition know they never stood a chance
Five elections I whip them on their conscience
In my Party I am absolutely boss
Who defied me I simply tell them get lost
With brain, intellect and charisma
My visions were always superior
Anyone who attempted to move me from the head
I just raised mih hand and they politically dead

The Williams persona of Penguin's "Betty Goaty", calling out from a place referred to simply as "down here", gloats over his new-found freedom from responsibility for irresponsible subordinates. The use of the child's taunt, recalling Williams' tantrum throwing, suggests that the child in him was too often master of the man; now, removed by death from the game of politics from which he could not free himself in life, he can jeer at those 'playmates' he had needed and despised:

To build up this Nation I try my best
End up in mess
Men I give rank and fame
Do things to make me shame
Pillage and rape the land
And leave me a sad frustrated man

Betty Goaty, Betty Goaty
I doing well

Is them in Hell
Tell all them cross
Is them who loss
You know how I was softie
And 'fraid to give men jail
Well now I hope somebody
Lock up some of them tail
Betty Goaty, Betty Goaty
Ah just watching and laughing ho-ho-ho
Betty goaty tho'

This reflects the schizophrenia of the man who saw himself simultaneously as master of his polity and victim of his politics, the poles indicated in Sparrow's "Get to Hell Out" and Chalkdust's "Bring Him In".

Given the satirical turn of mind exhibited by Crusoe ("Politicians" 1974) and by Penguin ("Look the Devil Dey" 1980 and "Doggie Look a Bone" 1981), one is chary of accepting their offerings at face value, yet the idea that their work may be informed by sentimentalism cannot be discounted. Also, both compositions resemble in the matter of Williams' confessions of his sincerity and integrity, the positives his supporters and others believe that he embodied. One cannot help concluding that they may be sincere tributes by calypsonians of African descent to an Afro-Trinidadian giant.

Explainer's "Chambers" (1982) lists Williams' negative qualities in an "open word" to his successor in office. Promising loyalty provided that George Chambers remain true to his mission as champion of the poor, Explainer cautions the new prime minister against developing several particulars of political vice:

Don't be a recluse
Don't display arrogance
Or let ego create any turbulence
Call for peace and do something for Labour
Also rap to those delinquent employers
Don't put horses before houses
And make mistakes like your past bosses

The cruel irony in this is that although Williams had displayed such king breaking vices for a long time, voters had remained true to him and he may have confidently expected re-election in 1981. It has been argued that his 'altruistic suicide' rescued the PNM[39] but such was the Williams mystique that his mere presence, or that of his apolitical daughter, as would be seen in 1991, may have guaranteed victory.

One obituary sung long after the fact needs to be mentioned. Delamo, one of the little children in whose school bags Williams had entrusted the nation's future,[40] makes an unflattering assessment of the "Father's" impact on the country:

'Suffer the little children to come unto Me
For they shall inherit my Kingdom'
So a certain Father to suffer his children really did he
You see, he left them a legacy of Sodom
Like sacrificial pawns on a chessboard of politics
He squandered his children's future with irresponsible antics
("Eric Williams Children" 1984)

Clearly, in Delamo's mind, Williams turned out to be not Messiah as some aver but false prophet. Delamo records his legacy as being a generation of "tief with jacket and tie, homosexuals and I and I man" together with a lost, abused race of youngsters seeking in drugs the self-respect which they had lost in Williams' schools.

Despite this, Williams remains our most cherished myth, a reference point in times of crisis, unsullied and untouchable. One is struck by the Delamo lines:

He freed our limbs but he never freed out minds
So how come after twenty seven years
Freedom from his freedom we cannot find

This is as much a comment on the psychological hold Williams exerts on the nation as on the calypsonians who, like Delamo, cannot get him out of their minds.

GENERAL ELECTION 1981

The PNM victory of 1981 produced two memorable songs, one by Kitchener, the loyal PNM defender, and the other by Sparrow, the 'defector' to the ONR. Kitchener, joyously echoing the PNM's slogan "Not a Damn Seat for Them" in a characteristic Road March styling, could not resist the temptation to tilt at Sparrow who was thought to be devastated by the defeat of the ONR:

Them ONR jump and wine
Making a big show
And they thought they had the crowd behind
Everywhere they go
So they thought that crowd was vote
They say they go cut we throat
Sparrow start to bawl
When he hear not a seat at all

Not a damn seat for them
Sparrow that's ingratitude
Not a damn seat for them

You bite the finger that give you food
Not a damn seat for them
Look how you hug up Dr Willie
Not a damn seat for them
People 'fraid you in this Country

Sparrow reacted predictably. In "We Like It So" (1982), he makes creative use of the traditional quarrel, that offspring of barrackyard/backyard life, but he disciplines and shapes the reckless energy and defiance to add a satirical overlay to his repressed fury and bitterness at the allegations of treachery made against him. Stanza one introduces the Sparrow persona, a rational voter, engaged in a futile quarrel with irrational neighbours:

Neighbour, look if I was a selfish man
I wouldn't be involved in this election
I done old already I ent want fame
Plus I ent looking for fortune again
All I'm asking is that you pay close attention to
The many problems we all face from day to day
You're intelligent, I think, and you should face issues
But behaving like a moron
Cussing me for where Ah born

But yuh pipe ent have no water
Yuh pay too much for butter
Take yuh steel beam and go
This terrible school system
Is such a bloody problem
Take yuh steelbeam and go
Agriculture is in a state
Planning is inadequate
Take yuh steelbeam and go
The northern and southern idol
The two kingpin of *bobol*
We know, we like it so
We like it so, we free

As they take the offensive and limit the voice of reason to brief statements, the unthinking 'neighbours', who have been trapped in the culture of poverty where the PNM met and left them, satirise themselves when they present arguments based on irrationality and insularity; the kind of 'reasoning' that has kept a corrupt and inefficient government in power:

Anything that's wrong he go put it right
Georgie Porgie tell we the other night
So instead of displaying impatience
Cool yuhself and give the fella a chance
How the hell you could say ONR go do better
We go send you back Grenada in a drum
We and Georgie going to put it together, yeah
We have freeness and freedom
Plenty roti, plenty rum

Skilfully, Sparrow has the diehard PNM supporters endorse their addiction to the political opium of "rum and roti". This acceptance on his part of the nature of PNM politicking demonstrates how far he has departed from his youthful assertions (compare "William the Conqueror" 1957) that the emergence of the PNM spelt the end of this kind of electioneering.

Stanza four testifies to the triumph of the propagandist art, dramatising how public opinion can be manipulated if collective fears are played upon:

It ent have a single thing you could say
Could make me abandon mih *balisier*
No steelbeam go fall down on top mih head
Sparrow, I'se a PNM till Ah dead
Birdie, you may be shocked when I tell you this
Hudson-Phillips is a Yankee CIA
And the whole of ONR is only Communist
They'll take Carnival away
And make people work each day

The diehard's dogged declarations of undying support are based on the privileged information of a plot to subvert the country, the conspiracy theory. The emotive letters "CIA" with their connotations of conspiracy gleaned from the movies, and the word "Communist" with its images of a way of life diametrically opposed to the Trinidad and Tobago *laissez-faire*, are critical in the manipulative process because the spectacle of a "Yankee CIA" heading a party of "Communists" defies probability, but to the nativist mind the accumulation of negative images is enough. The last couplet clinches the argument:

They take Carnival away
And make people work each day

Trinidadians were horrified when it was reported that the revolutionary Cuban government of Fidel Castro had postponed Christmas festivities in order to mobilise labour to expedite the vital sugar-cane harvest. This one act inspired more collective fear and outrage in the minds of Trinidadians than any other attributed to Castro. For them, the reasons for his actions were not important; it was enough to know that it had been reported to be true. To be made to miss Christmas is a frightening prospect; to have to *work* on *carnival day* is the ultimate nativist nightmare. Significantly, Kitchener's "Not a Damn Seat for Them" attributes the PNM victory to the panic caused by the mention of an ONR – Cuban connection:

> Trinidadians got a hint
> They heard of the plans
> The ONR had blueprint
> To bring the Cubans
> People took it on of course
> Say their freedom would be lost
> Before this problem
> Better put back the PNM
>
> This is what PNM do for we
> Not a damn seat for them
> They give we freedom and liberty
> Not a damn seat for them
> Freedom to walk, freedom to protest
> Not a damn seat for them
> Freedom to talk, freedom of the Press
> Not a damn seat for them

Apparently a PNM victory was enough to exorcise from Kitchener's mind the horror of repression voiced in his "No Freedom" (1973).

In the public mind, as the two calypsoes suggest, Hudson-Phillips was made to appear the destroyer of individual liberties and the willing agent of hostile foreign powers. In his campaign, Chambers had invoked the fascist bogey by recalling the infamous Public Order bill. He confided to thousands in a public place that the bill had been the work of a "certain kind of mind" and he hinted that it had been drafted without cabinet approval. He also referred obliquely to unnamed "Wicked and nefarious people" who, if given the chance, would introduce the concentration camp. There were, he intimated, "certain people" who had advised Williams to have undated letters of resignation from all senior public servants and to have all heads of departments and of the defence and protective services take an oath of allegiance to the party. "They are too wicked," he thundered in his peroration, "Not a damn seat for them!"[41]

Labelled a fascist and, paradoxically, linked to communist Cuba at the same time, Sparrow's hero Karl Hudson-Phillips lost to the jibes of the pro-PNM Kitchener, yet Sparrow himself scored a victory with "We Like It So" which is above all else an intensely personal statement. It is Sparrow's explanation for his 'desertion' of the PNM so shortly after Williams' death because, despite his public identification with Hudson-Phillips before Williams' death (compare "You Mad" 1980; "Karl Say" 1981), the public remembered the Chagville photograph in which he is captured embracing Williams. Sparrow therefore needed to convince people that he was not a turncoat opportunist.

"We Like It So" also reminded the public that although Sparrow was past his prime he had not quite 'gone through' as Trinidadians are quick to write off popular and public figures. The couplet, "This concern you showing here for we/Could well cost you your popularity" in addition to stressing Sparrow's sense of being an outsider, also tells that he was aware of the fickle ides of popularity and of the effects of PNMism on same. The days of "If Sparrow say so is so" being long over, Sparrow anticipated an ebb in his popularity because of his affiliation to the ONR which was thought to be antagonistic to the lower classes. His association with that party was read as a sign that he was losing his mind, as the 'neighbours' had advised " . . . you need psychiatric aid/To be in them bourgeois motorcade". Sparrow had risen from the lower classes and his calypsoes of the early 1960s document the dialectics of his alienation from his parent group to whom he remained 'we boy' in spite of everything. His alignment with his new friends and sponsors[42] was seen as a temporary aberration, something like his discharge of a firearm[43] and the public 'cussing' at the Savannah in 1975.[44] These were considered minor excusable weaknesses or lapses in one who was great. One can note the complexities of race and class in a mobile society where Sparrow, the reputed millionaire, and Williams, the hermit leader, continue to be considered men of the people because of his origins, in the case of Sparrow, and because of what was perceived as his earlier identification with the lower classes, in the case of Williams, whilst Hudson-Phillips, son of a black millionaire, is always seen as a middle class person instinctively hostile to the masses.

Anti-Sparrow reaction did materialise in the persons of some PNMites who took it upon themselves to heckle the calypsonian but so powerful was the calypso and so sincere the performance that many who came to jeer remained to cheer thus giving Sparrow and the Calypso a hard-fought victory over narrow political partisanship.

The last word on the election is Merchant's mature "Build a Nation". An incredibly gifted composer – though an indifferent performer – Merchant's life and career have been plagued by quirks of character which continue to deny him the greatness corresponding to his outstanding talent. Living in the heart of Port of Spain after his eviction in the 1970s (compare "Who Squatting"), and exposed to the tensions of partisanship as the African based PNM was challenged by what to some extent was a splinter faction, Merchant shrugged off his usual apathy to politics to sing:

Now the election bacchanal pass away
In short this is what I have to say
Forget the fight, grudges and concentrate
Let us sit down and try to relate

'cause now more than ever we must show
Discipline, Tolerance and Production
To build a strong and better nation
That is the main foundation
So let's work now hand in hand
Because this is our Land
Come my brother, come my sister
Let us build a Nation together

As later events would show, this calypso suffered the fate of many a useful and inspirational song: it was applauded, it received some airplay from sentimental and nationalistic disc jockeys but the public promptly forgot its message.

"The Sinking Ship"
1982–1986

By the polls of 1981 George Chambers was confirmed in the position to which he had been nominated on Williams' death and mandated to direct the affairs of the nation. Chambers' election triumph signified that people were willing to accept him as a symbol of a revitalised party and government. Explainer's "Chambers" (1982) articulates the hopes for the "young vibrant leader/To replace a past political era":

An open word to our Prime minister
Your job is hard but I want you to remember
Come down from your heights
Meet the poor and the humble
Always be in sight
Any time they may grumble
Take up your role as chief disciplinarian
And use your sword on the evil called corruption

And if you true we go follow you
If you true we go follow you
If you true we go follow you
Treat the people as you ought to

His parting words combine encouragement and warning which, with the benefit of hindsight, could be termed 'prophecy', a typical Trinidadian form of reasoning:

Don't be annoyed when they call you dummy
But just avoid being called deafy
The Bible say a wise man is a good listener
The fool displays what he know more than ever
But prove yourself during your reign
And we the people would vote for you again and again

Unfortunately, Chambers lacked Williams' stature and charisma and never captured the public imagination in the way that his illustrious predecessor did. While Williams' achievements in founding the nation and providing stability outweighed in the public mind his numerous failings as a manager, Chambers was execrated for the recession which savaged the country and for the unbridled corruption – a legacy from Williams – which ravaged the treasury. Lost in the process of deifying Williams, people forgot his responsibility for the concatenation of disasters which overtook Chambers and the nation, and they claimed that were Williams alive and at the helm, he would have navigated a safe course through the storm waves then buffeting the ship of state. Early in his administration, Chambers had promised to "put right that which is wrong" and he had warned that the fete of the 1970s was over and that the nation must go back to work. He had tried to live up to his word by suspending work on the Malabar Housing Project and the Caroni Racing complex,[1] but his compromise with corruption[2] and the continuing deterioration in infrastructure redounded to his discredit and were pivotal in the devaluation of the image of the leader and the party.

"LYRICS TO MAKE A POLITICIAN CRINGE"

Calypsonians took a leading role in the avalanching anti-PNMism. From all perspectives and standpoints, in a variety of literary and musical styles, they discussed and dissected the weaknesses of the Chambers administration. Ironically, Chambers supplied them with the language, thus adding to the arsenal of verbal weapons which they have always used in criticising the shortcomings of political regimes.

Funny, was one of the first to take up Chambers on his promise to right wrongs and so on:

> Georgie, yuh can't see T&TEC they done fail
> Them road repairers and WASA should be in jail
> The motor car industry ripping off people
> Telco in a straight jacket
> And them labour unions need better direction
> And don't talk about black market
>
> Too much mismanagement
> In government department
> That wrong, Georgie, that wrong
> And when yuh not telling we
> How much cash we got in the Treasury
> That wrong, Georgie, that wrong

When yuh just let people take we money and go
When yuh just stay dey sitting down
And the thing about it is Georgie yuh know
That wrong, Georgie, that wrong, wrong, wrong
("Right and Wrong" 1983)

In March 1982, Chambers convened a National Consultation on Productivity and called upon the nation to produce more in the national interest. Some calypsonians thought that this call sounded farcical and they made suitable *picong* response in song.

Crusoe's "Productivity" (1983) tabbed the consultation as just another occasion for "ole talk and lime" by the seaside. Trinidad and Tobago, he concedes, is already the most productive country in the world because

We produce over fifty billion dollars in this Country in seven years
And then produce a one-track economy that collapse and leave we in tears
And then we produce a corrupted seta scamps that take we money and gone

Stanza four articulates the cynicism with which a jaded populace greeted the attempt to mobilise them in the national interest when government's actions tended in the opposite direction:

This country producing millionaires overnight
It will continue to do so anytime the money read right
We produce a seta foreigners, produce them the top jobs too
Now is only unemployment we have left for us to do
Poor people went and produce some shacks because no houses in town
We produce the men from the Regiment to move in and break them down
This productivity is the best that I've ever heard
Right now we are heading for the Guinness Book of records

Stalin's "Make Them Alright" (1984) ridicules the grand assembly:

They send out big invitation
They holding big consultation
They want to find the answer to poor production
They invite agriculturist
Lawyers and geologist
They even invite a prime minister of politics
But while they in Chaguaramas looking
Well the answer to more production right in town lying
You simply got to give better incentive
On top of which a contributor must live

Stalin's contempt is clear in the line "They even invite a prime minister of politics" which makes of the highest elected official a mere do-nothing public servant with nothing better to do than lend the dignity of office to a meaningless exercise. This calypso view departs radically from the truth that is was *Chambers* who had initiated the consultation, perhaps in the desperate hope of warding off a looming recession and the hovering IMF conditionalities. Stalin, annoyed at the insinuation that the nation's planners were blaming the Boxers for the general predicament, protests the treatment of Tubal Uriah "Buzz" Butler ("How you could call my hero a squatter?") and of the unsung heroes who collected "cardboard and sidewalk" as their gratuity. He also highlights the plight of those who had been pensioned off only to be exposed to harsh price increases which mock the pittance they receive. The calypso deplores the lack of institutionalised concern for those whose minds have been blown by the entire experience and now present a shocking vision of the naked truth.

The choruses detail the measures the government could take instead of passing Litter acts designed to remove from the towns the unsightly human wreckage, the flotsam and jetsam of the tides of PNMism. Stalin reveals in this calypso his private scheme of values, a simple humanistic philosophy which informs several of his Black Power and Rasta calypsoes:

> You pick up yuh mooma and popa
> Who work so hard for the colonial master
> And make them alright
> With yuh big seta billion dollars
> Run a better pay to yuh elders
> And make them alright
> Ah say, you cyar leave them on no corner
> Calling them no madman and beggar
> You got to show more appreciation
> For their contribution
> And then Ah know that the daily worker
> Would be glad to work eight hour
> 'cause he know when he come a elder
> He go be alright

Cardinal, up to this time a minor tent calypsonian, delivers the response of the man in the street who experiences daily the horrors of breakdown in essential services and who curses daily an improvident government:

> Ah sit down and Ah view the situation
> Currently existing in this Nation

That's why Ah say they only fooling
When they say they talking 'bout production
Every civic-minded person must agree
This whole Nation want productivity
But if we mind confused and in frustration
How the hell they want more production

But when WASA cut out we water
In the morning we can't flush we sewer
We can't brush we teeth, no food to eat
Just imagine how we house smelling sweet
Next thing we children suffering from gastro
No medicine in the hospital when we go
On top of that they damn bold to tell we
How they want productivity
("Productivity" 1983)

The Chambers regime then adopted the unfortunate practice of verbally
chastising its many critics and thus drew down the ire of the calypsonian who, as
the politicians should have known, are among the best at this kind of attack.
Sparrow's "Prophets of Doom and Gloom" (1983) responds to such an assault by
PNM ministers in general and specifically President Ellis Clarke's address at the
Pan Is Beautiful Two steelband music festival in 1982:

If you happen to see and know
When politics going wrong
With facts and figures prepared to show
It's better to bite yuh tongue
To them political boss
Who the people trust and get double-cross
You're an obstacle to be removed at any cost
A social conscience is really very dangerous to your health
The awesome strength of the powers that be
Most certainly will be felt
To tell them that their priorities and their performance is under par
They will proceed to describe to you who you are

A megalomaniac
A power-seeker
A crazy or a crack
Trouble in the maker
If you tell them that the economy
Is no longer in full bloom
Then you become a prophet of doom and gloom

"CORRUPTION IS A CALLALOO"

Even more reprehensible from the point of view of a public embittered by salary cuts and wage freezes which broke down their party of the late 1970s, was Chambers' reluctance to put right the wrong of corruption. For those whose fete had been stopped it was too much to see officials waltzing away with wealth which *vox populi* said was acquired dishonestly. This was the node of political dissent and many songs stand out for their imaginative use of the extended metaphor.

Sparrow's "Sam 'P'" (1984) flayed the political directorate and the public service, but not his friends of the private sector, for what he saw as collusion in the Sam P. Wallace affair; Wallace being the American contractor who had confessed to impropriety in the award of a tender for the construction of the grandstand at the Caroni Racing Complex.[3] Exploiting to the full the freedom of the calypsonian in performance, Sparrow represents the stench of corruption from that deal by using the appropriate image of a horse urinating and befouling all its handlers with its uniquely vile discharge:

> They bring down Sam and forced him to drink
> Now is time to urinate they can't take the stink
> All them big heroes in they fancy suit
> Covering they nose quaking in they boot
> Who make the contract
> Who get the kickback
> Nobody ent want to answer that
>
> Now the President
> 'fraid
> The whole of Parliament
> 'fraid
> The Permanent Secretary
> 'fraid
> Business and Industry
> 'fraid
> Corruption in high society
> Have them trembling in anxiety
> Everybody 'fraid Sam P[ee]

This calypso, which seems politically motivated, hence the absence of reference to the private contractors who may have supported the ONR, Sparrow's party of choice, records the government's attempts to stonewall the opposition, and it implicates every office holder imaginable in a sweeping allegation of complicity which, outside of calypso, would form the basis of many a lawsuit, but within calypso is accepted as the stuff of *mepris*.

Cardinal's "Band of the Year", the second of the tandem which took him to the national semifinal and made him a household name, employs the metaphor of the carnival band to designate that cluster of public and private citizens who have indulged in acts of mischief:

Carnival coming Ah bringing a band
The mas we playing is called 'Corruption'
We portraying all kinda character
From Government to private sector
Corruption as you know is a *callaloo*
So some of my characters I must call for you
Only to give a little idea
Of what you the public will have to hear

The King of the band we call him Amal
He portraying one big money scandal
So much of millions in we currency
He tried to embezzle out of this Country
When Burroughs ketch him was only *mamaguy*
You know he get 'way free, please don't ask me why
Just tell Wayne Berkley Ah say have a care
'cause Ah feel we could win the Band of the Year.

"Amal" is Cardinal's fictional name for Michael Amar, a local business tycoon who had been fined three thousand dollars for attempting to smuggle out four million dollars,[4] to the public mind a ridiculously disproportionate penalty. Valentino regards this incident – and others similar – as the genesis of the worldwide recession:

Check out the Trini who banking his money
And shopping in them foreign country
Contributing to crash we economy
They ketch a man smuggling out four million
And all they charge him was three thousand
So you see who causing this recession in the land

Amar's co-conspirator, Gilman Thomas Hussein, was fined seven million dollars the next year and depositors at the International Trust Company of which he was chairman thought it prudent to withdraw their investments thus occasioning a run of panic in the world of the nonbank financial institutions.[5] Valentino, who is certainly no banking expert, may have felt himself vindicated. Stalin's "That Is Head" (1983) viewed the Amar incident as one of the characteristically weird actions on the part of the élites who normally act so irrationally that the casual observer is convinced that they operate under the influence of potent hallucinogens. He contrasted the leniency granted Amar with the stern punishment meted out to a man of the lower classes for a much lesser offence:

> They hold a brother in Piarco
> Carrying a little weed to Tobago
> Ten thousand dollars they charge he
> Take 'way he weed immediately
> But then they hold a big-shot businessman
> With ten million dollars carrying out the island
> Yuh know is three thousand dollars they charge to he
> And give he back he money
> Yuh talk 'bout head
> That is head

While a private citizen, Amar, was crowned and satirised for his sophisticated and bloodless crime, a senior state official was crowned and condemned for her 'crime' of showing off and squandering public resources on frivolous display. PNM stalwart, Mrs Muriel Donawa McDavidson, in her capacity of chairperson of the Festivals Committee, had authorised a scheme to have trees around the Savannah decorated with lights and 'sold' to private citizens and firms. This was her way of celebrating the 20th Anniversary of Independence – and the trees were to remain lit until Republic Day (24 September). She persevered in this willow of the wisp idea in spite of the facts that the nation had suffered massive power outages from March through May, and that the electricity authorities were dead set against the idea.

Stalin found in McDavidson's actions the proof that the élites operate on a different level of consciousness:

> If a man give a man money for something
> And the man ent give the man the something
> The police going to come and hold him
> Give him a charge called embezzling
> But T&TEC have me in darkness nightly
> September, Muriel put up Christmas tree
> And doh care how Ah fight, doh care how Ah fret
> Randy ent lock up Muriel yet
> Yuh talk 'bout head

Cardinal felt that McDavidson's actions were sufficiently reprehensible to warrant her elevation to the throne of 'Corruption':

The Queen of the Band name McDavidson
This Queen doh think, she have no reason
In the band people suffering from load-shedding
Here wha' McDavidson portraying
People bawling for months no electricity
But she going round the Savannah to light up tree
So you see why Ah telling Berkley have a care
Ah just feel we could win the Band of the Year

References to the smuggling and to the tree lighting crop up in many other calypsoes but it is remarkable how Cardinal and Stalin, two singers of such dissimilar backgrounds, are agreed as to the seriousness of their implications and how they fuse these two unrelated incidents. Even more important is the treatment of the persons involved. Neither singer calls Amar by name, although they may safely have done so because the matter for which he had been convicted was public knowledge; both singers, however, gleefully castigate the politician by name. It seems that the calypsonians think that private sector millionaires are averse to criticism and condemnation in calypso and may safely do the calypsonian some harm while the public official, sensitive to the image of office, has to suffer in silence or lose face publicly.

Among favourite public service targets for the calypsonians' slings and darts are police officers. Cardinal's "Band of the Year" and Stalin's "That Is Head" provide evidence of the deep-seated antagonism between calypsonians and policemen, a social phenomenon pointed out earlier.[6] Externals had changed somewhat, but the permanent basis of the conflict remained as is explained in Eagle's tidy syllogism:

The rich ones control the law
The law controls the ones wha' poor
So the law and the poor always in a war
("Law and Poor" 1984)

The calypsonian, regardless of his socioeconomic status, aligns himself with the underclass and defends their privileges and peccadilloes against the interference of the superstructure and its agents. Policemen, the frontline agents of what the calypsonian sees as the conspiracy between class and law, normally come in for rough handling in song, and the 1982–87 period is no different. Monkey's "We Cyar come" (1984), taking off on Chambers' refusal to participate in what is called the American-led rescue mission to restore law and order in Grenada in the wake of the assassination of Prime Minister Maurice Bishop, satirises the inability of the protective services to contribute meaningfully to serious military operations:

We soldiers will go to Grenada if is football they have up dey
We police will go to Grenada if is music they want we play
We go help them tune pan
Lend them money by the million
But when it come to invasion
Caricom people you have it wrong

As far as he sees, the Regiment is a gang of *badjohns*:

Soldiers is to break houses down and hold naked people in Toco
Invade the College bar and beat people til they head bus'
And terrorise poor villagers like what they do in Cedros

Policemen are either ceremonial figures or entertainment personalities:

To carry the President races is the work of a policeman
Police is to drive taxi and to play music for calypsonians
And to act in Better Village and play on television

While Monkey indulges in bitter satire, Cardinal's "Band of the Year" recounts an incident which shows that the police service remains the police force:

If you see the Brutality section
Reynold Ganesh playing in that one
With he head well pound up like a tenor pan
Is a inspector wha' do that in the Band
Going to work early one morning
He and the inspector they start quarrelling
The inspector feel he big and hot
Beat up Ganesh head with he revolver butt

The incident in question is the assault on Reynold Ganesh, a motorist who had committed the 'crime' of crashing into a vehicle owned and driven by Inspector Rudolph 'Scorpion' Regis of the Flying Squad. It is alleged that an irate 'Scorpion' drew his service revolver and pounded Ganesh about the head with it causing injuries which led to Ganesh's death. 'Scorpion' was duly arrested and charged with manslaughter, but like Dasent before him,[7] he was cosseted by his colleagues and was later acquitted in court.

In the Stalin scenario of "That Is Head", the policeman-businessman axis discriminates against the "rootsman", and the police function as willing instruments of their allies. "That Is Head" engages Randolph Borroughs, Commissioner of Police, with a familiarity which masks heavy irony:

Now Randy, Ah really know that you trying
Yuh utmost best to do something
But how yuh moving nothing happening
All police train to fight guerrilla
Bank robber and dope-pusher
So we end up with no investigator
And all them headmen having a field day
With nobody to carry them down
Because all you arresting people for is marijuana and gun

Burroughs had long been vilified in the calypso (Cypher's "Calypsonians in Politics" 1972; Chalkdust's "Ah Fraid Karl" 1972; Maestro's "Mr Trinidadian" 1974 and "Yuh Fooling" 1977; Dacron's "Sponsorship" 1975), and Stalin's stanza cited above implies that Burroughs' Monday morning disclosures of caches of narcotics and arms, his public relations campaign to convince the public that the service (and especially his Flying Squad) was fearless, conscientious and incorruptible, had not fooled Stalin at least. Therefore, when the calypsonian focuses on the structural defect in the training of police officers which allows the service to produce arresting officers by the score but comes up short in the department of investigations, he is satirising the institutionalised omission which allows insider 'headmen' like Burroughs, Commissioner of Police, to escape detection.

"MORALITY GONE"

Turning briefly from the realm of the purely political, one is overwhelmed by the tremendous volume of calypsoes testifying to the deterioration of social life. Many singers hardly cared to distinguish between the breakdown in the political sphere and the disintegration in private and public morality. Social life had degenerated to the point that the citizen at home, the student at school and the worshipper in church, all sought the security of protective bars. Penguin's "We Living in Jail" (1984) examines this anomaly of prison in freedom, an entire society imprisoned by the boldness and savagery of a criminal few:

Everybody talking 'bout freedom
But is like everybody blind
If you think we living in freedom
This freedom only in your mind
Everywhere I look
Criminals and crooks
Terrorise as they run amok
While poor you and me

Behind lock and key
Walking round like if we in shock

We living in jail
We living in jail
While criminals out on bail
Honest men ketching they tail
In they home-made jail
You 'fraid to open yuh door
Like we fighting war
We living in jail
We living in jail

To some calypsonians it seemed that madness had triumphed (Chalkdust's "Learn to Laugh" 1985 and "Port of Spain Gone Insane" 1986) while others felt that the last days were upon us (Stalin's "In a Earlier Time" 1981; Delamo's "Sodom and Gomorrah" 1982). Roaring Lion and Chalkdust, two Roman Catholics, shared the hope that the January 1985 visit of Pope John Paul II would apply the brake to a runaway society. Lion, who was chosen to perform before the Pontiff, sang in welcome:

His Holiness John Paul the Pilgrim Pope
Came just when we have lost courage and hope
We've sunken low spiritually
And lost all sense of Christianity
There is so much maliciousness, wickedness and selfishness
Our Nation is plagued by sheer lawlessness
So we need his blessings in Trinidad
("The Visit of His Holiness Pope John Paul II" 1985)

Chalkdust, performing at the first Biggest Universal Calypso King Show (BUCKS) later that year, deplored the wretched state of the nation. As is his wont, he develops a dramatic situation using as 'respondent' Roman Catholic Archbishop Anthony Pantin. "Pantin" in explaining his reasons for inviting the Pope confesses that, "Too much evil thing happening":

The Country have a light
It needs a blessing to change it and remove the blight
For everywhere is mad people, coke, Herpes and AIDS
Dropouts from school, pushers in the marijuana trade
And like them criminals want to take over the Nation
("Our Only Hope" 1985)

A major theme at this time is the nation's obsession with sex. Calypsonians, now in the vanguard of defining a new morality where once they stood defending the *jamette* amorality, voiced deep concern with the nation's plunge into permissiveness and promiscuity. Penguin's "Games" (1984) deplores the addiction to games, especially the skin game: accompanying and underlying every transaction is the barely disguised sexual inference "Let me play with you/I want to play with you." Even more disturbing is the evidence that aberrant sexual behaviour is on the increase. Chalkdust's "Pantin" is appalled at the unseemly boldness of the male homosexual:

> A big, big priest like me Ah cyar walk through the city
> If some homosexual ent send sweet eye for me
> Ah send for the Pope because them homosexual are a threat
> This year they take over the Carnival fete

Cardinal's "Band of the Year", which includes public and private corruption, refers to the degradation of school children:

> Is murder, rape, tief, *bobol* and bribery
> For who want to play, sex is the band fee
> When we reach in town go be bacchanal
> We have some twelve-year boys go be homosexual
> Doh play you ent see when we start to jam
> 'cause we have some Junior Sec playing lesbian

"Morality gone," Duke mourns in "A Point of Direction" (1980) and many calypsonians agree.

"CAPTAIN, THE SHIP IS SINKING!"

Searing satire of the kind delivered by Crusoe, Cardinal, Stalin and others must have contributed to the *reductio ad absurdum* of Chambers' position because the perceptions of power, duty and responsibility hold a prime minister accountable for the shortcomings of his subordinates, for the working of his administration and for the state of the nation in general. The "deaf-dumb-blind" label first hinted in Chalkdust's "Three Blind Mice" (1976) attached itself to Chambers with a vengeance.

Plain Clothes' "Chambers Done See" (1985) uses clever word play to indicate at one homonymic level ("Chambers done see", that is, Chambers has already seen) that Chambers knew what was going on, thereby implying incapacity or worse; at the other level ("Chambers done see", that is, Chambers is a dunce) that the prime minister was incapable of understanding what was going on under his very nose and eyes. Chambers riposted angrily and Plain Clothes explained that he had meant no disrespect.

Chambers' popularity was at an ebb when Gypsy performed "The Sinking Ship" (1986). In his zeal to scapegoat Chambers, Gypsy testifies inaccurately to the stability and viability of the Williams era:

> The 'Trinidad', a luxury liner
> Sailing the Caribbean Sea
> With an old captain named Eric Williams
> For years sailed smooth and free
> But sadly Eric Williams passed away
> The ship hit rough water that day
> Somebody turn the bridge over
> To a captain named Chambers
> Mih blood crawl
> Things start to fall
> Hold mih head when a sailor bawl
>
> 'Captain, the ship is sinking!
> Captain, the seas are rough
> We gas tanks almost empty
> No electricity
> We oil pressure reading low
> Shall we abandon ship
> Or shall we stay on it
> And perish slow
> We don't know, we don't know
> Captain, you tell we what to do'
>
> (ii) The 'Trinidad', oh she was a beauty
> With wealth that few surpassed
> And in her day she sailed majestically
> There were few in her class
> Faithfully she fulfilled her sailors' needs
> Some were overpowered by greed
> And so they pilfered slow
> Some took by bulk and go
> Now she looks dull, she's at a lull
> She can barely sit on her hull
>
> (iii) The 'Trinidad', in her days of sailing
> She was a friend to one and all
> She never once hesitated
> To answer all SOS calls

And yes, well she always did her best
To help out those in distress
Now it's so sad to see, she's in difficulty
Some she helped, jeer, some of them cheer
And sarcastically declare

(iv) Now there's a lot of fingers pointing
Suspicion is running strong
Who's to be blamed for all her failures
Who's to be blamed for doing her wrong
But please remember I'm warning you
For thirty years she had the same crew
Who hold the keys to her vault, so we know who's at fault
Now it's up to you, it's up to me
To make her worthy to go back to sea

"The Sinking Ship" testifies to the demigod status that Eric Williams now enjoys. Although he was captain for 25 of the 30 years that some of the crew plundered the ship, no blame or breath of taint attaches to his memory. Gypsy does not even suggest that Williams was a bad captain for being ignorant of the fact that there were pirates among his crew; or if knowing, for being unable, for whichever reason, to toss them overboard. According to the logic of his calypso, Williams was either knave or fool but Gypsy does not go so far to accuse him of one or other. One wonders if he would have been so lenient with any other prime minister.

"The Sinking Ship" became the centre of political action. The main opposition party, the National Alliance for Reconstruction (NAR), advertised its meetings with the opening words "The Ship is sinking" while PNM jerseys flaunted the message "The Ship is not sinking". Chambers is quoted as saying, "When I'm ready I will tell him [Gypsy] and all Trinidad what to do,"[8] a pointed rebuttal of the line "Captain, you tell me what to do". He wisely refrained from quarrelling in public with Gypsy, and the PNM contrived to minimise the damage wrought by the calypso: they paid Gypsy to perform at their annual carnival fete. There he and Chambers exchanged fraternal embraces and greetings. Chambers admitted later that "The Sinking Ship" was a "damned good calypso" – which it was – while Gypsy in the same spirit of friendship confessed that his calypso was "not derogatory of any political party or individual although it did give the opposition a platform to work on the ruling party". He did express the hope that the PNM "would use the song as the basis to get out of its mood of apathy".[9] Despite this diplomatic gesture, Gypsy later declared for the NAR who rewarded him with high honours in the 1988 Independence Awards Ceremony, ostensibly for his 1988 victory in an international competition held in Barbados. In the hostile anti-NAR climate of 1989, however, the platforms of 1986 and 1988 became a scaffold for Gypsy's public execution at the semifinals of the National Calypso Monarch Competition in San Fernando.

Perhaps the most intriguing feature about "The Sinking Ship" was that it provided a symbol which many could appropriate, each for his own purposes. One can only speculate that the probable cause for the universal acceptance of Gypsy's symbol lay in its timely encapsulation of a dominant mood and its presentation in an attractive musical package which allowed for protest in party, and thus linked the two poles of the modern calypso.

By this token, one can appreciate the reasons for the obscurity of Valentino's slow minor "Trini Gone through in they Consciousness" (1984), a despairingly bitter satire on the people's lack of seriousness as understood by the solitary and disillusioned prophet of the early 1970s. Valentino's final stanza, summarising all the negative things which were being voiced in the calypso of the day, predicts danger:

> And so I see this Nation
> Heading in the wrong direction
> The Nation sinking in corruption
> Old and young, rich and poor, everyone
> In confidence there's a leak
> Aboard the ship of the mighty and meek
> With them attitudes you might get stick
> And end up like the 'Titanic
>
> They have no discipline, little tolerance
> So their production can't support their Independence
> All they have is this party mentality
> From in '56 and the days of Dr Willie
> Since 1970 I and I notice
> Oh Jah! Trini running last in they consciousness
> In partying and feteing they stay the hardest
> But Trini gone through in they consciousness

This calypso raises several points besides the likening of the "Trinidad" to the "Titanic". First, Valentino wrenches the nation's watchwords from their optimistic 1962 setting to rework them in the bleak setting of the 1980s. Secondly, he dates the 'rum and roti' syndrome of national politics to 1956, inaccurately. Thirdly, he turns into a taunt the PNM's boast of being the force to initiate party politics. Finally, Valentino sees 1970 as the beginning and end of consciousness and he somehow seems to have trapped himself in that time and space thus contributing to his own decline as a popular artiste.

At the end of 1986 Trinidad and Tobago found itself in crisis. Clearly the PNM was intellectually incapable of government, psychologically and physically unable to guide the country out of the morass into which it had led it, morally unable to redress wrong; the citizenry was cowed and afraid for the future, reverting to the primal as defence against encroaching others. If the calypso Jeremiahs speak true, many citizens had lost direction and were literally grasping at straws (of cocaine) and at skirts (sometimes of reluctant women, or, sadly, willing men). Given that there reigned the notion that the political directorate and direction were responsible for all our wrongs, the nation embarked on a grail quest which could revive the wasteland.

A concerted movement of the people was needed to realise this noble objective. This seemed achieved in the union of four parties which brought together races and classes in an alliance for national reconstruction. A leader was needed – not D'Alberto's cosmic Rambo the Avenger ("Rambo" 1987) – but a politician of courage and vision who could rescue and enlighten the twin-island republic. Believing that the many symptoms of disorder and disease in the body politic and social were part of the syndrome of bad government, and with childlike trust in the efficacy of a political purge, the public turned once more to a general election.

GENERAL ELECTION 1986

By 1986 the wheel had come full circle for the PNM. In 1956 they had blamed the country's troubles on colonialism. "Colonialism," Williams had declared dramatically, "There's the enemy."[10] By 1986 PNM had completed the Orwellian transformation to become that enemy. The calypsonian had long urged the ballot and in 1986 he felt that the public finally listened.

Calypsoes blared from loudspeakers as the political parties awoke to the power of the political Calypso in mass communication. PNM mobile units blasted out the Machel Montano song "I Love My Country" (1985), thereby hoping to attract the vitality of youth (Machel was a mere 11-year-old when he made the national finals in 1986) to what was largely a gerontocracy. NAR adherents jammed frantically to Gypsy's "The Sinking Ship" and Deple's "Vote Dem Out".

Before 1986 Deple was a comedian. He claims that he was asked by an NAR member to write a campaign song and this he did, secure in the belief that the public would have forgiven him if the NAR had lost.[11] When Deple admitted this he was the chairman of a constituency arm of the NAR, but when interviewed one year later at the inaugural public meeting of Club '88, a breakaway faction of rebel NAR parliamentarians en route to becoming the United National Congress (UNC), Deple renounced party affiliation.[12] His political career produced his only major song.

"Vote Dem Out" met all the specifications of a campaign song: its aggressive *kalinda* antiphony could be sung, chanted and danced; it convinced the voter of the power of his vote; and it did not make any electoral promises of its own. It did not endorse any party either, but the NAR, knowing that it was written in its name (it was probably financed by the party too) used it as a battle hymn. It is impressive in its directness and simplicity:

> Your vote will decide
> Our destiny
> Your vote will decide
> What you want to be
> Your vote can foretell
> Our Country's fate
> Go and use it well
> Before it's too late
>
> If it is that who you vote may be on a doubt
> When you voting vote them out, vote them out
> If it is they proving to be only full of mout'
> When you voting vote them out, vote them out
> If it is the time is now that this should come about
> When you voting vote them out, vote them out
> Register and
> Vote them out
> If they duncie
> Vote them out
> Stain yuh finger and
> Vote them out
> Show them no mercy
> Vote them out
> Vote them out with total scorn and utter disdain
> Let's put our Country together again
> Vote them out of power, terminate their reign
> Let's put our Country together again
>
> (ii) If for thirty years
> You voting them in
> And is only tears
> As soon as they win
> They giving you big words
> And enslave your souls

Promising you roads
And giving potholes

If they are the reason why the economy won't sprout
When you voting, vote them out, vote them out
If they passing laws that them alone could flout
When you voting, vote them out, vote them out
If it is they building eyesores east, west, north and south
When you voting, vote them out, vote them out
The same way you vote them in
Register and
vote them out
Stain your finger and
vote them out
Rescue the Country
vote them out
Vote them out with tempo
They have we in pain
Let's put our Country together again
Vote them out with Calypso and joyous refrain
Let's put our Country together again

(iii) If their policy
Is a fallacy
If their bureaucracy
A catastrophe
If they cannot cope
And you seeing so
Then your only hope
Is for them to go

If it is fabrications the statements that they spout
When you voting, vote them out, vote them out
If it is that frustration does make you want to shout
When you voting vote them out, vote them out
Before they misuse out, tief out, sell out and digs out
When you voting, vote them out, vote them out
If is you who vote them in
Vote them out
Register and
vote them out
Stain your finger and
vote them out

Vote them out in Scarborough and in Port of Spain
Let's put our Country together again
Vote them out in Cumuto and in La Romain
Let's put our Country together again

(iv) People must come first
Citizens by right
None of we ent worse
Yellow, black or white
Food, shelter and clothes
Free movement and speech
A garden that grows
And one law for each

If it is that injustice is what they always show
When you voting, vote them out, vote them out
If it is that avarice is all they seem to know
When you voting, vote them out, vote them out
If it is their politics is just a *pappyshow*
When you voting, vote them out, vote them out
When election day come, all bandits must go
Register and
vote them out
Stain your finger and
vote them out
Vote them out with total scorn and utter disdain
Let's put our Country together again
Vote them out of power terminate their reign
Let's put our Country together again.

A December carnival needed a road march all its own and this Deple supplied using the double chorus technique of Kitchener's immortal "Rainorama" (1973).

As Deple recommended, the electorate voted out the PNM "with calypso and joyous refrain". After the battle, PNMites lamented their dolour to the tune and revised lyrics of Merchant's "Pain" (1986), thus linking their distress to the international horrors detailed by the calypsonian. On the other side, NAR members cavorted and whooped in the first flush of victory, but when they faced the enormity of their achievement they sobered up. Aware of having created a power vacuum and fearful for the future, they resurrected Sparrow's "Lend a Hand" (1971), which many Trinidadians then thought was a new song, as a rallying cry for the nation as a whole.

Surprisingly, the volume of election commentary which had been drying up since 1962, almost in tune with the decline in voter participation, was reduced to a trickle although the voter turn-out showed that many considered this a crucial ballot. More surprisingly, despite the scope of victory, paeans of victory were rare with Sparrow's "One Love, One Heart" being the best known. One probable cause for this is that by 15 December when the election was contested, most calypsonians would already have recorded their new offerings for the next season, and so would either have had to write new songs or wait for the results thus risking loss of air play in the early season. Sparrow, preoccupied with restoring his faltering image with remixes of past glory, had rerecorded hits like "Jean and Dinah" on his *Party Classics* album whose success delayed the release of his second album *One Love, One Heart*, the title track of which did receive some air time before wilting in the carnival heat, it being a feeble song at best.

Most election commentary was unflattering. Quasar, a practising attorney, took issue with the declaration "all ah we tief", the most significant single statement of the entire campaign. PNM Minister Desmond Cartey had made it in *picong* response to heckling from an amused crowd and perhaps with the meaning that the average citizen was not above chicanery in some form, but he was represented as confessing to PNM corruption. Quasar, reacting to the newspaper article in which the Cartey statement appeared, dissociated himself from the grand larceny allegedly practised by the PNM:

All ah we tief
This big man declare
All ah we tief
And people splitting like Fred Astaire
But you ever see me Piarco leaving under escort?
I doh even have a diplomatic passport
All ah we tief
Me cyar take that so
I doh have no Chinese garden nor no tower in Toronto
So the next time you feel like speaking, speak for yourself, Chief
I ent know 'bout you
But I know . . . I ent tief

Quasar's references are to the flight of John O'Halloran which was made possible by the grant of a diplomatic passport. O'Halloran's name had been bandied about in nearly all the major scandals involving improper financial deals since the early 1960s and it was felt that only his closeness to Williams protected him from prosecution. When public opinion finally mounted against this man, Chambers, reneging on his promise to "put right the things which are wrong", granted him a diplomatic passport and had him escorted to safety. The "tower in Toronto" forms part of the O'Halloran Foundation. The "Chinese garden", known otherwise as the

Japanese garden, decorated the palatial home of Errol Mahabir, another senior PNM cabinet minister. Interestingly, Quasar's two references are the same as Delamo's in "Apocalypse".

Quasar's calypso singing career seems to have consisted of this one song. One cannot help thinking that this lawyer, debarred by the ethics of his profession from making statements difficult to prove in a court of law yet offended by the impunity with which suspected miscreants escape their just deserts, may have been using the calypso as a medium of protest and for therapy. The evidence he tenders is the calypso, although supported by the witness of other calypsonians, is clearly not of justifiable quality as the lawyer in him would caution. Therefore, like the singers in West Africa[13] and the calypsonians in the Caribbean, Christopher Grant sought to use the song tradition as the medium for venting his dissatisfaction.

One of the more successful commentaries was Bally's cynical and mordant "Party Time" which sees the election as one big fete. Designed and constructed for the dancehall where it scored enviable success, "Party Time" ridicules the manoeuvres of the politicians and power brokers:

It was party time once again across the land
Anywhere you pass people they get out of hand
With DJ George and Robbie in front the band
All because of party time, party time
Them promoters, all ah them had silver tongue
They make you feel their fete was the best around
With promises of Utopia in song
All because of party time, party time

You shoulda hear them
Jump high, jump low
Shake yuh manifesto
Ramajay, come leh we *ramajay*
The five years nearly done
Is time to have some fun
Ramajay, come leh we ramajay
Ah-ha
Was a Carnival
Ah-ha
If you see ramgoat
Ah-ha
Join the bacchanal
Ah-ha
Just to get your vote
RAN, NPM
Begging you to fete with them
Party time, party time

The PNM is satirised through the dancing movements of the buxom members of the League of Women's voters ("And the Fat Brigade I ketch them shaking glass"). The well-endowed anatomies shaking at public occasions make them targets for Bally's cheap shot.

Hidden away in the exciting music is snide criticism of how and why the NAR (RAN in the calypso) came into being:

> There was one DJ called Robbie the Tax Wizard
> For mixing tunes, well he was the hardest hard
> He mix up four, construct into one real bad
> Just because was party time

A.N.R. Robinson, who had promised to revise the system of PAYE to provide exemption for lower-income groups, becomes in the party idiom "Robbie the Tax Wizard", a take-off on DJ Papa Rocky the Wax Wizard, one of the country's leading operators. The necessary DJ skill of 'mixing' describes how Robinson took four unitary organisations and formed out of them "a party of parties". The calypso suggests, however, that the NAR elected under the same conditions of fete as was the PNM, would behave in like manner and that the 1991 election would be just as that of 1986.

Bro J.'s "The Advice" cautions Robinson against squandering the excellent opportunities presented him by the overwhelming victory. Politicised to a high degree because of his antecedents, he is the son of old Butlerite, A.P.T. James, and because of his trade union background, J. sees the election triumph as the culmination of all the progressive forces in the country and not necessarily the work of a few politicians. He looks at the victory as earnest of a thrust towards a bold new world and, accordingly, his advice contains elements of encouragement and warning:

> You promise we a spiritual rejuvenation
> As you marched across the land
> Saying, 'It's time for reconstruction'
> If you don't deliver these goods to the people
> Then Arthur Raymond Robinson your backside in trouble

Written during the Christmas holidays 1986, "The Advice" was meant to be a backup song to "National Unity", but early in the tent season Bro J. witnessed the large scale demonstrations against the suspension of Cost Of Living Allowance (COLA) which the NAR government had announced in its first 'budget of sacrifices'. J. thought it better to sing "The Advice" to suit these new developments – not to mention that "National Unity" was not doing as well as he had anticipated.

A practitioner of extempo, J. created lines during performance. The key couplet "Robbie, this ent no jive/But I don't feel that you could make five" does not appear in his original manuscript and J. is at a loss to place it in his revised script. Other lines written before the first NAR crisis, assume different significance in the changed mood to the extent that when J.'s tent, Culture House, visited Tobago, the leader of the band was loth to play fearing violent reaction on the part of Tobagonians who doted on Robinson who was born on that island. Valentino, no doubt remembering his own experience of 1971 when Kitchener tried to bench him when Williams visited the tent, supported J. in using backstage language to convince the musician. J. wisely inserted the couplet "We know you from Castara/That is why we choose you as Prime Minister" and the crowd loved his performance. "The Advice" was the lone bright spot in a tent which folded in mid season, fortunately after J. had qualified for the national semifinal of the Calypso King competition.

THE SCOTT DRUG REPORT AND THE "TESORO SCANDAL"

Two sensational exposés rocked the nation in 1987. February witnessed the publication of the report of the Commission of Inquiry into the extent of the problem of drug abuse in Trinidad and Tobago, and March brought the news that former prime minister Chambers had been implicated in a scandal during the 1970s when he had been PNM's finance minister.

The first intimation that the Scott Drug Report was political dynamite came indirectly in the fall from grace of Police Commissioner Randolph Burroughs. Rejoicing in the borrowed name and image of television cop 'Kojak', this egregious personality had dominated the political scene as the enforcer arm of the PNM government until his political masters, embarrassed by the wealth of evidence against him in the then unpublished report, had him charged with misconduct in office and with drug trafficking. He was cleared in 1987 but it was obvious that 'Kojak's' time was up. Rudder's "Kojak" represents his departure in typical innuendo:

Kojak was the hardest
Kojak was the baddest
He was the baddest man to walk through the TV land
But one day the programme director
Say, 'Out with the inspector!'
And they take him off with just a wave of the hand

The town say
'They take Kojak off the TV
But what about Dallas and Dynasty

They take Kojak off the TV
But what about Dallas and Dynasty'

Kojak had a lollipop
And every day you could see him suck
The flavour wasn't cherry or vanilla
The flavour was power
So one day the programme director
Say, 'Out with the Inspector!'
Too much of crime on the screen
So they take him off for the hour

In a land addicted to television and feasting on American programming, reality becomes a television fantasy. If "Kojak" is removed from the screen then other high profile soap operas should also be taken off. In his unique way, Rudder queried the nonremoval of other highly placed figures commonly thought to be involved in the drug trade.

Chalkdust's "Scapefox" (1987) insisted that Burroughs was sacrificed for the sins of others and for the collective crimes of the Police Service which he headed. By using the term "Scapefox" ("the Fox" was one of Burroughs' nicknames before "Kojak" appeared on our television screens), Chalkdust suggests that Burroughs was no helpless innocent dragged to the altar, but a wily operator finally brought to earth by hunters. Despite this, the calypso is more intent upon showing up the cynical exploitative nature of the PNM government which had allowed Burroughs free run until 1986:

You filled his hands with power until it overflow
You gave him authority and machine guns for so
You gave him the right to search any man's bungalow
You gave him the right to kill prisoner, friend or foe
You made him judge and jury, hangman and boucanier
You laughed when bereaved ones shed a tear – in fear
Despite all the evidence that the people disclose
You waited years to hold Burroughs

You made him a god now you calling him a devil
You done know the score
What you holding the man for
The Flying Squad killed so many people
You done know the score
What you holding the man for
Who killed Kenneth Tenia

Police
Joel de Masia
Police
Buried Guy Harewood bones
Police
Who killed Beverly Jones
Police
All these people die
Not one word, you just close yuh eye
You done know the score
What you holding the man for
It have plenty more
Who does play jigsaw with the law
You done know the score
What you holding the damn man for

"Scapefox", one in the continuing series of calypsonian-policeman conflict which had not been seriously affected by the presence of calypsonian/policemen such as Johnny King, provides a detailed list of those who had died at the hands of the police since 1972, but Chalkdust makes the additional protest at the political use of the service against his party NJAC:

You make him Commissioner to keep you in power
When the Black Power men were threatening to take over
You make him train policemen with hand grenades and then
So that they will hit and wipe out all them NJAC men
You make him pay criminals as police informer
Then make him Trinity Cross holder – like Butler
You worshipped his machine gun, all his misdeeds you endorse
Now you want to nail him to the cross

As a member of NJAC which reveres Butler as the father of the nation, Chalkdust is understandably horrified that the PNM government equated the chief servant with the nation's chief executioner, Burroughs, being regarded as merely an extension of his smoking gun. Burroughs was awarded the nation's highest honour, one that Butler had to wait so long for despite his lifetime of struggle and sacrifice.

Anxious to underwrite the hypocrisy of the PNM, Chalkdust juggles the sequence of events because Burroughs had been appointed commissioner in October 1978, long after NJAC ceased to be a system-threatening mass movement, and long after NUFF, not NJAC, had been destroyed by police gunfire. Also the "you" is deliberately and dishonestly vague: Williams was the "you" who had made possible the rapid ascent of his protégé (who, curiously enough, did not represent the service at his funeral); Chambers was the "you" who withdrew the protective mantle. Chalkdust must have known this because his calypso reflects the phases of Burroughs' Williams-sponsored omnipotence and his public relations created omnipresence since 1970.

As said before, the trial of Burroughs was the first ripple from the inquiry into the drug problem. The commission, appointed in 1984, had presented its findings in February 1986, but the continuing silence of Prime Minister Chambers on the contents of the report aroused the worst suspicions. On the campaign trail, Robinson had promised to disclose the contents but once in office, he too manifested reluctance until the publication of sections of the report in Caribbean media forced his hand. Reactions ranging from screams of outrage to knowing smiles of confirmation greeted the airing of the report but its contents were largely ignored in the calypso. Chalkdust's "Calypso Drug Report" exulted at the vindication of the lowly calypsonian and crowed at the fall of members of the glamour professions. Valentino, too, revived the idea of the People's Court, a notion deriving from NJAC's heyday, and of the Kaiso Court of the mid 1970s to try those named in the drug report. Apart from these, calypsonians ignored the claims which in some cases simply substantiated assertions they had made in song many years before (Cypher's "Calypsonians in Politics" 1972; Chalkdust's "Ah Fraid Karl" 1972; Maestro's "Mr Trinidadian" 1974 and "Yuh Fooling" 1977; Dacron's "Sponsorship" 1975).

Greater interest was taken in the news of the alleged suborning of former Prime Minister Chambers by the Tesoro Corporation, and the revelation that a blonde prostitute had been procured for him at a cost to the corporation of some three thousand US dollars. For purposes of background, it is necessary to summarise reports of allegations appearing in the newspapers.[14] In 1974, then Finance Minister Chambers attempted to impose a new tax regime on the Trinidad Tesoro Company which protested, citing arrangements agreed to by John O'Halloran who had signed for the government when the joint venture between the state and the Tesoro Corporation was established. Not trusting legalities, Tesoro president, Robert West, a man versed in intrigue and subterfuge, arranged for a prostitute to entertain Chambers at his hotel suite in Ottawa whither he had travelled for a meeting with international financiers in January of 1975. By June, the government caved in to demands by Tesoro for special treatment. The tip of the "Tesoro Scandal" iceberg, Chambers' 'business mating', was disclosed in a Texas court where West was being indicted for stock manipulation. Although Chambers denied the allegation, he did not secure a retraction as had happened earlier when a journal apologised for publishing a statement reproducing an allegation that he had received illegal payments from Tesoro.[15]

In the normal course of events, the public would have had to wait until the next season, that is, January 1988, to enjoy the calypso interpretation of this salacious detail, but the staging of a calypso competition to mark the 25th anniversary of independence provided the calypsonian with a forum for public comment while the exposé was still fresh in the mind. Chambers and his blonde would form a subtheme in that competition as the calypsonian, amused and intrigued by (one hopes, not jealous of) this Congo Man relationship, zeroed in on the encounter.

A point of interest in the 1987 calypsoes is the absence of comment hostile to the NAR, except for Bro J.'s reaction to the removal of COLA. Granted that COLA was removed after the tents were opened, one still expects that any calypsonian worth his salt would find ways of making calypso comment on this measure and its far reaching implications. Conjecturally, it seems that the calypsonian was unsure of the reaction on the part of a public which had shown massive solidarity with the NAR government in the voluntary clean up of January 1987, a campaign in which the calypsonian may well have participated. And yet while the calypsonian hesitated, the calypso going audience took the lead in venting anti-NAR sentiment by booing Robinson at the 1987 Calypso Fiesta. It was explained that the fiesta, staged as usual at Skinner Park, San Fernando, was swarmed by residents of Pleasantville, heartland of the constituency hardly won by new PNM leader, Patrick Manning, who was warmly applauded. This explanation seems specious at best.

It is thought that the calypsonian leads the nation into vice and racial conflict, vilification being his usual meed in spite of his sterling efforts to instill national pride and overarching national ideals including racial harmony. The rise and fall of the NAR government gives one the opportunity to study the role of the calypso and the calypsonian in shaping public opinion. As seen above, the calypsonian did not initiate the anti-NAR pogrom: he simply grafted his protest onto an existing and very obvious dissatisfaction. Even when it was clear that the NAR had forfeited popular support, the calypsonian hesitated until, with the encouragement of the public, he attacked with full force.

The Mighty Explainer

The Mighty Chalkdust

The Mighty
Stalin

Lord
Valentino

El Maestro

Calypso Rose

Lord Shorty ▶

Black Stalin
and Cro Cro
COURTESY OF
THE GUARDIAN
NEWSPAPER

◀ Sparrow and
Dr Williams

Happy Anniversary:
The 25th Anniversary of Independence
Calypso Monarch Competition

The date 31 August 1987 marked the nation's 25th anniversary of independence. In the history of any nation, such an event serves as occasion for celebration of achievement, as cause for assessment and rededication to the national service, and as assurance of continuity or tradition which is a source of strength and inspiration in facing the future. While all this can be ritualised by means of parades, awards ceremonies and the like, Trinidad and Tobago has the added advantage of the calypso which can articulate the aspirations and immortalise the achievements of the people in their own language.

One can only wonder at the curious fact that the decade after 1962 witnessed no national independence calypso competition. Perhaps it was that those who should normally have seen to this, felt that the calypso segment at the annual PNM Buy Local Jamboree was enough, but when one recalls that the national government never thought of national awards until forced to respond to Granger's Pegasus initiative,[1] one may well conclude that the organisers of the independence celebrations had simply forgotten about the calypso. As it was, the second independence calypso competition was realised at the 10th Anniversary of Independence celebrations, that is 1972. There, singers performed two songs, and Chalkdust, the winner, offered his "We Are Ten Years Old", a trenchant critique of a decade of statehood, a comprehensive catalogue of nonachievement. Perhaps the popularity of this excellent song, coming in the wake of a Buy Local Competition which, though moribund at this time, had taken an increasingly critical tone, convinced the several independence celebrations committees that they should spare themselves embarrassment at the hands of the calypsonian. This may explain why in 1977, the 15th anniversary of independence, there was no competition although the state coffers were awash with oil dollars. It may also account for the omission of the Calypso from the 20th anniversary of independence celebrations in 1982 when the "total breakdown fete", as Stalin calls it in "Breakdown Party"

(1980) was on its last legs, or before the lights went out, if we bear in mind Mrs Muriel Donawa-McDavidson's tree lighting *pappyshow*.[2] Perhaps the local Arabs who feted away the nation's god-sent, or more accurately, OPEC-sent, revenue, overlooked the calypso; perhaps too, they instinctively feared the element of unpredictability or cynical realism personified by the calypsonian. Whatever the reason 1972–87 produced no competition, and even that of 1987 was privately organised, as we shall see.

Before discussing the songs performed at the 25th anniversary of independence competition, we must consider calypso commentary on intergroup social relations and especially Afro-Indian affairs which, as several calypsonians had indicated in 1962, were critical to the development of nationhood. One can begin by pointing out that most of the major controversies of the survey period had to do with the question of race relations.

In 1973 the Hindu community sent two clear signals that it was displeased at the overt disrespect towards it as was manifested in the calypso. On the morning following the Calypso King Competition at the St Augustine campus, protest action by the Society for the Propagation of Indian Culture forced a cancellation of classes for one day as students debated the issue of respect. What precipitated the brouhaha was Rawle Aimey's wearing the costume of an Indian dancer and singing:

Ram Ram Sita Ram
Salaam babu Salaam
Am a true true Indian man
Salaam babu salaam

Aimey's target was his wayward lecturer, Lloyd Best, who on the campaign beat, had worn what looked like a dhoti at a meeting with Curepe taxi drivers.[3]

Later that year, the Pawan Sajeewan Hindu Cultural Organisation urged cabinet to ban Shorty's "Indrani" which they thought to be a denigration of East Indian womanhood.[4] Cabinet did not agree that it was.

Nineteen seventy-nine witnessed what one of the protagonists, UWI social psychology lecturer, Dr Ramesh Deosaran, called "the most animated and pervasive calypso controversy in Trinidad and Tobago's history"[5] (until then, that is). Stalin's "Caribbean Unity" had advocated a coming together of the Caribbean people on the basis that

Is one race
The Caribbean Man
From the same place
The Caribbean Man
That make the same trip

The Caribbean Man
On the same ship
The Caribbean Man

Stalin won his first Calypso Monarch title with this song (and "Play One"), to the infinite delight of his numerous supporters and many of the Afro-Trinidadian community. When he clarified, for the benefit of a television audience, that by "Caribbean Man" he meant the Afro-Caribbean man, he was roundly criticised by Deosaran and others, including Afro-Trinidadians, and was defended as vigorously by journalists, academics and others.

Earlier that year, Shorty's performance of "Om Shanti" had offended the Hindu community. The Sanatan Dharma Maha Sabha, horrified at the spectacle of The Love Man's 'wineing' to a sacred mantra, and aghast at the possibility of this unholy act being replicated thousands of times on the streets over the carnival, appealed to Pan-Trinbago and to the CDC to keep the calypso off their programmes and further made the formal request to have it banned from the Carnival streets.[6]

In 1980 the Hindu Vishwa Parsad successfully petitioned cabinet for the withdrawal of the line "Hindu priest raping school children and all" from Scrunter's "Take the Number", on the grounds that the matter to which the calypso alluded was still sub judice, and that the line "tended to show Hindus in a bad light."[7]

In the 1980s it was the turn of the Afro-Trinidadian to condemn what he perceived as antiblack sentiment in the calypso. In 1982 Afro-Trinidadian feminists attacked Sparrow because his "Maharajin" proposed marriage to a *doolahin*, an honourable act which his many songs on encounters with Afro-Trinidadian women never considered. By way of response, Sparrow, who is happily married to an Afro-Barbadian, offered "Maharajin Sister" (1983) and "Maharajin Cousin" (1984). The feminists got the point; so too did the Indo-Trinidadian purists who had bristled at the mere thought of a mixed marriage.

Johnny King received a baptism of fire because his "Nature's Plan" (1984) identified the blacks in South Africa as a people doomed to servitude by design of nature. Several Afro-Trinidadians responded in anger to this suggestion and to the lack of race pride demonstrated by those unthinking descendants of Africa who, ignoring the lyrics of the stanzas, as so often happens, revelled to the melody of the chorus. Natasha Wilson's "Reincarnation Wish" (1985) triggered off angry response from the Afro-Trinidadian who was as disgusted with the content of the song as upset with the fact that it brought Natasha the National Junior Calypso Monarch title.[8] By contrast there was no furore over the bizarre CDC decision to disqualify Chalkdust's "Grandfather Backpay" (1985) from the finals on the grounds that it was divisive and "could spread racial strife in the country".[9] Surprisingly, Chalkdust, who is normally very vocal on his exclusion from the finals, took this absurd decision very well.

The manifestation of tension within the national community and the perception that the calypso contributes to the escalation of those tensions are part of the background against which we must evaluate the 25th Anniversary of Independence Calypso Competition.

This competition was sponsored and organised not by the NAR government which was still reeling under the impact of inheriting an empty treasury, but by the National Brewing Company (brewers of Stag lager beer) and the Fernandes Distillers Company (manufacturers of Vat 19 rum), both of which had prospered during the recession. The Stag/Vat 19 National 25th Anniversary of Independence Calypso Competition was launched solemnly at the Fernandes Industrial Centre in the presence of the NAR Minister of Culture. Innovative prizes were offered, including the imaginative incentive of 40 hours of recording time for the winner, a prize so attractive that it lured most of the top singers in the land. Unfortunately, several monarchs still active in calypsodom, chose to abstain from the competition: Sparrow, seven-time King, eight-time Road March winner and reigning BUCK's King, did not participate, neither did three-time Monarch, Stalin, who, revelling in his 1987 success, had gone off in high good spirits on his first European jaunt; Kitchener, the Grand Master, ten-time Road March King and Calypso King of 1975, and David Rudder, the thrice-crowned rave of 1986, had both forsworn competition. But calypso royalty was well represented in the persons of Chalkdust, three-time national monarch and defending Independence King (having won in 1972 when the competition was last staged); Melody, King of 1954; Pretender, the ageless King of 1957; Lutha and Bally, Young King of 1985 and 1987 respectively; Valentino, an uncrowned king, if ever there was one; Shadow, the 1974 Road March King and Francine, the oft-crowned National Calypso Queen. The original field of 100 plus had been whittled down to 12 for the finals on 22 August at the National Stadium.

The technical problem of having to evaluate 25 years of significant happening is summarised succinctly in Rio's opening lines: "Twenty five years of History/ Five minutes to explain". But calypsonians responded with enthusiasm and ingenuity to this challenging invitation. Lutha's "Trinbago" personified the state, which then presented an autobiographical sketch, while Bally delved into the archives, there to discover Williams' oft-quoted Independence message to the youth, and he entered in his "School Book" what he thought had been the main developments since 1962. Valentino, honoured by Chalkdust as one of the few remaining "spin bowlers of Calypso" ("Calypso Cricket" 1987), employed a cricketing metaphor: "On a wicket that's sticky and very tricky/ You stood there and made a quarter century" in his "I Salute You". This song is distinguished musically by the appropriate use of marching rhythms which marked Valentino's return to the lyrics of commitment, and thematically by its judicious avoidance of the political and social issues he had been at pains to discuss since 1971. De Fosto's "The Flag" likewise avoided the thorny problems of human failing by settling for a rededication to the ideals symbolised by the national flag. Several singers used the imagery of the family so that the competition produced a number of Mother Trinidad and Sister Tobago and similar family-type relationships. Chalkdust's "Granny's Advice", for example, presented the 25-year-old Trinidad complaining to his grandmother Africa about the "little boy" status he still enjoyed in the eyes of "others" although he was married to Miss Tobago and had a "deputy" in Miss Grenada.

The competition differed markedly from that held on 15 August 1962 in its lack of unanimity of approach to the subject matter. There were several songs of praise along conventional lines; several reserved statements reflecting their authors' dilemma of wanting to keep faith with the celebratory nature of the competition while retaining vivid memories of the missed opportunities and the misdirection of the era; and there were still others which frankly admitted the failure of the independence experience. The mood of unbounded optimism and euphoria of 15 August 1962 was tempered by the sobering acceptance that the country had not progressed as much as it could and should have.

Despite this, the declarations of love still held sway as did the declarations of commitment to the land which is still described as a model nation. The racial unity theme, the most beloved national myth, was resurrected for public adoration; state-sponsored heroes of the period, Hasely Crawford, Claude Noel and Leslie Stewart (the first being the nation's first Olympic gold medallist, the others world-title holders in professional boxing) were given their due praise. Only Chalkdust remembered the calypsonian and the steelbandsman among the nation's nurses together with Cipriani and Gene Miles. Winners of international beauty pageants, Miss Universe 1977, Janelle "Penny" Commissiong and Miss World 1986, Giselle LaRonde, were toasted. Rio sang ecstatically:

We have lovely women here like crazy ants
To make Mona Lisa look like Jack Palance

thus uniting in a *cosquel* cluster the homely ("crazy ants"), the classical European ("Mona Lisa") and the American ("Jack Palance", the big white ugly of Western movies). To this, Short Pants ("Leh We Show") responds sourly that if Trinidad's women are so desirable why would someone want to "flock around with Blondie", an unkind but typically calypso reference to the alleged Chambers affair.

Shadow's "From Then to Now" typifies to some extent the conventional praise song heard at the competition:

There was a change in the region
One of intelligence
From colonialism
Straight to Independence
Grand celebration
From country to town
We became a Nation
And still going strong

From then 'til now I've seen progress
I've seen distress
I've seen a multiracial society
Living in total harmony
The African, the Indian man
The China man, the Syrian
Yet we don't have racial confusion
That's what makes us a model nation
Trinidad and Tobago, my king and my queen
Trinidad and Tobago, a paradise in the Caribbean

Stanzas two and three synopsise the history of the period showing how Williams in his father/founder role:

. . . led us like Moses
Led the children to the Promised Land
He built us the stages
Then left us to perform

This singular adulation which echoes Dougla of 1962 finds no response in other songs, and one may note here that veneration of the leadership, a significant feature of 1962, is absent from 1987 and is replaced by cynical references to venery and venality. In point of fact, the singers of 1987 call upon the citizenry to make independence work as if the leadership mattered not at all. Returning to Shadow's effort, his story takes the listener through the stages by which Port of Spain progressed from a 'colonial fancy' to become a modern city. In his inimitable way he lumps together the nation's prized resources into the irreverent melange "gasoline, kerosene, healthy beings and beauty queens".

But the unease underlying the composition emerges in the final stanza when Shadow exhorts the nation to concerted effort in order to exorcise the atavistic demons of race and class:

Now let's get together
We've got work to do
You got to remember
The future depend on you
Unity is strength
And strength is what we need
And if we combine our strength
Together we will succeed

From now 'til then I hope to see
A unity
They say Faith can move a mountain
And unity can do the same thing
Like making peace
From West to East
Feed hungry mouth
From North to South
And when we conquer this situation
We shall become a super-nation

Seventy-year-old Pretender begins with an assessment which concedes some degree of failure but rejoices in the nation's stability and its adherence to the rule of law:

Looking back down the corridors of Time
I began to reminisce
So I make up mih mind
I have to come and tell you this
From the past twenty five years or so
We ent really reach where we want to go
But I think I can tell you with assurance
That we have come a long way since Independence

No nation in the world cyar come close to we
When talking about racial equality
No matter what your nationality
You living in a Land of true-true democracy
So if you from St Clair or quite Castara
You could be President or Prime Minister
Let's raise our hands to the Almighty
On our 25th Anniversary

He describes the meaning of independence as a personal experience, thus affording a perspective that is largely unknown to later generations who take for granted the blessings – such as they are – of an independent state:

> First things first, so I have to let you know
> I was born many years ago
> I was living in that cruel time
> When poverty was really a crime
> That time I didn't even have the privilege
> To carry a message inside the college
> But today every Tom, Dick or Harry
> Could go to college or university

"Our 25th Anniversary" conjures visions of the exultation that the black urban proletariat must have felt in 1956 and in 1962. Listening to Pretender, one understands the unswerving loyalty of the Afro-Trinidadians of his generation to the PNM even in decadence, and one appreciates especially the deification of Williams by that group.

Thirty-four-year-old Cro Cro, singing in the very next position, reflects the disillusionment of the offspring of Pretender's generation, those children into whose school bags Williams had entrusted the nation's future:

> I didn't want to sing
> 'cause I ent like this thing
> I does sing facts
> And I does end up getting the axe
> You see, they does wilfully keep me down
> Now they invite me to sing for they Independence Crown
> I start to frown
> I tell mih girl I ent singing none
> But she tell me if you don't sing up there
> She say, Cro Cro, John Public wouldn't hear
> The evils them vultures do
> Since Independence 1962
>
> It had PNM niggers and DLP coolies
> Is them what instil that racialism in we
> For twenty five years
> Them politicians give we tears
> I go be stupidee
> To come here and sing 'Happy Anniversary'
> Ah go be happy, happy

To see Gene Miles arresting Kenneth Tam in a gas station
With Pat Solomon and a policeman
Ah go be happy, happy
And Ah go sing sweetly
'Happy Anniversary'

According to this first generation Trinidadian, independence has only brought racism, corruption and the victimisation of those who sought to sing out against these evils. Cro Cro refers first to the Solomon Affair and to the Gas Station Racket, both of which happened when he was in his early teens, and both of which, according to the song, would have to be put right before he can celebrate independence.

Stanza two recalls the glorious post-1973 scramble for wealth:

Trinidad was nice
Was a paradise
Oil flew freely
Ministers fix theyself and they family . . . independently
They thought that the oil woulda always flow
They used to say Trinbago is El Dorado
They shoulda know
That some good day it wouldna be so
They wheel and they deal over the years
Who plant Japanese gardens, who make fares
Now the whole of Wall Street laughing at we
Ki-ki-ki, three thousand dollars US for a blondie

Curiously enough, the trajectory of this calypso at once converges on and diverges away from Pretender's. Both congratulate the nation for its maturity in effecting a peaceful transfer of power following the 1986 general election, but it is at this point that the two philosophically different songs seem to alter course with each adopting the line followed earlier by the other. Pretender, perhaps regretting the decline of the PNM, voices reservations for the future ("As regards the outcome of the future/Well that is a matter of conjecture"), while Cro Cro expresses confidence that the future will produce a reality which will enable him to sing lustily "Happy Anniversary!" Differing starkly in tone, focus and style, these two calypsoes achieve consensus in one matter and this is in their determination that the country urgently needs a collective effort in the national interest.

Looking at Shadow's "From Then to Now", Pretender's "Our 25th Anniversary" and Cro Cro's "Happy Anniversary" one understands the diversity of approach caused by the differences of attitude to the past; calypsonians regard the anniversary as occasion for celebration or commemoration, and yet they voice hope that the future can be more profitable and can give point to the ideals of 1962.

The undisputed success song of the competition was Funny's "How Yuh Feel?". Funny, as the sobriquet so correctly implies, had started his career as a humorist, but a social conscience had propelled him into the arena of politics ("Ah Soul Man" 1981; "Right and Wrong" 1983). In August 1987, needing to reconcile the expectations of a praise song with the memory of shame and blame, and reluctant to compromise memory in favour of sentimentality, he did a masterful balancing act which adroitly transfers the onus of decision from himself and onto the audience. The very structure of the calypso reflects the balancing, the weighing of options: the stanzas make assertions, the choruses present choices.

Trinidadians and Tobagonians
This land belong to everyman
And since we got Independence
It means hard work for you and me
Independence means unity
It means you got to fight
It means we need co-operation
Fight with all yuh might
It means if yuh have to work
Work yuh fingers to the bone
It means that yuh on yuh own

Twenty five years have gone, how yuh feel
Yuh feel yuh put yuh shoulders to the wheel
Yuh feel yuh perspire and achieve
Yuh feel yuh clean up the mess
Yuh feel yuh could stand up proud and say yuh feel that yuh did yuh best
Yuh feel that we just keep moving on or backing back on we heel
Twenty five years have gone how yuh feel

(ii) Independence means productivity
Yuh must produce to build the economy
It means we facing stormy weather
And the burning heat altogether
Independence doh mean fete with big-big celebration
It means that we are one people building a nation
It means if you are asleep wake up from yuh sleep
It means what yuh sow you shall reap

Twenty five years have gone how yuh feel
Yuh feel is joke we joking or for real
Yuh feel we work hard and we produce

Yuh feel that things going fine
Yuh feel we reaping the benefits
Or yuh feel we on the decline
Yuh feel exporting was really good and we make the proper deal
Twenty five years have gone, how yuh feel

(iii) A multi-racial society
With every creed and race living in unity
The mecca of steelband and Calypso
We could be proud of anywhere we go
We must set an example for the children to follow
For they are the future leaders, children of tomorrow
And if we don't maintain the ship, the ship is going to sink
For a chain is as strong as its weakest link

Twenty five years have gone, how yuh feel
Yuh feel we have things covered and well seal
Yuh feel that them leaders pave the way
Yuh feel that we produce champs
Yuh feel that honesty was a must
Or yuh feel was a seta scamps
Yuh feel that things looking shaky to fall
Or we standing solid like steel
Twenty five years have gone, how yuh feel

(iv) A blessed Country that's rich with oil
And much more produce coming from the soil
With beautiful women with skin like spice
And sweet Tobago a tourist paradise
We got men and women with brain, people with integrity
Plenty skill and constructivity, we got the ability
And nowadays, my friends, we must be smart
For a fool and his money will soon part

Twenty five years have gone, how yuh feel
Yuh feel the facts was reveal or concealed
Yuh feel financially things was good
Yuh feel money was well spent
Yuh feel the people responsible could account for every cent
Yuh feel that justice was really done
Or yuh feel you could appeal
Twenty five years have gone, how yuh feel

The audience, offered the twin choices of judging the independence experience and of judging the calypso, chose to do the latter and they acclaimed it the best on the theme of independence, a decision with which the judges concurred. Funny, however, placed second in the overall standing, a result which annoyed Kitchener who felt that an Independence competition should consist of one song on that theme,[10] something Kitchener should have insisted on before the preliminaries and not after the finals. As it turned out, Cro Cro was a popular winner with "Happy Anniversary" and "Botha", a stinging satire on the hypocrisy of those who condemn the Afrikaner while doing comparable things in Trinidad. By a curious chance, this victory, Cro Cro's first in a major competition, was the springboard to success. In the next year, he won the Young King and the Monarchy, which last he repeated in 1990 and 1996; he also went on to become the most controversial calypsonian of the post-1987 period, a period unfortunately not covered in this study. He, at least, looking back on 31 August 1987 can sing "Happy Anniversary" as he was celebrating his happiest birthday as a calypsonian.

A fly in the ointment was Chalkdust's tirade against the winners and judges. Earlier that year, apropos of the public comments of a National Carnival Commission (NCC) judge, he had explained the technique and structure of his "Calypso Drug Report", and he had added that Stalin, Rudder and himself had entered the realm of the metaphysical where the language of the calypso was concerned.[11] This must have come as a surprise to his confrère Duke who had submitted earlier that the topicality of Chalkdust's "Calypso Drug Report" qualified it for a higher place in the Calypso Monarch Competition than second-placed "Calypso Music", Rudder's metaphorical and metaphysical masterpiece.[12] Duke, who seems to have fronted for Chalkdust in the past,[13] and may well have been doing so in 1987, clearly and for obvious reasons could not anticipate his colleague's self-description as metaphysician.

Chalkdust, the historian, wrote two articles on the Independence Competition. In the first, written after the finalists had been announced, he declared himself pleased that the official slate corresponded with his private list because it seemed that, "The finalists got in because of lyrics." He did express some disquiet at the noninclusion of Penguin and he was a bit apprehensive that the judges would similarly misunderstand his "Grandma's Advice". He anticipated a fight for himself from Cro Cro, De Fosto and Funny (in that order).[14] Eight days later, having lost to Cro Cro, Funny and Shadow (in that order), he declared the competition "a waste of the nation's time". He was severe on the judges from whom he had expected better because, judging from their names, he had been confident that "for the first time calypsonians would be judged according to criteria and not just by crowd". "The judges," he argued, "did not know what Independence was about." They did not understand his song, and they were "probably more accustomed to Cro Cro and Shadow, having heard them before". In closing he volunteered his own unsolicited solipsist verdict that Cro Cro's song was entertaining, as was Funny's, but "when it came to seriousness himself, Short Pants, Pretender and De Fosto had it".[15]

Chalkdust's comments are regrettable. Any responsible study of the modern calypso must of necessity acknowledge the quality of his endeavour and success qua calypsonian. His energy, imagination and courage guarantee him a place in calypso history. One wishes that a *kaisonian* of such experience and standing would take a more educated view of competitions and their place in the development of the Calypso.

Ars Poetica

One of Ruth Finnegan's criteria for poetry is "local classification of a piece as 'poetry'"[1] and it is in this category that the calypso 'fails' as poetry because the local public, schooled to European models, considers poetry to be the verse presented in school primers, the work of Derek Walcott and the erudites, and latterly, the work of the public poets Abdul Malik, Lasana Kwesi and the rapso artistes. The notion that "the poem is perfect only when it becomes a song; words and music at once"[2] is alien to this nation, and only dimly understood. Curiously, several calypsonians seem to understand perfectly. C.L.R. James relates that Sparrow answered the criticism of one of his lines with the musing reflection that he would have to change the music. When the critic protested that nothing was wrong with the music, Sparrow replied, as if stating the obvious, that if something was wrong with the words then something had to be wrong with the music.[3] Unfortunately, most of Sparrow's public do not share his inspiration; to them a calypso is "jes' a calypso".

A major irony of the political Calypso is that its aesthetic is generally overshadowed by the very elements which give it shape and form. Imaginative use of 'facts', inventive discourse on personalities, issues and positions, a high level of allusiveness, the ubiquitous 'I', and the pervasive presence of humour combine at once to give the political calypso its literary dimension and to prevent listeners from appreciating its literary quality. Audiences are already familiar with the content of the songs thanks to the conventional media, a slew of yellow tabloids, and the "*Gazette Negre*", as Max Ifill[4] so elegantly terms that which the vulgus loosely refers to as *niggergram*. No audience is ever satisfied with the dismal recital of things already known and this suggests that an audience's delight in a particular song is in the artistic treatment of the common reality. Ironically, discussions turn to what is being said rather than how. This chapter dedicates itself to analysing the poetic art of the political Calypso, with a view to highlighting the elements which audiences take for granted.

The independence experience has forced the progressive calypsonian to find a communicative medium: he needs to open a three-way channel of communication between himself, an alienated leadership, and an increasingly hedonistic audience addicted to the anodyne of pop music and alternating between periods of consciousness and *comesse*. He needs to search restlessly for a medium by means of which he can relay to these parties his panic at his invisibility and inaudibility insofar as he struggles to sensitise the remote and the giddy to the reality of a nation in danger of losing its soul and its capacity to survive.

Having wrestled unsuccessfully with immovable forces in the persons of messianic leaders and their devoted constituency, the calypsonian found it necessary to seek creative uses of language, drawing upon all the elements provided by a dynamic volatile society.

THE ARTISTIC ELEMENTS

The political calypso traverses two dimensions: the one artistic, dramatic and literary; the other thematic and attitudinal. This makes for a broad spectrum created by the tirelessly creative manipulation of literary and musical forms for the exploitation on many levels of the numerous possibilities afforded by developments in the political sphere. A major variable in the construction of this matrix must be the personality of the singer (or composer): how he or she perceives and responds to stimuli, what choices he or she makes in terms of theme, content and form.

Choice is facilitated by the availability of constants like group sensitivity to verbal display and the well-known receptivity to humour. Jourdain has noted that, "The use of creole reached perfection by virtue of its poetic quality of speaking directly through images and its peculiar humour which is inimitable as it is untranslatable."[5] Relator's "Take a Rest" illustrates the complex interplay of Jourdain's two elements. Apropos of recommending that "Dr Williams and the PNM take a rest," Relator declares that those opposed to this timely advice are so inclined because, "They get accustom to they free *cokieoko*," meaning that they have grown to be carried by the PNM giant, *cokieoko* being the local term for piggyback. Relator sings his phrase "free-co/kieoko", thus conveying the idea of *freeco*, Trinidad's premier entertainment which offers pleasure without cost. When one considers election campaigns as seasonal *freecos*, and the PNM as sponsors of continuous postelection *freecos*, as Stalin suggests in "Breakdown Party", then Relator's message is fully deciphered.

Mention of the PNM's clientelism brings to mind the way in which the PNM symbol, the *balisier* (Heliconia Bihar) has been treated in the calypso. Brought from the forest in 1956, it entered the Calypso as a symbol for nationalism and nationalist practice. Sparrow, who in "No Doctor, No" (1957) had complained that Williams' first budget was forcing citizens to imbibe the then despised Vat 19 rum, a beverage of local manufacture, proudly endorsed the very product in "Drink Your Balisier" (1960). After 1956 Vat 19 became known as *balisier* and Sparrow's song of 1960 promoted the beverage as indispensable to the Christmas festivities. By the 1980s, however, the *balisier* had acquired negative connotations. Several of Penguin's devils find it a ready and effective disguise ("Look the Devil Dey") while Delamo's first horse sprouts a *balisier* instead of a tail ("Apocalypse").

Delamo's "Ah Want a Wuk" (1986) adds another dimension of meaning to the PNM symbol. The narrator (clearly not Delamo himself, because he was employed on an oil rig offshore) exclaims to Chambers:

> Ah want a wuk, Ah doh care wha' you say
> Ah doh mind if Ah have to plant *balisier*

The *balisier* luxuriates in the wild, thriving in moist ground and in places where it can be protected by tall trees. Its pod like flower provides shelter to young snakes and this creates the association between the plant and the animal which holds inordinate terrors for Trinidadians.[6] Because of the snake association, few care to cultivate the *balisier* in domestic gardens. Interpreted in this light, Delamo's protagonist is begging to be employed even if his labours constitute an exercise in futility or even contribute to the increase in dangerous creatures. Additionally, it could be Delamo's way of suggesting that many people in the shadow of the *balisier* engage in futile exercises and may well be menaces to society. Shadow's "Snakes" (1984), exploiting the snake-*balisier* connection more directly, claims that "Snake in the *balisier*. . . bite up the Treasury."

The symbols of other parties have not been taken seriously except for the ONR's steelbeam which assumed a Damoclean threat (Sparrow's "We Like It So" 1982). Even its successor, the NAR's A-beam, was regarded with some suspicion. Funny, wondering at the mettle of the NAR government, questions, "You feel things looking shaky to fall or you feel we standing solid like steel?" ("How Yuh Feel?" 1987). This curious comment on a government which had swept to a landslide victory a mere eight months before that calypso was performed testifies to the disenchantment which had set in after the 'budget of sacrifices' was approved in parliament and condemned on the streets.

THE USE OF THE CHORUS

Abrahams gives as the three most important aesthetic tropes of the British West Indies, the importance of the performer, the tendency to dramatise and to argue, and the total involvement of the performer and audience in the enacted drama.[7]

Calypsonians involve audiences by using the 'hook', that is, a simple chorus or choric line which the audience can sing at the appropriate time and which then becomes their common property; indeed, the public, never overly concerned about the official names of calypsoes, renames songs after their 'hook' lines. "Caribbean Unity" thus became "Caribbean Man" and even its composer refers to it as such. 'Hooks' sometimes originate in the political culture, for example "Get to hell outa here", and are thus ready-made mnemonics.

Calypsonians create other engaging devices. Chalkdust invites assent to his 'facts' and approval of his skill and courage with the formulaic "Am I wrong?" which clearly demands a reply in the negative. Composer, his tentmate at the Regal 1972–77, structures audience response into his "True or Lie" (1976):

Our politicians say this time next July
Every workingman will have work so anything he could buy
And you know every politician is a truthful guy
True or lie?

The lessons of experience conspire with the facts of rhyme and metre to encourage the one answer possible: "Lie!" Chalkdust adds a master's touch to crowd manipulation when he premiered "Calypso Drug Report" at the 1987 Dimanche Gras. For three choruses he had the audience supporting the paid choristers as they chanted alternately "Not he" and "Drug Free" as he named singers who have not been linked to drug abuse, but when in the final chorus he unexpectedly named four calypsonians widely thought to be drug users, the massive crowd fell into a stunned uncomprehending silence from which they awoke several seconds later to give Chalkdust a tremendous ovation for his skill.

It may also happen that the singer may turn out to be too clever for his audience. Valentino employs a line from a calypso of the 1940s to satirise the masses who chant in their ignorance "Trinidad is nice, Trinidad is a paradise," a chorus, the calypso says, best sung by businessmen and their political confederates. After three chorus sequences of this, with chorus and crowd singing along enthusiastically, Valentino suddenly turns on his faithful choristers, and on an unsuspecting audience, with the accusation:

But this song I singing
Like if I hearing
Mih chorus singing
'God save the King'

By interpreting the chorus to be the national anthem of the former colonial master, Valentino is hinting that this country has returned to hated bygone days thanks to the acquiescence of a Carnival-loving people many of whom, unaware of his subtle mockery and his sober warning, chant as merrily as before, "Trinidad is nice, Trinidad is a paradise."

PERSONIFICATION, PERSONALISATION AND THE MASK

The tendency to dramatise has resulted in the proliferation of "I" narrations by means of which the calypsonian speaks his own mind in his own voice, 'enters' the minds of others, and creates scenarios which add to his credibility as an eyewitness or a man with inside information. Many calypsoes are commentaries in which the calypsonian presents his own interpretations or opinions on matters either known to or speculated on by the general public; these are straight cases of plain talk. Often, though, the singer would create dramatic monologues or dialogues using as 'I' narrator or respondent, personae drawn closely from real life. Many 'I' narrators share their creator's name, personality and attitudes and this persona is so psychologically credible and consistent that he/she is accepted as real. This causes the distinction between person and persona to become blurred and some people accept the artistic as the actual.

Williams was the prime choice for this kind of treatment because of the forbidding silence with which he hid his private actions and the motives for his public actions from all, including his political associates.[8] Denied discussion, the calypsonian sought to invade the castle of Williams' mind to engage him in dialogue or to have him explain himself through monologue. Critical moments, especially after 1970, inspire this kind of activity. Composer's "Different Strokes" (1974) and Superior's "Why I Left, Why I Returned" (1974) sought to make sense of the resignation/return of September–December 1973 via this approach, while Crusoe's "I Eric Eustace Williams" (1982) and Penguin's "Betty Goaty" (1982) allowed the deceased Williams his own funeral oration. Chalkdust, who seems ever eager to understand Williams, tried to 'enter' his mind on several occasions ("Two Sides of the Shilling" 1971; "Bring Him In" 1973; "Let the Jackass Sing" 1974) until even he reconciled himself to failure ("Eric Williams Loves Me" 1980).

Perhaps the most intriguing instance of the monologue is Sparrow's "Get to Hell Out" which purports to be a dramatisation of Williams' final statement on the Solomon Affair. This calypso employs suitable embellishments, not the least of which is the creditable imitation of Williams' voice delivering the infamous threat, and this technique stamps an imprimatur onto the ritualistic boasting of the Midnight Robber which Sparrow uses as the main referent and analogue to Williams' real-life utterances. Many who missed the Bourne's Road meeting may well have thought that Williams did say:

I am going to do what I feel to do
And Ah doh care less who vex or who get blue
And if you want to test how Ah strong in a election
Let we bet some money, Ah giving odds ten to one
I control all the money

That pass through this country
And they envy me for my African safari
I am the weight of town
I am politically strong
Don't argue with me
You can't beat me in John John

Who's not with me is my enemy
And dust will be their destiny
And if I say that Solomon will be Minister of External Affairs
And you doh like it
Get to hell outa here

This sounds very much like what Williams would say in public, but that master of Robber Talk could not use rhyme so fluently even at his eloquent best. Clearly "Get to Hell Out" is the work of a creative consciousness crystallising Williams' utterances into diamond-like hardness and brilliance. What compounded the problem of inability to distinguish between Williams, the person, and "Williams", the persona immortalised in song, is probably the personality of Sparrow himself. Sparrow had twinned his public self with Williams' and the composite of artistic and actual characters presented in the calypso mirrors the real Sparrow – and the real Williams. Many can be forgiven for believing that Sparrow rejoices over his hero's triumph over his enemies. Crusoe's "I Eric Eustace Williams", which purports to be Williams' self-eulogy, accepts and endorses the bona fides of Sparrow's inimitable and memorable persona.

Standing in inverse relationship to Sparrow's Midnight Robber is the protagonist of Commentor's "Opera of the Midnight Robber" (1981). Singing in the shadow of the Peter Minshall creation, which was the unchallenged King of the Bands 1980, and in the more sinister cloud of allegedly corrupt PNM hierarchs, Commentor fuses the artistic fantasy and the alleged reality into a single figure who, in the vein of the traditional Robber, challenges Minshall's "mas of bone" and brags about his own dastardly deeds:

Throughout this land I rape and plunder but I get 'way scot free
So how you could be so bold to boast you is more bandido than me
When people try to expose my game
They fail in they argument
The Speaker say they can't reveal my name
In the House of Parliament
So surrender your crown to me
Peter Minshall, your king is petty
Cause if he step out of line
Ah knock him down with mih DC-9

Commentor's degenerate robber cannot capture the flourish of his more illustrious master who is celebrated and satirised in the Sparrow calypso, because his rhetoric is but a sorry recital of sordid theft.

Of a still lower order is the mean-spirited defiance of the sneak thief. Loyal as ever to his PNM party and to the stalwarts who came under pressure in the early 1980s, Kitchener essays the 'defence' of "Soca Corruption" (1983):

If I have a few million
And they want to link it with corruption
Is mih damn business
If is true how they describe
Ah get mih money by taking bribe
Is mih damn business
If they say I gone abroad
To get away from a charge of fraud
Is mih damn business
If they say it is a fact
I have no intention of coming back
Is mih damn business

There is no attempt here to reproduce the ritualistic grandiloquence that derives from the Robber's erudition and pseudoaristocratic origins because Kitchener's persona is no princely Midnight Robber, the aristocrat of masqueraders, but a common midnight robber, a debased character on par with the despicable 'fowl tief', formerly a contemptible figure in real life and a comic masquerade.

Chalkdust is a master of the mask and this technique is a trademark of his political songs. In a remarkably short time he progressed from the simple disguises of "Reply to the Ministry" (1969) and "Ah Fraid Karl" (1972) to the sophisticated mask of "Somebody Mad" (1973) and "Bring Him In" (1973) to give only two of the more outstanding examples.

"Bring Him In" features "Chalkdust" as the subject of discussion among the middle level of the PNM. It had been reported in the print media that an application for membership in the name of Hollis Liverpool had been received and considered by the PNM. Chalkdust uses that story as the basis for "Bring Him In" which is supposedly an account of the deliberations as leaked to him by persons present at the meeting in an official capacity:

Somebody in PNM loves me
And want me join the Party
So they sign up mih name upon a form
And send it to the Secretary
Ah hear the whole General Council vote for me

Except Merritt the PRO
He say I love Chalkie as much as you do
But rain might fall and wet we coca

Merritt say
If you love him, bring him in
If you love him bring him in
But be prepared for anything
Like allyuh want the public to get to know
We fire Gene Miles from up in Whitehall just so
Because she slap up a Minister who try to kiss her
Bring him in
If you want the Nation to know the truth
How Robbie win Eric in his libel suit
And Eric have to pay him plenty money to boot
Well then, Merritt say, it ent no big thing
Bring him in

The General Council insists on voting in Chalkdust because they do not regard him as an enemy (which is this writer's opinion). They seem rather to believe that he would be a reformer and a ferret and that his presence would curb the abuses of the PNM's higher-ups (which all of his calypsoes were never able to do). Defeated, Merritt scampers off to inform "Williams" who immediately vetoed Chalkdust's application on the grounds that, "History teach me that I must keep incompetent men in high position." Then "Williams" confessed why he too was afraid of Chalkdust:

Like allyuh want the Police to get to hear
Ah moving Bernard to put Ernest Pierre
And is not Chalkie alone, pal
I and all 'fraid Karl
Bring him in
If the Nation now to hear
I make tailor Blackman, city mayor
Because although mih clothes does look *obsoquie*
He does make them free

The calypso thus ends with a *fateeg*, that is, a light-hearted jest, which takes away any bitterness created in earlier lines.

"Somebody Mad" seats the 'I' narrator, "Chalkdust" next to "Dr Bharath", an eminent local psychiatrist, at the football match between a national team and Santos of Brazil, a game that formed part of the 10th Anniversary of Independence celebrations. The Oval was packed to capacity with fans anxious to see the legendary Brazilian Pele in the flesh and so "Bharath" finds himself trapped next to an implacable inquisitor posing as a perplexed citizen seeking a professional opinion on the mental health of the national leadership. "Bharath" is invited to diagnose obvious cases of lunacy and the inquisitor's relentless logic forces him to conclude that the conduct of national affairs is no different:

> I ask him
> Doc, what would you say if I should throw a dead dog on Frederick Street
> I'll say you mad, I'll say you mad
> And if I give a dead *corbeau* to everyone I meet
> I'll say you mad, I'll say you mad
> Well then, if a man could watch the La Basse right dey
> And build houses so near for people to stay
> To take in that stinking stench whole day
> Somebody have to be mad
> Doc, somebody have to be mad

"Bharath's" immediate response is the hurried downing of "three straight rums on the rocks" and a hasty objection to being drawn in a conversation of that nature, but his interlocutor traps him by insisting that inability or unwillingness to identify insanity is de facto proof of same. The reference to "Bharath's" drinking is almost like a clever *picong* aside because Bharath was known to be a heavy drinker, a fact which Chalkdust uses to suggest as a probable reason that the unnamed person in Whitehall escaped clinical attention for so long; the psychiatrists could not certify him because they too were in need of attention, witness being their addiction to alcohol.

Chalkdust's mask is meant to be transparent and designed to be seen through by all; it is the thinnest of literary fictions to protect the composer from charges of libel and slander. Evidence of the transparency of this mask is adduced from the statement by the Trinidad and Tobago League of Women's Voters who protested the "wanton disrespect for the principles of decency and respect" arguing that, "The office of Prime Minister is one of dignity and this office must be treated with the dignity and respect it deserves."[9]

Chalkdust's achievement is that he found innovative ways of enumerating the many sins of the PNM regime 1968–86 without causing lasting bitterness. It is not my intention to isolate the elements of his antimanifesto towards determining what was truth, half truth or untruth; still less am I concerned with tracking down the sources of his information. Such exercises will, at best, reveal that for John Public 'truth' is an attractively edible goulash of fact, misinterpretation, innuendo, distortion and fiction, the whole a product of national characteristics of excitability and sensationalism. It should be noted, however, that many PNM faithful seemed to accept Chalkdust's "facts" as gospel and disliked him for holding up the party's leadership to scrutiny. Williams himself sagely adopted the public pose of aloofness. He is alleged to have said dismissively of Chalkdust, "Let the jackass bray," this when the League of Women's voters drew to his attention the lèse-majesté of "Somebody Mad".[10] Still later, he is reported to have "laughed for so" when he heard "Let the Jackass Sing"[11] which is Chalkdust's response to his belittling comment. When one considers the traumas of later Prime Ministers Chambers and Robinson, one must agree that Williams' attitude was clearly the most politic response to political *picong*.

Chalkdust's technique has been the subject of some discussion. Short Pants agrees with Tanifeani that Chalkdust's work is deficient in literary craft and that it too closely resembles and imitates the leaflet.[12] Tanifeani and Short Pants (who incidentally is the calypsonian closest to Chalkdust in technique of catalogue) both ignore the many Chalkdust scenarios and the masterful handling of the mask and other devices which contrast with the bluntness of his nationalistic songs such as "We Is We", "National Pride" and "Ah Love Trinidad".

On the other side of the coin, Eric Roach attributes Chalkdust's skill to his university education and recommends that future governments "disbar [sic] educated people from composing calypso".[13] While Chalkdust's mastery of satire is beyond dispute, Roach's theory is highly questionable for several reasons. First, Chalkdust's patent overelaboration at Calypso Monarch finals bespeaks either a misguided sense of theatre, overanxiety, or worse a lack of confidence in the quality of his work. Secondly, his scholarly work does not reflect the level of artistry of his calypsoes and does not do him the justice that other creative souls do themselves in critical writing. Chalkdust may have thought that satire was natural to the art form, a notion derived from his attending to the calypso masters, none of whom was university trained. Crediting mastery of satire to a university education while denying similar competence to the "illiterate vagabond singer", as Roach terms the 'ordinary' calypsonian, more in defence of his argument than from observation, does tremendous injustice to the master satirists Sparrow, Cypher, Relator and even to those minor figures like Happy.

This Tobago-born singer played on the coincidence of Chambers' Christian name being the same as the stage name of British pop star Boy George, the androgynous seeming idol of Trinidad's pop oriented youth. In performing his "Boy George" (1985) which co-opts the melody of Boy George's "War", Happy disguised himself in Boy George style costume, and he refutes any attempt to mistake himself, the impersonated George of pop music, for the other George, he of unpopular politics:

Are you George who torture people
In where the people dead

Ah say no, no, that is heartless George
Are you George who went to Kapok Hotel
With he wife, she chile and she boyfriend as well
Ah say, no, no that is brass-face George
Are you George that run up a bill sky-high
Still come and tell the people lie
Ah say no, no, no, that is disgraceful George
Are you George that does go out the country
To meet folks and squander money
Ah say no, no, no that's wasteful George
Ah tell you I am Boy George, Boy George

Happy is not Chalkdust and Chambers is not Williams, and so this brilliant calypso won for Happy only a place in the national semifinal and no other mention. On the credit side, it did not win him the antagonism of the PNM women but minus the negative publicity the calypso was doomed to obscurity, controversy being necessary to visibility – especially if one is previously unknown.

USING THE "ENEMY'S" LANGUAGE AND TECHNIQUE

Williams liked to boast of his successes in founding 'The University of Woodford Square' and in training a cadre of politically educated adults. To support his claim he cites Gordon Lewis who marvelled at "the relationship which PNM has been able to work out between the intellectual and the masses".[14] Williams retails an anecdote in which a young PNM lady puts off a proposing young man because he lacks the discipline which is essential to qualification for someone educated at Williams' Open University.[15] This anecdote or its apocryphal parent is dramatised in the mildly satirical "Political Girl" (1962), which was composed by "Rocky" McCollin and sung by Nap Hepburn:

Last week I took a chance
And went to a PNM dance
I saw a girl looking so lonely
So I decided to work on she
I tried to drunken she with beer
But she know more politics than the Premier
Whilst dancing the twist we tumble and fall
Politically the young girl bawl

Chorus
No, No, no, the premier say
You can't fight down dey

And you can't bribe me
To fight in this constituency
I know you in a drunken state
And you'll like to be my candidate
I don't care how much money you show
Let me see your manifesto

(ii) I tried to influence she
To allow me to join she party
I start to beg on mih knees as man
Why you reject my application
She have a lot of brain and plenty tricks
I never knew one woman know so much politics
She watch me in my face, she laugh and then declare
I'm a student from Woodford Square

(iii) You could imagine how I drafting mih plan
To fight this election
Like a little schoolboy I started begging
She said you ent got no discipline
She said if you want to join this party
You got to have some behaviour and decency
She say I don't care how much politics you know
You can't fight this election so

One notes how skilfully and subtly the calypso communicates the underground feeling that in the breasts and hearts of the PNM women there nestled for Williams feelings maternal and other than maternal. The narrator claims that he took a chance to go to the dance, implying that he was not one of the flock, and that by going there with conquest on his mind he was poaching.

According to this calypso, too, politics has intruded into normal courtship patterns giving the woman a politically active reason for rejecting a casual relationship. Generations later, however, the preoccupation with the business of politics would be blamed for its disastrous effect on family life and on the nation as a whole.

Delamo's "Eric Williams Children" (1984) faults the political girl-become-mother for her role in contributing to social disorder:

You might say to me that a hand never clap alone
That if the Father was so cruel then why did the mother condone
But she formed herself a free brigade to fraternise with this and that Minister
And she sold her children's birthright for bread without butter

But woe unto that woman who commits treason on her womb
She is like a ten-days worker on a highway of doom

So when you hear daughter cussing mother and mother saying
'You feel you is a big woman'
Ah want yuh stop, listen, understand
That these are the fruits of the Father, the products of his system
They are all Eric Williams children
You see, at convention and at party group meeting
She didn't have time to give her daughter training
They are all Eric Williams children

Williams' platform style impacted on the political Calypso. For a long time, his pamphleteering style, and especially his fondness for cataloguing and accumulation of example and instance, seemed the perfect vehicle for singing his praises and the pre-1962 Calypso is replete with examples of this. Even as late as 1971, Gibraltar sought to demonstrate that Williams was uncontaminated by his participation in the "dirty game" that is politics:

Yuh mean them house and school that he buil'
They say that ent do nothing still
The road to Carenage and Diego Martin
They say that he ent do nothing still
He buy BWIA and Angostura
He pay for students in Canada
They had a lot of parties long before he
Tell me who do more than Dr Willie
("Politics Is a Dirty Game" 1971)

Gibraltar expresses here his incredulity that citizens could dare calumniate Williams who had done so much, but an age of irreverent singers had long begun to catalogue Williams' nonachievements and his more spectacular – albeit unpublicised – failures. Chalkdust compiles litanies of Williams' sins of commission and omission, and the popularity of the Chalkdust antimanifesto paved the way for calypso attacks on Williams' credibility as politician.

Stalin's "Plan Your Future" (1980) appropriates for that calypsonian the role of corporation sole to warn the people about a recession which Williams, the official corporation sole, should have anticipated and prepared the nation to meet:

This is my message to my people for the 80s
Trinidadians, learn to live with small monies
Because today you up, tomorrow you down
While you up you better start making preparation

In case of famine or flood we could make
If is hurricane or flood we could take
So if today something nice happen to you
Listen what Ah think we should do

Sit down and plan carefully how allyuh spending
This big seta oil-bread that they say Trinidad running
Like who you lending and who you giving
And in which direction you have the bread investing
Because if oil drilling here and the cost of gas so high
Then wha' go really happen when the oil well run dry

Stalin may have been inspired to write this calypso by Williams' critique of his "Caribbean Unity" and this calypso is to some extent asking Williams to mind his own business. Recalling the public put-down of 1979, Stalin picks up the statistics of PNM failure remembering Williams' flair for statistics:

10 million for one boat ride to Tobago
5 million little coppers for Piarco
40 million for bus from India without spare
For a plane that ent drive yet, Douglas charge you so dear

Each of these represents a classical case of the corruption and mismanagement which had become so endemic that they passed into the "folklore of corruption", a fusing of fact and fantasy which makes the incredible seem typical and natural. By the early 1980s the Williams regime had achieved that distinction, perhaps eclipsing the Albert Gomes regime of 1950–56 which they had replaced partly because they were able to campaign on the platform of morality in public affairs.

Just as the irreverent parodised the official style and approach, so too did they make capital of the official rhetoric. Leveller's "Juvenile Delinquency" (1966) is bitingly critical of the inability of the intelligentsia and of the religious mandarins to deal with the wildcat street violence of the early 1960s. He strings together the hypotheses advanced by the cognoscenti, delivering them in the fast-paced spiel favoured by the practitioners of the rhetorical recitative of yore who revelled in the magical power of the words which imparted to them the real power denied them in ordinary life. Leveller's calypso seems to be suggesting that there has been a dramatic reversal of roles in that the 'intellectual government', having come to power on the strength of command of language, now hides behind the sound and fury of academic pronouncements:

Blame the slum environment
Parents' mismanagement

Teachers' intolerance
Complex psychology
Colonial inequity
Racial recalcitrance

Traditional linguistic bluff now becomes evidence of incompetence to deal with reality.

The same preoccupation with word as mask or as concealing device informs Valentino's "Bills and Acts" (1976) which examines the deliberate obfuscation of legal terminology with specific reference to the Anti-Sabotage Bill (1 of 1975). Valentino's gift for snide wordplay is evident in the opening lines:

Sometimes they introduce a Bill
When you survey the price could make man blood chill
Sometimes they introduce an Act
The Act-man is the man I really attack
After five hundred years is some weird weird laws
Is drafts, paragraphs and section and plenty clause
Mr Amender, amend the Amendment Bill
Because the price of the Order alone could kill

Constance has observed that Valentino juggles the words "price" and "order" to have them sound "like jargon from the market or grocery; yet it could also be the price one has to pay in human terms for the 'order' that must be maintained by the use of things like the Public Order Act which protects a certain order of things or system."[16]

Valentino is claiming an experiential knowledge which allows him to see through the engineered confusion of "drafts, paragraphs and sections and plenty clause" – the harsh reality glossed over by the legal verbiage:

Now the paragraph could never conceal
What the chapter would soon reveal
The kinda clause I see in this book
Is what my cause could never overlook
Speaking broadmindedly, these Acts really act on me
And the men who hand down these Bills they show no mercy
Massa man like he really come out to kill
Check out the Anti-Sabotage Bill

You cannot protest neither demonstrate
If you march for your rights licks could be your fate

A very brutal Act I care to remonstrate
So you see clear what's their intention
And from here you got the solution
My people, A C T I O N really spells 'action'

Censors blessed with supersensitive hearing took pre-emptive action of their own: they cunningly insinuated this calypso into a list of smutty and drug endorsing songs and banned the lot from the airwaves.

In an age of openly declared censorship, however, it was still possible to revert to parody. Some calypsonians mocked Williams' words. His famous pronouncement, " money is not a problem", uttered in tribute to returning Olympic gold medallist Hasely Crawford, was ridiculed in Bomber's "Money Is No Problem, the Problem Is No Money" (1977), Chalkdust's "Money Ent No Problem" (1977) and Shorty's "Money Eh No Problem" (1979), all of which, taken together, paint a detailed picture of privation and poverty in the midst of squandermania promoted by political patronage. Equally significant is the consensus achieved by these singers of dissimilar backgrounds and attitudes.

The Chambers administration suffered like treatment. In his uphill task of rallying party and people, Chambers coined – or publicised – morale-boosting slogans which unfortunately provided ammunition for his detractors. Funny's "Right and Wrong" (1983) had pointed out in an extremely serious tone the many obvious things which Chambers apparently did not recognise as being wrong. Stalin's "Better Days" (1983), adopting the Williams approach to statistics, offers the sobering logistics of Chambers' "better days":

6 million for school and 19 for bombs
8 million for house and 16 for gun
That is the type of budget they making
They getting ready for this better days wha' coming
18-year old joining up military
To kill 18-year old that he never see
That is the kind of preparation
It take to live in this beautiful Promised Land

"Better Days" includes ironic codas which mock the hope which Chambers tried to inspire in the people:

Better days are coming
Get your bus pass and wait
Better days are coming
Get your food stamps and hang in there

> A better day is coming 'round the corner, man, just sit down and wait
> It coming, it coming, it coming

Chambers' National Consultation on Productivity provoked Crusoe into belabouring the key word "produce" and into hammering out of being whatever fetishistic properties Chambers sought to invest in it. What Crusoe perceives as the "link-up between productivity and corruption" illustrates a novel interpretation of the word "produce" as it functions in the local context:

> We produce a man who produce one seta money and hide it in Panama
> Then produce a man who produce a law saying we cyar bring the man back here
> So he gone all over the world having fun 'cause he know he cannot be caught
> Because before he leave we produce the man with a diplomatic passport

Sparrow counters President Clarke's verbal offensive launched against those antigovernment doomsayers who were prophesying dire future for the nation based on the PNM's dismal showing in the domain of planning. Clarke chose as his stage the finals of the Steelband Music Festival (1982), introducing an element of the unlovely into the "Pan Is Beautiful Two" scenario when he demonstrated political partisanship by publicly echoing sentiments trumpeted by PNM ministers. Many were offended by this gaucherie, none more so than Sparrow who saw himself as being singled out for his "We Like It So" which was bitterly critical of the PNM's lack of achievement over 25 years. In his counterattack which is defiantly named "Prophets of Doom and Gloom", he personifies the common sense view of reality first seen in "We Like It So", and he reacts to Clarke's verbal bombardment and to the aggressive epithets hurled by other PNM potentates, by displaying a linguistic capability of his own. The PNM barrage had included terms like "nefarious", "megalomaniac", "disciple of Judas" and "counterrevolutionary" to which Sparrow responds:

> In this Land of steady power failure
> People houses in darkness
> But on every tree round the Savannah
> Display of luciferous politics
> You have to ask yourself which is worse between a schizophrenic baboon
> A megalomaniac and a prophet of doom and gloom

Sparrow had once made light jest of the relative popularity of Williams, Lord Hailes (governor general of the short-lived federation) and himself ("Popularity Contest" 1963). Twenty years later that jest has become bitter invective, the raw insult "schizophrenic baboon" sounding a jarringly discordant note in the comparative civil political *picong* of the day.

THE LANGUAGE OF THE DRUG SUBCULTURE

For the calypsonian, the drug subculture provides substance for escape as well as symbolism for appropriation in his conflict with the status quo. Explainer's "Is Grass" (1978) challenges the view that cannabis is the bane of the younger generation:

The old people saying
This tampi smoking
Killing the young man
And having him mad in St Ann's
They prefer liquor
To lick up they liver
When I smoke ganja
Explainer don't need magnesia

Whey I get the inspiration
To write 'Mr African'
Is grass
'77 composition
'Caribbean Integration'
Is grass
Now the police, doctors, the nurses, lawyers
People from the highest class
Smoking they grass
And they wouldn't lock up they arse

While Explainer considers cannabis to be his source of inspiration, Valentino sees it as the vehicle for his flight through fantasy. "Third World" (1972) creates that link between a fantastic view of a new world and the drug trip. This is quite clear in the opening couplet:

Meditating in mih house just the other day
Is like Ah charge up mihself and Ah trip away

Stalin elevates 'the weed' into the purifying incense, the cloud of smoke that protects the minds of the righteous user against the seductions of the vampires who are habituated to beguile the alcohol-befuddled ("Vampire Year" 1981). The vampires of local politics are helpless against the chalice of burning marijauna.

"Not That Man" (1982) and "That Is Head" (1983) convert it into a weapon of race and class consciousness. "Not That Man" endorses the several varieties of cannabis while pointing out the greater dangers of cocaine, the evil product of contemporary white civilisation and the metaphor for white civilisation itself:

He lick up Brother Jimi Hendrix sad, sad, sad
He deal with Sister Billie Holliday hard, hard, hard
He take out a whole piece of Charlie Parker head
If Ray Charles dint ketch heself, he to end up dead
Early one morning on a subway station
He pass the sword on brother Monty Williams[17]

Calypsonians began to perceive marijuana as the poor man's drug, a harmless natural intoxicant when contrasted with the more potent man-made alcohol and cocaine which were preferred by those substance abusers of another generation and of another class. Delamo's "Six Years Hard Labour" (1979) raises the idea of class discrimination in the practice of law and police procedure where cannabis is concerned because his 'I' narrator is unceremoniously hauled down to the police station and haled before a magistrate on a mere suspicion arising from his living in a government flat. Valentino's "Recession" (1983) explains the actions of the "Men in business/And the political exploitists" as the doings of men crazed by the use of artificial hallucinogens:

Ah smelling something
Like them big boys up they smoking something
Allyuh ent smelling
Like them big boys up they smoking something
After they done occupy the state
They bring a bankruptcy in the place
After they done get high on they millions
They create a world recession

The men in business
For their own interests
And the political exploitists
Is them who have this place in this financial crisis
Although recession killing the Country
Max Senhouse still needs the money
So you see who bring this recession on we

Stalin's "That Is Head" (1983) charges that the actions of the élites of society are so weird, so irresponsible and so bizarre that the sober, rational mind can consider them only to be the work of hardened hard drug users, no other explanation sufficing:

Now, Randy, something funny happening
And I only hope that you noticing
The thing I smoking

Is not that them smoking
It can't be the boo from in Sangre Grande
Or the shake-off from Guayaguayare
Them fellas importing that thing
From some foreign country
And when you hear the pusher-man in town
And you hear they get they nice head
Well, Randy, they doh care who live or dead

Listen
A man bounce a man in Tunapuna
Gone and report the matter in Arima
They take 'way he book and charge the brother
Say he report the accident too far
But then a big-shot Member of Parliament
Say he didn't know to report accident
You know is thirty dollars they charge to he
And set the Minister free
Yuh talk 'bout head
That is head

After spending one Friday in the chamber where the House of Representatives was in session, at least according to "In Parliament They Kicksin" (1979), Explainer concludes, "Like them fellas high up on cocaine." Listening to several presentations during the campaigning for the 1986 general election, Chalkdust is forced to come to the same conclusion ("Calypso Drug Report" 1987).

THE LANGUAGE OF THE FETE

The absorption of the fete is evidence of the political calypso's most remarkable powers of assimilation and resilience. The fete mode and that of the political commentary had grown apart and were increasingly thought of as being mutually exclusive if not antagonistic, a dichotomy that was emerging with the coming into prominence of singers who concentrated on slow songs of commentary. This latter group defended its stance in terms of the 'truth' that the original calypso was a protest song; they thought that their confrères had deserted their true vocation and that they, the standard-bearers in the unending conflict, folk versus superstructure, were in truth the only true opposition. Survivalism dictated that they adjust their beat and this generated the 'serious fete song', the working synthesis which could appease the traditional spirits of community while appealing to the newer gods of commercialism. This last has been achieved by using the language and music of the fete for political commentary.

Stalin's "Breakdown Party" (1980) represents the nation under PNM rule as a "total breakdown fete"; his language and music draw upon Swallow's "Don't Stop the Party" (1979), the standard for fete songs during the early 1980s. "Breakdown Party" notes that party and nation were revelling in the anarchy of the oil boom era and that all involved mocked Williams' belated and ineffectual efforts to arrest the breakdown in national will that he himself had initiated by patronage and by inability to discipline his subordinates. Therefore Stalin, who was already aggrieved by Williams' public criticism of his "Caribbean Unity" thesis of 1979, presents himself as a viable alternative:

> But if this was my party
> Ah woulda stop the damn thing already
> When Ah say 'Stop!' stop the jam
> Else Ah break a DJ hand

While this is good as the rhetoric of the *badjohn* and in many ways is typical of Williams' intemperate language in pressure situations, it is clearly unworkable in a complex political situation which has taxed the ingenuity of generations of leaders.

"Wait Dorothy", Stalin's prize winning classic of 1985, shows that the talented composer can make the music of the fete as a means of mocking the facile catchcalls of dance calypso while reaffirming his own dedication to the calypso as a medium of instruction, and as a vehicle for raising the level of consciousness of affairs national, regional and international. One hesitates, however, to ascribe the tremendous success of "Wait Dorothy" to the skilful accommodation of serious lyrics to party music or even to the imaginative turning of a song of defiance into dance music. Stalin may have been up to calypso tricks. Stanza one refers to his "You Ask for It" (1983), a sly 'slack' song about his refusal to sing soca. Calypsonians were making capital of the homonymic similarity between "soca" and "suck her" and Stalin wrote a soca song exploiting this similarity. "Wait Dorothy" may have remained irreconcilable on two levels and it is possible that it is best remembered for the lines:

> Ah jam she
> In the party
> And Ah squeeze she
> In the party

which epitomise the very attitude and lyrics that the singer purports to be condemning.

While the truth behind the success of "Wait Dorothy" remains a matter for conjecture, the fifth stanza of Delamo's "Ah Cyar Wine" leaves no doubt that the singer was aware that members of the public had misunderstood the message of the earlier stanzas:

> They say get a woman to wine on stage and get full marks for presentation
> Apparently people don't mind if I soil my reputation
> The worst thing could happen to an artiste is when his fans declare him interdict
> So for short-term rewards, my principle I wouldn't contradict
> To create a balanced calypso was my only object
> Check mih words, mih music and you will find
> It is a party tune but it stimulates the intellect
> So it's not important if I could wine, cyar wine, should wine, would wine
> Shaking up this old behind
>
> Doh ask me to wine
> Ah cyar wine
> Doh ask me to wine
> Ah cyar wine
> All who feel this is a wine song go home and check your stereo carefully
> Delamo is giving this Nation a lesson in morality
> So doh ask me to wine
> Doh tell me to wine

Delamo's experience illustrates the point of the dubious success of those better-known calypsoes which attempt to mix the modes. If his friends, advisors and well-wishers could so far misunderstand his calypso (or understanding, put the Monarch title above all else) then one is forced to conclude that the appeal of the "hook" and the party music seem to have obscured the message that the singer thought was being transmitted *en clair*.

THE RELIGIOUS DIMENSION

Except for Mauricette's monograph,[18] the religious paradigm in the Calypso has been curiously neglected. This is quite surprising when one considers the volume of evidence testifying to the importance of religion in secular life. Trinidad and Tobago is officially a multidenominational nation recognising Christianity, Hinduism and Islam whose leaders turn out to sanctify secular gatherings of all kinds, a practice consistent with the pious hope devoutly expressed in the national anthem's "Here every creed and race/Finds an equal place." However, a generic acceptance of magic, which is termed obeah and is inextricably linked to the persistence of ancestral religions, especially *orisha* worship, not only coexists with but constantly threatens orthodoxy. Here, as elsewhere, the universal faith, the "truly Catholic creed, is a belief in the efficacy of magic".[19] Blue Boy underlines this in "Jingay" (1987) in which an itinerant preacher, dressed in blue gown and carrying a Bible, a candle and flowers – the habit and accoutrements for which Blue Boy's "Soca Baptist" was censored in 1980 – offers his wares to all and sundry, knowing that he has "a *jingay* for every creed and race". Another important sales pitch is that one "Can't survive today/Without a *jingay*".

The use of religious symbols as metaphor indicates that the calypsonian is aware of the involvement of the religious dimension in daily life, and is sensible and sensitive enough to appropriate it for use in the political calypso. History confirms the longevity of this tradition. In 1805, slaves on the eve of rebellion co-opted essentially Christian symbols as motifs and codes in anticipation of a bloody triumph over the Europeans who had tried to impress upon them the sacrosanctity of such symbols. A translated version of the slave songs reads like this:

> The bread is the flesh of the white man
> San Domingo
> The wine is the blood of the white man
> San Domingo
> We will drink the white man's blood
> The bread we eat is the white man's flesh
> The wine we drink is the white man's blood[20]

Many years later, Black Stalin gave his own value to Christian symbols. "Vampire Year", a free flow reinterpretation of Christian iconography, hints at the collusion of church and state in maintaining an unholy status quo. Stalin observes that "Trini vampires" emerging for their quinquennial blood offerings ally themselves with the church ("with crucifix and cross they could make the grade"); their enemy is the "chillum and loud smoke", the buckler and shield of the Rastafarian. In "Burn Dem" (1987), he rearranges the Judgement Day scenario to insinuate himself into the role of special assistant to St Peter in charge of "burning" selected enemies of the African race, disregarding the fact that St Peter is not usually cast in the role of burner of men. Stalin's symbolism contains features of unorthodoxy noted elsewhere, for example, in Funny's "Bacchanal in Hell" (1972) and Valentino's "The Invitation" (1972) which both celebrate a sublimated carnival in the other world.

The peculiar religiosity reflected in the calypso is often a consequence of a social reality. Squibby, for example, is the nephew of a former Roman Catholic Bishop of Grenada, but he is the son of an *orisha* worshipper, and he uses his knowledge of this latter system in "Shango" (1980), "Distant Drums" (1981) and "Steelband Running Wild" (1982), a trilogy dealing with possession by an insistent spirit of music. In "Shango", the narrator/protagonist accepts the incompetence of orthodox religion to deal with this formidable spirit:

Christian, Hindu, Moslem, Judaism, Buddhism
None of these religions cyar tell me what happen
It was in a Shango feast in Fyzabad the spirit turn to me and said
'The only man who could set you free is Papa Nizer [21] and he dead'

It is not surprising that the calypsonian exposed to numerous religions and even more magicoreligious practices would cultivate a mindset which tends to explain the otherwise unaccountable in these terms, and as the political kingdom offers countless examples of what to the Trinidadian mind seems inexplicable, it is only natural that the calypsonian should use religious metaphors to account for such phenomena. One needs to note too, that in the modern era, religion has been the handmaiden of politics: it was used to rally and politicise Hindus;[22] to consolidate the Roman Catholic vote in the face of Williams' godlessness;[23] to assure Williams support as a means of encouraging him to stay in 1973;[24] to give coherence and resolve to Williams' political industrial enemies in 1975; to rally Spiritual Baptist animosity against the ONR in 1981; to mobilise the Roman Catholic Church militant in support of the ONR in 1981; to restore the integrity of a fragmenting NAR in 1988; and to ward off the depredations of the "Anti-Christ" Imam Yasin Abu Bakr who represented himself as an arrow in the bow of his God launched against a satanic foe.

It seems even more natural that our greatest political phenomenon should be accorded supernatural status. PNMites, ignoring the fulminations of the Roman Catholic hierarchs and their journalistic allies at the Trinidad Publishing Company, considered him god sent. "The Master couldn't come", proclaimed one placard held up at a public meeting "so he sent Williams". Dougla echoes similar ideas in his independence calypso 1962:

Dr Williams come like Moses in biblical history
And he led us like the children of Israel to independency

This vision and voice are reflected and echoed in Shadow's "From Then to Now" (1987). Apropos of the events of September–December 1973, Scraper hails Williams as "the greatest obeahman" ("The More you Live, The More You see" 1974), while Crusoe's "Politicians" of the same year suggests the same ("like he working obeah") as the reason for Williams' escape from the disasters overtaking other world leaders. Chambers, assuming Williams' place, is credited with his predecessor's mystical powers. Kitchener's "Not a Damn Seat for Them" (1982), rejoicing in the accuracy of Chambers' 'prediction' bestows on that worthy the accolade of seer ("Chambers is a obeahman"), voicing an opinion natural in the circumstances.

But a shaman evokes as much fear as reverence since he is simultaneously a negative and a positive force. Chalkdust seemed fascinated by Williams as a malevolent power and a source of infinite danger to his enemies. "Goat Mouth Doc" (1972) masks his concern for his own safety in the warning of Trinidad-born international spiritualist, Harribance Lalsingh. "We Blight" (1974) ascribes the troubles assailing the country to the vengeful ghosts of Williams' vanquished foes and to the effluence from numerous malefactors, including those holding high office. The protagonist of this calypso, a Roman Catholic woman, appeals to a priest at the Abbey of Mt St Benedict to effect an expulsion of public evil:

> Father, if you say some masses for we
> We'll remove the blight from those who guilty
> So say one for Hyatali
> Another for Karl and Lord Shorty
> But poor Chokolingo, he needs three
> Five for Abdul Malik and Azard Ali[25]
> But Father, say six high masses for Deafy
> Like somebody blight this Country

Chalkdust, who has not abandoned the Roman Catholicism of his childhood, creates a near-heretical persona who, although herself a devout Catholic, utters the blasphemy that all priests indulge in obeah, a thought natural to local religious philosophy but one which would have been censored immediately if voiced publicly in song in the 1930s.[26] Chalkdust further exploits calypso licence in "Our Only Hope" (1985) which has Roman Catholic Archbishop Pantin enumerate the many ills afflicting the society, acknowledge the insufficiency of his prayer, and justify his sending for an external and more powerful "obeahman". "Pantin" confesses miserably that he has fasted and prayed like the prophets of old, and he has even offered two high masses, all to no avail. So, unable to cope, and running out of hope, he had no alternative but to send for the Pope.

Chalkdust seeks masks from other religious systems. In "Shango Vision" (1977), a "PNM Shango man" chortles over the 1976 general election victory and chronicles the developments that would surely have followed upon an ULF win. Credibility is given the persona by the known and feared power of the *orisha* priest, but one wonders if Chalkdust, hiding behind this convenient mask, is expressing his own delight and is perhaps asking PNM members and clients to give thanks and praise. By this token, and given Chalkdust's ambivalence towards Williams, the line, "Give thanks, my brethren, that Raffique Shah didn't win" may be the evidence of the mask slipping – deliberately? – to expose the manipulator, and the calypso itself may be a masterpiece of bricolage that in the survey period was the usual vehicle for dealing with Afro-Indian relations.

When Chalkdust finally admitted in song ("Eric Williams Dead" 1987) that his *alter ego* was dead, he fabricates a dialogue between a protagonist "Chalkdust" representing a hard-headed view of reality, and a Rosicrucian woman who is convinced that Williams could not be numbered among the shades and who finds "Chalkdust's" reasoning pitifully naive ("You mean they fool you too, Chalkie?"). The choice of persona merits closer examination. The much-maligned PNM Women's League worked wonders in their campaigning for Williams and it is the uncharitable mind that insinuates that their devotion was actuated by a more than maternal love for the little man. He himself was thought to be a Rosicrucian, membership in that exalted society with its carefully shrouded mystique of occult wisdom and esoteric rituals recommending it to those wondering minds which held that the mysterious prime minister must needs be of a higher order than the rather familiar secret orders which flourish in these islands.

The many masks employed by Chalkdust's fertile imagination (spiritualist, Roman Catholic devotee, Roman Catholic Archbishop, PNM Shango man, PNM Rosicrucian woman) bear witness to the symbiotic relationship existing among beliefs locally as well as to their use for definition of and comment on the political kingdom.

From the mid 1970s onwards, a growing number of calypsoes addressed the malaise in society as a religious problem as calypsonians focused on the spiritual dimension of the hurtle towards chaos. One is struck by the sense of despair which succeeded the mood of revolution; it is as if the calypsonian, frustrated with temporal politics, surrendered to the feeling that man was too debased to resist the onslaught of the seven deadly sins. Stalin's "Money" (1980) creates terrible images of the all-conquering Mammon: the internationalism of godless materialism, its domination of corporate thinking, and its corruption of interpersonal relationships ("Calculator take the place of wife"). Of particular importance is the total debasement of the Christian ethic and the confusion of God with Mammon:

> Trust in the Creator one was a must
> Nowadays it turn around to in gold we trust
> Man write out cheque to big institution
> To pay for a seat to pray for he salvation
> And man giving man extra set of money
> To say a special prayer for he
> To get onto money they will do they utmost
> Money is Father, Son and Holy Ghost

> Ah tell yuh
> No time for the Master, no time for Jah Jah
> Is just money money, they want all the money

No time to give thanks to the Man who have them around
Is the dollar note in town

Monkey's "Vengeance of Moko" (1981) charts the degeneration of the church militant and its capitulation to Mammon, and it prophesies a "spirit lash" for the decadent society:

We jump outa bed to warm we car engine
Before bed that night is blue films we watching
Children on dope and vice, parents committing adultery
For the love of money every one into corruption
For the love of money Man killing Man
We joining pyramid games, we all money crazy
We pray to win in *whe whe*, bingo, horse-racing and lottery
We just praying for luck just to win money
And the right things we need to pray for we just put it off
Rain bring flood, water wash 'way livestock and crop
When it have sun the place hot hot hot
Disaster is near at hand we better take stock

No time for praying, no spiritual value
Religious teaching in school, well, that gone through
Religious occasion is now turned into fete
A little respect for the Master, He just can't get
Bazaar and harvest in the churchyard, DJ music and gambling must play
No time to say thanks for the things that come our way
A Nation youths who worship Michael J, Boy George
A Nation of lesbians and homo
What go fall on the Nation is the vengeance of Moko

Despite this, the Caribbean calypso man living in a world where the gods stand ready to do man's bidding, once properly invoked, does not sojourn too long in an existential hell, and he often presents the possibility of rejuvenation as the other side of the apocalyptic vision. This too is expressed in terms of diverse religious philosophies: Shorty's "Om Shanti" (1979) points to traditional Hinduism as a way out of the spiritual wasteland; Stalin's "In a Earlier Time" (1981) invokes Rastafarianism as the only escape from the certain destruction of "Babylon culture"; Lion's "The Visit of His Holiness Pope John Paul II" (1985) promises hope along Roman Catholic lines and Delamo's "Sodom and Gomorrah" (1982) and "Visions" (1987) reflect pentecostal type faith.

"Sodom and Gomorrah" employs the austere imagery of the Old Testament prophet in linking the biblical and modern wastelands:

An Angel of Death visited Abraham way back in Scripture
And said, 'I will visit death and destruction to Sodom and Gomorrah
But if in the cities I find ten righteous men there
Paraventure my spirit will be pacified, both cities will I spare'
But if that very Angel should come visiting here in my country
Tell me if it could find ten men of integrity
'cause avarice, greed and corruption is in control of this blessed land
Social ethics forgotten, honesty downtrodden
The Angel may not find one man
In this whole Island

'cause we are living in this modern Sodom and Gomorrah
And one day soon the Angel will visit we here in the near future
And if your wife turn into a pillar of salt
Ah want you know it is your fault
And if fire and brimstone fall down on we
We are all guilty

Unlike "Apocalypse" which blames the PNM government for its ill-advised decision to construct the Caroni Racing Complex, "Sodom and Gomorrah" interdicts the entire decadent society singling out effete politicians, supine ecclesiastics, venal practitioners of abortion and infanticide, and the arriviste black capitalists who had marched in 1970 for economic dignity only to retrogress to the condition of the nonblack exploiters they had earlier condemned.

For all its grimness of tone and language, "Sodom and Gomorrah" offers a vision of hope that a new system of morality can arise out of the ashes of this moribund society such that when an Angel of Light passes over the bright new world it will see a paradise on Earth. This patriotic hope is the basis of "Visions" which attempts to preclude the bitterness felt by adherents of the PNM at being ousted by a coalition of enemies and parties they had crushed easily in earlier polls. The calypso deals mainly with economic and moral reconstruction but the final stanza offers "the peculiar vision" of a "new Jerusalem" in which a genuine "one love" prevails and the political firmament is "supported by both a *balisier* and an A-beam in loving harmony". Curiously, Delamo offers this hope tentatively and without the confidence with which he projects the new economic order. It is as if he is suggesting that the diversification of Caroni or the rational development of Tobago is much easier to realise than the constructive coming together of the two major political parties.

This chapter would not be complete without a discussion of Natasha Wilson's "Reincarnation Wish" (1985). Natasha, a tiny pupil of St Dominic's Roman Catholic School, Port of Spain, created a highly volatile situation when she emerged in the colourful costume of an East Indian dancer to sing:

They say after death
There is reincarnation
If that is the case
I would like to change my race
To be a Negro
Is to live in misery
So when I return
An East Indian I want to be

Reincarnation is a contribution of Hinduism to religious philosophy in Trinidad and Tobago, and in point of fact, the teacher/composer, George Martin, was inspired to write the calypso by the comments of a child during class discussion of this subject.[27] A subtle form of mockery underlies the statement that for the Afro-Trinidadian reincarnation into an Indo-Trinidadian represents a transformation into a higher form of life. The traditional warning that the Afro-Trinidadian look to himself is encoded in religious terms, ironically, the religion of the feared other, as the calypso suggests that even the philosophical and religious foundations of race pride, the basis of racial ontological security may be threatened. A more skilful use of calypso irony it is difficult to find.

CONCLUSION

Describing the political landscape necessitates a process of encoding which can convert worlds of meaning into words of delight and vice versa. Valentino's couplet "The word is the code/As we pass along this road" ("Visions" 1985), captures the essence of the importance of calypso comment in helping to orient one through the interlocking mazes of race, class, colour and creed which comprise the political culture. The calypsonian's achievement can best be appreciated when one has to explain the subtleties of single utterances which the initiated take for granted. Maestro's "Mr Trinidadian" is a useful example. In listing the grounds on which the electorate disqualifies the aspirants to high office, Maestro needed only quote the common talk:

You call Robinson a traitor
You say worse than that about Granger
You say Kamal seeking he own interest
You call Millette a Marxist-Leninist

A.N.R. Robinson never outlived the 'traitor' image diehard PNMites had of him and they felt vindicated in 1990 when Abu Bakr did to him what they remember, fancifully, he had planned to do to the beloved 'Doc' in 1970. The worst that could be said about Geddes Granger was that he was a 'Black Power advocate', but so frightening was this that the mainstream rejected his brand of politics despite the upgrading and sanitising of his public image.[28] Kamaluddin Mohammed, certainly the most senior of Williams' three deputies, was passed over when Williams died without nominating a successor. It was felt that the country was not ready for an Indian prime minister, but even more importantly, in a season of public morality Mohammed's wealth was cause for concern.[29] James Millette, Marxist-Leninist and obviously a spawn of the red devil, never had a prayer of a chance of becoming prime minister of Trinidad and Tobago.

One important observation that needs to be made vis-à-vis the political Calypso of this period is the dignity of its language. Certainly there has been abuse and bitterness, but humour acts as a palliative, modifying the quarrel and the reproach. In 1977, for example, Chalkdust, embittered by the elevation of Basil Pitt to Ambassador Plenipotentiary after the voters of Tobago West had rejected him at the polls, declared in "Singing Protest":

I would like to tell Basil to try
And kiss my upper thigh

a euphemism anatomically close enough to what is a mild obscenity in polite conversation. Statements like these which evoke laughter and mute bitterness can create space for dialogue and even make for friendship, as happened to Williams and Chalkdust – if truth be the latter's.[30] The dignity of the language is also noted in the absence of vituperation and contumely and in the respect for the antagonist, features which distinguish the calypso of this period from the acrimony of the post-1987 songs. The control demonstrated by the singers is a vital element: in attack, vehemence is tempered by humour and restraint, and when attack seems to have failed, withdrawal is dignified. Stalin, for example, concludes his argument against posturing politicians with the equable farewell words:

You just stay steady on your course
I stay with mine and is no love lost
("Show Your Works" 1984)

Afterword

After 1987 the tone of the political calypso changed dramatically. New and different voices articulated artlessly the anger of an intolerant age which clamoured for an expression that was appropriately raw and direct, harsh and unforgiving. Between 1988 and 1991 the main target of this anger was Prime Minister A.N.R Robinson.

Professor Gordon Rohlehr's excellent article, "Apocalypso and the Soca Fires of 1990", which analyses the scapegoating of Robinson, examines the process by which the society ignited its anger against the leader it had chosen in fair and free elections open to all. Rohlehr observes that the process of seeking a sacrificial victim originated in the collective need for someone to suffer publicly for the horror of colonialism and the failures of independence. History was too abstract, the descendants of the white colonists too untouchable and Williams too long dead to be flogged, but Robinson was well within reach. His first 'budget of sacrifices' was but the first in a series of austerity measures which angered the masses, his rigid authoritarianism annoyed his confederates, his expulsion of undisciplined ULF populists alienated the Indo-Trinidadian voters and his obsession with demolishing the Williams godhead antagonised the Afro-Trinidadian voters. Different groups cultivated private grievances, some manufactured, others magnified, and the aggregate fury of the real and the perceived fell with triple vengeance on the once putative saviour. Calypsonians featured prominently in the anti-Robinson blitz.

Cro Cro, Sugar Aloes and Watchman lead the main assault and others launched flank attacks or sniped from cover. Stalin's "We Can Make It If We Try" (1988) and Shorty's "Righteousness Exalts a Nation" (1989) essayed defences but the general tendency was to flay Robinson and the NAR. To their credit few of the protest singers of the 1962–87 period joined in this practice and when they did voice dissent their song never degenerated to the level of the prevailing anti Art. Chalkdust's "Chaffeur Wanted" (1989) and Stalin's "Nah Ease Up" (1990) represented the old style, the style that had become passe since 1988.

When the Jamaat al Musilmeen stormed Parliament on 27 July 1990 and effectively put paid to Robinson's demolition of Williams, calypsonians delighted in ridiculing Robinson who had borne himself with dignity and courage despite the humiliations imposed on him by the insurgents. Very few singers thought to reflect deeply on the Musilmeen's exercise in tragicomedy.

Then in 1991 the PNM again took office. Criticism was slow in coming despite the fact that Patrick Manning was continuing the policies of his predecessor, policies which had seemingly offended many calypsonians. While calypsonians gave the new-look PNM a chance to prove themselves, they found other 'villains' in Dr Morgan Job, the NAR apologist, who fulminated against the tribalism which engendered ignorance and facilitated the emergence of a variety of 'swine', and Ms Hulsie Bhaggan, the UNC Member of Parliament for Chaguanas, who declared that Afro-Trinidadians were raping Indo-Trinidadian virgins in her constituency. Both came under attack in song.

Manning's popularity ebbed quickly following several decisions which were ill considered – if considered at all. "De driver driving good," Luta commented sarcastically flaunting Chalkdust's "Chaffeur Wanted" in the faces of the calypsonians who seemed to be able to find nothing bad to say about Manning's many mistakes. Interestingly enough Luta's "Good Driving" was good enough to earn him a tie for the 1994 Calypso Monarch title with Delamo one of whose songs, "31 Years Old" criticised Manning's slogan "Let's go down the road and get the job done."

In 1995 Manning called a snap general election. His party won 17 seats, Basdeo Panday's UNC won 17 and A.N.R. Robinson's NAR won the two Tobago seats. Robinson chose to enter into coalition with Panday, making one love sweeter the second time around to paraphrase the sentiment of the new prime minister. Cro Cro's "All Yuh Look fuh Dat" chastised Afro-Trinidadian voters for letting the atavistic enemy in the door and made harsh references to the sexual harassment for which the new prime minister had been charged prior to 1995, charges of which he was cleared after assuming office. To the absolute horror of many, Cro Cro was crowned Monarch ahead of Bro Marvin, whose "Jahaaji Bhai" was considered by the Indo-Trinidadian community to be a national unity song. It was said by many an Indo-Trinidadian commentator and several of African descent that racism was rewarded.

Worse was to follow in 1997 when Prime Minister Panday, referring to the 1997 edition of the Dimanche Gras show, declared that his government of national unity would not stand by while racism was celebrated and while innocent citizens were denigrated in song. Panday promised that measures would be put in place to prevent taxpayers' dollars from being misused to reward those who would subvert national unity. Characteristically, he did not say which songs gave him offence and the public chose to fault Aloes' "Unity", GB's "Jahaaji Blues", Tigress' "Two Nations", Ella Andall's "Say My Name" and even Gypsy's "Little Black Boy". Taking cue from this, the attorney general promised to introduce legislation to prevent the venting of racism in calypso.

We are in for stirring times.

Notes

1. Eric Williams, "My relations with the Caribbean Commission 1943–1955". In *Forged from the Love of Liberty: Selected Speeches of Dr Eric Williams*, comp. Paul Sutton (Port of Spain: Longman Caribbean 1988): 269–80.

2. Chalkdust |Hollis Liverpool|, "From the horse's mouth: an analysis of certain aspects in the development of the calypso and its contribution to contemporary society as gleaned from personal communication" (Caribbean Studies Thesis, UWI, St Augustine 1973): 20. Superior informed Chalkdust that, "You sure to get a twenty dollars from him." This is far less – and far more believable – than the princely handouts with which Blakie credits Williams. See Carlton Herbert |Blakie| as told to Aldwin Primus, "The Doc would give us $3,000 of his own when we were broke," *Bomb*, 15 June 1990: 11.

3. *Trinidad Guardian*, 4 January 1957: 7.

4. "Dr Williams is married", *Trinidad Chronicle*, 5 December 1958: 1.

5. "Tiger quits over 'C.M.' ", *Trinidad Guardian*, 10 January 1959: 1. See Rawle Gibbons, *No Surrender: A Biography of The Growling Tiger* (Tunapuna, Trinidad and Tobago:
Canboulay 1994) 83–88 for a fuller treatment of the issue.

6. "Calypsonians complain of propaganda", *Sunday Guardian*, 24 January 1960: 10.

7. C.L.R. James, *Party Politics in the West Indies*, 2nd printing (Port of Spain: Inprint 1984): 14.

8. Eric Williams, *Inward Hunger: The Education of a Prime Minister* (London: Deutsch 1969): 201–202; 248. Williams claims that "P.A.Y.E" and "Federation" represented public opinion. In 1980, apropos of Sparrow's celebrating 25 glorious years of calypso performing, he sent a message to the tent reiterating the sentiments of *Inward Hunger*, and adding that Sparrow had come to his assistance with "Leave the Damn Doctor" during one of his most difficult moments – he did not say which. See "PM praises Sparrow's inspiration", *Express*, 6 January 1980: 3.

9. Liverpool, "From the Horse's Mouth": 16.

10. Sparrow (Slinger Francisco), personal interview, 24 January 1991.

11. Eric Williams, "*Massa Day Done*": A *Masterpiece of Political and Sociological Analysis* (Port of Spain: PNM Publishing Co. 1961): 1–2.

12. Selwyn Ryan, *Race and Nationalism in Trinidad and Tobago: A Study of Decolonisation in a Multiracial Society* (St Augustine, Trinidad: ISER, UWI 1972):265.

13. James, *Party Politics*: 162. James' perception of Sparrow as a political personality is demonstrated by his inclusion of the Sparrow vignette in the section "Personality and Politics" 151–72, a chapter which discusses only one other figure: Williams.

14. Gordon Rohlehr, "'Man talking to man': Calypso and social confrontation in Trinidad, 1970 to the present", *My Strangled City and Other Essays* (Port of Spain: Longman Caribbean 1992): 326.

15. Francisco, personal interview. Sparrow did not say who called him in for consultations, neither does he say whom he met.

16. Ryan, *Race and Nationalism*: 182.

17. James, *Party Politics*: 162.

18. Harold McCollin (Rocky), *Cristo: The Man, His Life and Times*, Radio 7.30 AM, Port of Spain, 20 January 1985. Rocky uses in his programme a tape recording of the 1962 Dimanche Gras show which includes the frenzied applause which greeted Sparrow's performance of "Federation".

19. Ivar Oxaal, *Black Intellectuals Come to Power: The Rise of Creole Nationalism in Trinidad and Tobago* (Cambridge, Mass.: Schenkman Publishing Co. 1968): 23.

20. Shiva Naipaul, letter to V.S. Naipaul, "The brothers Naipaul", *Sunday Guardian*, 22 February 1981: 31. Winston Mahabir, *In and Out of Politics: Tales of the Government of Dr Eric Williams from the Notebooks of a Former Minister* (Port of Spain: Inprint 1978): 36 tells of the disparaging response of a rural Indian villager to the PNM. Winston Mahabir describes a campaign meeting in the largely Indo-

Trinidadian town of Chaguanas, ending his account by quoting the words of an Indo-Trinidadian that . . . "no true Indian go vote for that nigger party."

21. "Dems used race", *Trinidad Guardian*, 2 April 1958: 1. This report summarises Williams' postelection address "The dangers that face Trinidad and Tobago and the West Indian nation" which he delivered at Woodford Square, Port of Spain. Mahabir, who arrived while Williams was in full flow, recounts the consternation of the non-African PNM leaders. See Mahabir, *In and Out of Politics*: 78–79.

22. Gordon Rohlehr, "Sparrow as Poet", *David Frost Introduces Trinidad and Tobago*, ed. Michael Anthony and Andrew Carr (London: Deutsch 1975):192.

23. John Grimes, "Tonight is the night for calypsonians. Who will be '61's king?" *Sunday Guardian*, 12 February 1961: 21.

24. Martin Sampath, letter to the editor, "Dangerous influence deplored in words of some calypsonians." *Trinidad Guardian*, 27 February 1961: 8. Sparrow's "Thanks to the *Guardian*" (1962) comments ironically on the role that the newspaper played, inadvertently, in making him, the loser, more popular than Dougla, the winner.

25. McCollin, *Cristo*. Brigo placed first, but Rocky did not preserve his calypso. This may have been oversight or even a technical fault in the recording system. It seems more likely, however, that Rocky, who had written "The Mad Scientist" (performed by Nap) was not impressed by Brigo's song and so condemned it to obscurity.

26. Ryan, *Race and Nationalism*: 266–70.

27. Ryan, *Race and Nationalism* 269. In a footnote to the page, Ryan confirms "a clear PNM bias" on the part of *The Guardian*, a new *Guardian* line deriving

from the policy of its new owners who were interested in securing rights to television.

28. Mahabir, In and Out of Politics: 109–12 presents a vignette on Capildeo, his close childhood friend. Mahabir notes among other things Capildeo's all-consuming desire to become premier – he was willing to join the PNM but Williams would have to step down. Mahabir, a psychiatrist by calling, noted that both Williams and Capildeo "exhibited signs of sporadic emotional balance". Of Capildeo, he continues, "had he, by any miracle, achieved political victory, the devastating pestilence of his power might well have polluted everything it touched": 111.

29. Ryan, Race and Nationalism: 268.

30. Ryan, Race and Nationalism: 269.

31. Nation, 27 October 1961: 2. According to this report, Williams had referred to Capildeo as a "mad scientist" during a campaign meeting at St Joseph on 24 October 1961.

32. Gerald Wight, "Sir Gerald sees danger ahead", Sunday Guardian, 8 January 1961: 1. Wight, a white Trinidadian and one-time leader of the DLP, recalls Williams saying in 1958, apropos of Louis Rostant (a prominent French Creole) being returned to the Port of Spain City Council, that PNM bulldozers were "digging deep into the hillsides" and "God help any minority group that gets in the way."

33. 1960 Census of Trinidad and Tobago (Bulletins no 1 and 2) cited in Ivar Oxaal, Black Intellectuals and the Dilemmas of Race and Class in Trinidad (Cambridge, Mass.: Schenkman 1981): 22.

34. "Independence crown to Brynner", Trinidad Guardian, 16 August 1962: 1.

35. Oxaal, Black Intellectuals Come to Power:175.

36. "Independence crown to Brynner".

37. Janet Reid, letter to the editor, Trinidad Guardian, 28 August 1962: 10.

38. K.V. Parmasad, "The Indian problem", Pelican (St Augustine: Guild of Undergraduates 1971): 17–20.

39. Gordon Rohlehr, Calypso and Society in Pre-Independence Trinidad (Port of Spain: Gordon Rohlehr 1990): 179–82.

40. Atilla the Hun (Raymond Quevedo), Atilla's Kaiso: A Short History of Trinidad's Calypso. ed. Errol Hill (Port of Spain: UWI Dep't of Extramural Studies 1983): 55–64.

41 Ranjit Kumar, Thoughts and Memories of Ranjit Kumar (Port of Spain: Inprint 1981): 236.

42. "'Mr Calypso' chosen: 36 auditioned out of 180 entries say Independence Calypso Competition Sub-committee", Trinidad Guardian, 10 August 1961: 1.

Chapter 2

1. Three statements may suffice. Ivar Oxaal, Black Intellectuals Come to Power: The Rise of Creole Nationalism in Trinidad and Tobago (Cambridge, Mass.: Schenkman 1968): 147 opines that the PNM had become a "charismatic autocracy within a sycophantic oligarchy"; Selwyn Ryan, Race and Nationalism in Trinidad and Tobago: A Study of Decolonisation in a Multiracial Society (St Augustine, Trinidad: ISER, UWI 1974): 224 notes the "gradual shift away from the politics of principle towards a more Machiavellian emphasis on the principles of politics"; Ryan, Race and Nationalism: 177 records the reappearance of nepotism and corruption "if indeed they had ever disappeared".

2. "The calypso and the realities of independence", Government Broadcasting Unit, Port of Spain, 3 June 1973. #19 of the 26-part radio

series *From Atilla to the Seventies* researched, scripted and narrated by Gordon Rohlehr.

3. Carl Jacobs, "Now Birdie speaks his mind", *Sunday Guardian*, 2 March 1969:13.

4. *Daily Mirror*, 2 January 1964: 9 reproduces a photograph of the "Applejackers peculiar creed" inscribed on a city wall.

5. "Sparrow runs for Police", *Trinidad Guardian*, 31 January 1961: 19.

6. Gordon Rohlehr, *Calypso and Society in Pre-Independence Trinidad* (Port of Spain: Gordon Rohlehr 1990): 373.

7. Blakie |Carlton Herbert| as told to Aldwin Primus, "The Doc would give us $3,000 of his own when we were broke", *Bomb*, 15 June 1990: 11.

8. Susan Craig, "Background to the 1970 confrontation in Trinidad and Tobago", *Contemporary Caribbean: A Sociological Reader* 2 (Port of Spain: Susan Craig 1982): 391 claims that the PNM had "gained the allegiance of the urban unemployed especially those who had created the steelbands . . . " Steelbandsmen became the unofficial army of the PNM in 1956. Darcus Howe and Bukka Rennie, "The unemployed and the special works", *Contemporary Caribbean*: 128 claim that "Only the Bad-Johns got work" and that some of the conflict was caused by *Bad-Johns* being employed outside of their territory and in that of others.

9. "Calypso and political criticism after 1965", Government Broadcasting Unit, Port of Spain, 10 June 1973. #20 of the radio series *From Atilla to the Seventies*.

10. *Guardian* newspapers, June–July 1963 carried accounts of the trial. According to *Trinidad Guardian*, 4 July 1963: 11, one witness testified that the soldiers sang revised lyrics to the melody of Sparrow's "The Gunslingers".

11. S. Hylton Edwards, *Lengthening Shadows: Birth and Revolt of the Trinidad Army* (Port of Spain: Inprint 1982): 51–52.

12. Anthony de Verteuil, *The Years of Revolt: Trinidad 1881–1888* (Port of Spain: Paria 1982): 44–115.

13. Rohlehr, *Calypso and Society*: 28–29.

14. Rohlehr, *Calypso and Society*: 237–38.

15. Rawle Gibbons, Sing De Chorus prod. Canboulay prod., Queen's Hall, Port of Spain, January–February 1991.

16. Chalkdust |Hollis Liverpool|, "From the horse's mouth: an analysis of certain aspects in the development of the calypso and its contribution to contemporary society as gleaned from personal communication" (Caribbean Studies Thesis, UWI, St Augustine 1973): 16.

17. *Guardian* newspapers February–June 1963.

18. Arthur Calder-Marshall, *Glory Dead* (London: Michael Joseph 1939) footnote to 164–65.

19. "This Young Killer is a bit nervous", *Daily Mirror*, 6 February 1964: 12.

20. Warrior (Wilfred Sylvester) told me part of his story during the late 1970s when he was holed up at Ste Madeleine. Other details were supplied by Squibby (Stanley Cummings) who is a gold mine of information about calypsonians, especially his southern contemporaries Maestro, Stalin and Shorty. Squibby also provided invaluable insights into the operations of city tents, especially the Revue of the mid and late 1970s. This information was gleaned over an extended liming period from 1975 to 1991.

21. "The calypso and political criticism after 1965".

22. One example of the police's attitude to defeat begs to be included here. In the early 1970s, Southern Division officers raided a Pleasantville apartment,

reputed to be a 'weed house', and the hangout of several members of Valiants Sports Club, one of the better teams in the San Fernando area. By coincidence this raid happened on the morning of a crucial Police-Valiants fixture and that evening at Skinner Park, I distinctly remember a nonplaying policeman express surprise that Valiants could still field a team. His words, if memory serves me right, were, "I thought we did lock up all ah dem."

23. "Minister took prisoner away", *Trinidad Guardian*, 10 September 1964: 1.

24. Max Ifill, *The Solomon Affair: A Tale of Immorality in Trinidad* (Port of Spain: People's Democratic Society 1964).

25. Patrick Solomon, *Solomon: An Autobiography* (Port of Spain: Inprint 1982): 234–38.

26. *Guardian* political reporter, "Solomon quits the Cabinet: Williams accepts the resignation", *Trinidad Guardian*, 15 September 1964: 1.

27. "Sparrow's calypso on Dr Solomon", *Trinidad Guardian*, 30 September 1964: 3.

28. Rohlehr, "The calypso and the realities of independence".

29. Ryan, *Race and Nationalism*: 269.

30. "James tells of fisticuffs in Cabinet", *Trinidad Guardian*, 19 February 1961: 1.

31. "The Uses of Adversity", editorial, *Nation*, 18 September 1964: 6.

32. George Harvey, "A job for Solomon: I have the power, PM tells Arima crowd", *Trinidad Guardian*, 21 September 1964: 13.

33. Wayne Vincent-Brown, "Solomon back again", *Sunday Guardian*, 11 October 1964: 1. The report quotes Williams as saying " . . . and those who don't like it could go and live abroad", a watered-down version of the truth offered in deference to the genteel sensibilities of *Guardian* subscribers.

34. Ralph Henry, "The state and income distribution in an independent Trinidad and Tobago", *Trinidad and Tobago: The Independence Experience*, ed. Selwyn Ryan with the assistance of Gloria Gordon (St Augustine, Trinidad: ISER, UWI 1988) 477–79.

35. Rohlehr, "The calypso and political criticism after 1965".

36. Rohlehr, "The calypso and political criticism after 1965".

Chapter 3

1. "The calypso and political criticism after 1965", Government Broadcasting Unit, Port of Spain, 10 June 1973. #20 of the 26-part radio series *From Atilla to the Seventies* researched, scripted and narrated by Gordon Rohlehr.

2. Alfred Tennyson, "The Lotus Eaters", *Tennyson: A Selected Edition*, ed. Christopher Rich (Longman: Essex 1984): 71–79.

3. Edward Brathwaite, "Didn't he ramble", *The Arrivants: A New World Trilogy* (London: Deutsch 1969): 23.

4. Eric Williams, *Inward Hunger: The Education of a Prime Minister* (London: Oxford University Press 1973): 230–35.

5. Susan Craig, "Background to the 1970 confrontation", *Contemporary Caribbean: A Sociological Reader* 2 (Port of Spain: Susan Craig 1982): 405. James Millette, "Towards the black power revolt of 1970", *The Black Power Revolution 1970: A Retrospective*, edited by Selwyn Ryan and Taimoon Stewart (St Augustine, Trinidad: ISER, UWI 1995): 69–70.

6. Leigh Richardson, "Requiem for a mad(?) scientist", *Sunday Guardian*, 7 February 1982: 8.

7. According to the *Nation* 4.4, 17 November 1961: 3, Williams, at a press

conference, requested civility of all involved in the soon to be contested general election. However, beginning with that very issue which carried Williams' statement and continuing until the election, The Nation carried on its front page in two insets, one on either side of the masthead, the message, "Send the mad scientist . . . into outer space."

8. Gordon Rohlehr, Calypso and Society in Pre-Independence Trinidad (Port of Spain: Gordon Rohlehr 1990): 210–11.

9. Selwyn Ryan, Race and Nationalism in Trinidad and Tobago: A Study of Decolonisation in a Multiracial Society (St Augustine, Trinidad: ISER, UWI 1972): 137.

10. Nyahuma Obika, An Introduction to the Life and Times of Tubal Uriah Buzz Butler (Point Fortin, Trinidad: Caribbean Historical Society 1982): 188–90.

11. Nyahuma Obika, Gene Miles: Our National Heroine (Point Fortin, Trinidad: Caribbean Historical Society, n/d): 10.

12. Jack Harewood, "Racial discrimination in employment in Trinidad and Tobago (Based on data from the 1960 census), Social and Economic Studies 20.3 (3 September 1971): 267–93; Acton Camejo, "Racial discrimination in employment in the private sector in Trinidad and Tobago: a study of the business elite and the social structure", Social and Economic Studies 20.3 (3 September 1971): 294–317.

13. Raoul Pantin, Black Power Day: The 1970 February Revolution: A Reporter's Story (Santa Cruz, Trinidad: Hatuey 1990): 25–28.

14. Sparrow is credited with the statement "I love Dr Williams like a god and a half and most of the Ministers are first class, none better," Bomb, 21 January

1969, quoted in Glen Roach, "Calypso and politics 1956–1972" (Caribbean Studies thesis, UWI, St Augustine 1972):16.

15. C.L.R. James, Party Politics in the West Indies 2nd printing (Port of Spain: Inprint 1984): 63–77 hints that Williams feared his growing influence in the party and set up members to attack him. It must be noted that James occupied a strange place in the PNM in those early years. Winston Mahabir, In and Out of Politics: Tales of the Government of Dr Eric Williams from the Notebooks of a Former Minister (Port of Spain: Inprint 1978): 70 observes that Williams imitated James' ideas, gestures, mannerisms and so on. Ivar Oxaal, Black Intellectuals Come to Power: The Rise of Creole Nationalism in Trinidad and Tobago (Cambridge, Mass.: Schenkman 1968): 147 notes that A.N.R. Robinson and Wilfred Alexander refused to attend meetings when James was present.

16. "Ministry queries Chalkie's dual role", Trinidad Guardian, 26 February 1968: 1.

17. "Teacher by day – kaisonian by night", Express, 24 January 1968.

18. Roy Mitchell, "The quest for independence and the making of Makandal Daaga", Trinidad and Tobago Review, vol 9.11, 12, 10.1, September–October n/y. This extract, which was sold on the streets by NJAC members, is the source for all the information in this paragraph.

19. Chalkie alleges that he was fired and only reinstated after he sang "Reply to the Ministry" (1969). See Hollis Liverpool, Kaiso and Society (St Thomas: Virgin Islands Commission on Youth 1986): 50. His allegation does not seem to find support elsewhere. Nation, 10 January 1969 notes that he was

careful to request permission for the next season.

20. "Regiment warned of Marxists", *Express*, 24 October 1968. Montano has been described by Winston Mahabir, *In and Out of Politics*: 49 as a man who saw red everywhere. What could have kindled his ire was the local agitation over the decision by the Jamaican government to refuse re-entry to Guyana-born Walter Rodney, the popular UWI history lecturer who had been 'grounding' with the Jamaican masses. This agitation, coming on the heels of the Trinidad government's decision to declare persona non grata Trinidad-born Black Power activist, Stokely Carmichael, aroused indignation locally and perhaps generated Montano's fiery speech.

21. Eric Roach, "A night of triumphs and disappointments", *Trinidad Guardian*, 7 February 1967: 7.

22. Karl Douglas, "In this calypso, the psychology of the slave mind", *Sunday Guardian*, 20 January 1963: 8.

23. Dena Epstein, *Sinful Tunes and Spirituals: Black Folk Music to the Civil War* (Urbana, Chicago: University of Illinois Press, 1977): 281.

24. Edward Brathwaite, "Leopard", *The Arrivants: A New World Trilogy* (London: OUP 1973): 244–47.

25. Ibn Battuta (1304–1369) was one of the greatest medieval travellers. He had travelled extensively through East, West and North Africa in addition to Asia and Arabia.

26. Yosef A.A. Ben Jochannan, *The Saga of the "Black Marxists" versus the "Black Nationalists": A Debate Resurrected* 1,2,3 (New York: Ben Jochannan 1976): xi.

27. Elridge Cleaver, *Soul on Ice* (London: Panther 1970). The section "White woman, black man": 143–72 features four essays, two of which, "The allegory of the black eunuchs": 143–59 and "The primeval mitosis" 160–72 discuss the psychology of black-white sexual relationships.

28. Gordon Rohlehr, "Sparrow and the language of the calypso", *Savacou*, 1.2 (September 1970): 94–95. The difference in perception between the scholar and the masses has to do with notions of what is 'good' in the calypso and is itself the subject of perennial debate. As far as "Congo Man" is concerned, the whole issue involves ideas of the responsibility of the artiste, his level of development and the level of the collective consciousness of his audience. Sparrow, it must be noted, is enamoured of "Congo Man" and rerecorded it in 1989. It may well be that he just likes it as a calypso.

29. "Mentacide" is "the destruction of the mind, a term created by Dr Bobby Wright (psychologist)". See Ben Jochannan, *The Saga of the "Black Marxists"*: x–xi.

30. "Dear Mr Prime Minister", editorial, *Nation* 12.32, 2 May 1969: 1. This editorial attacked an unsigned lead in *Moko*, 25 April 1969 entitled "The bus workers strike – labour must show the way". It singled out *Moko* editors, UWI lecturers James Millette and Gordon Rohlehr in its protest against the "indoctrination of our young citizens with violence, disorder and rebellion under the pretext of university education and academic or intellectual freedom and inquiry . . . "

31. *Nation* 12.50, 5 September 1969: 6.

32. Dave Darbeau, "Black students on trial in racist Canada", *Vanguard*, 7 March 1970: 3.

33. Gordon Rohlehr, "The dilemma of the West Indian academic in 1970", *The Black Power Revolution 1970: A Retrospective* edited by Selwyn Ryan and Taimoon Stewart (St Augustine, Trinidad: ISER, UWI 1995): 394.

34. Khafra Kambon, *For Bread, Justice and Freedom: A Political Biography of George Weekes* (London: New Beacon Books 1988): 192–93.

35. Pantin, *Black Power Day*: 33–36. During the 1960s and 1970s the *Express* earned PNM disapprobation for what the regime rated as adversarial journalism. *Express* coverage of the Country Club affair and its criticism of the Country Club caste provoked the affronted élites into withholding advertising support for the newspaper until they were appeased by a carefully calculated flattery of their wives.

36. Eric Williams, *"Massa Day Done": A Masterpiece of Political and Sociological Analysis* (Port of Spain: PNM Publishing Co. 1961).

37. Khafra Kambon, "Black Power in Trinidad and Tobago February 26–April 21, 1970" in *The Black Power Revolution 1970: A Retrospective* edited by Selwyn Ryan and Taimoon Stewart (St Augustine, Trinidad: ISER, UWI 1995): 220–21 lists the following: "1001 white devils" played by St James Village Drummers; "The truth: before, then and now" played by Pinetoppers from East Dry River; and "King sugar" played by UWI students.

38. Pantin, *Black Power Day*: 44.

Chapter 4

1. Eric Williams, *Inward Hunger: The Education of a Prime Minister* (London: Deutsch 1969): 311.

2. Khafra Kambon, *For Bread, Justice and Freedom: A Political Biography of George Weekes* (London: New Beacon 1988): 44–45.

3. Zin Henry, "Industrial relations and the development process", *The Independence Experience 1962–1987*, edited by Selwyn Ryan with the assistance of Gloria Gordon (St Augustine, Trinidad: ISER, UWI 1988): 48.

4. *Vanguard*, 3 May 1969: 2–3.

5. "PM pledges a battle to the end", the *Express*, 18 May 1969: 1. Williams is reported as having warned that, "The confrontation will be fought to the finish and the forces of law and order will prevail."

6. Kambon, *George Weekes*: 175–79.

7. Figures vary. The *Express* reported on 22 May 1969: 1 that 690 workers were turned back. On 25 May, however, it ran the headline "Agony of the 800".

8. *Nation* 12.33, 9 May 1969: 1. The PNM caricatured the strike by labelling it an NJAC-TIWU production "The Lawless Breed" a la Italian Western then in vogue. (TIWU stands for Transport and Industrial Workers Union.)

9. Kambon, *George Weekes*: 197–98.

10. Bill Riviere, "Black Power, NJAC and the 1970 confrontation in the Caribbean: an historical interpretation" (typescript, UWI, St Augustine 1972): 22.

11. Ivar Oxaal, *Race and Revolutionary Consciousness* (Cambridge, Mass.: Schenkman 1977): 15.

12. Raoul Pantin, *Black Power Day: The 1970 February Revolution: A Reporter's Story* (Santa Cruz, Trinidad: Hatuey 1990): 59.

13. Kambon, *George Weekes*: 204. Ken Parmasad, "Ancestral impulse, community formation and 1970: bridging the Afro-Indian divide", *The Black Power Revolution: A Retrospective* edited by Selwyn Ryan and Taimoon Stewart (St Augustine, Trinidad: ISER, UWI 1995): 314–16 details the advance

work done by members of SPIC to counter the mischievous propaganda of those opposed to the march.

14. Kambon, *George Weekes*: 225–26.

15. Eric Williams, *Forged from the Love of Liberty: Selected Speeches of Dr Eric Williams* (Port of Spain: Longman Caribbean 1981): 161–71.

16. It had been Williams' main text throughout 1969. See "Build, baby, build – Dr Williams", *Nation* 12.41, 4 July 1969: 3. and "Political leader outlines party's progress", *Nation* 3 October 1969. It also formed the main message of his two nationwide radio and television broadcasts in early 1970.

17. Williams, *Forged from the Love of Liberty*: 168. In all fairness, however, it must be noted that some commentators have alleged that in 1970 something was afoot behind the street demonstrations. Deryck Brown, "The failed coup: The Jamesian connection", *The Black Power Revolution*: 1970: 543–78 alleges major conspiracy by the New Left while Candice Kelshall, "Mutiny or Revolution", *The Black Power Revolution* 1970: 419–39 alleges, implausibly, a plot involving most of the officer corps of the regiment. eg Raffique Shah, "Reflections on the mutiny and trial", *The Black Power Revolution* 1970: 514 confirms that there was a plot afoot.

18. Selwyn Ryan, *Race and Nationalism in Trinidad and Tobago: A Study of Decolonisation in a Multiracial Society* (St Augustine, Trinidad: ISER, UWI 1974): 460–61 gives a summary of Spencer's version of the story.

19. "Mr Q", "A politician recalls", *The 1970 Black Power Revolution*: 605 remembers that Williams remained calm and collected throughout.

20. Roy Mc Cree, "Joffre Serrette: Black man on a white horse", *The Black Power Revolution* 1970: 526.

21. Ryan, *Race and Nationalism*: 467.

22. Selwyn Ryan, *Revolution and Reaction: Parties and Politics in Trinidad and Tobago 1970–1981* (St Augustine, Trinidad: ISER, UWI 1989): 15.

23. Patricia Robinson, interview with Wayne Brown, *People*, 20 July 1986: 13. Mrs Robinson, one of the bright young people sharing Williams' vision in the late 1950s, gives valuable insights into the workings of his mind during the federation crisis.

24. Martin Sampath, *Search and Destroy* (Siparia, Trinidad: Arawak 1976) v. Sampath, a founding member of the PNM, had been one of the commissioners looking into the disturbances at Teteron. His minority report had counselled against the courts martial. He left the PNM in the early 1970s to become a member of Robinson's Action Committee of Dedicated Citizens (later Democratic Action Congress). Sampath, a medical doctor living at Siparia, had his house searched by the police who were ostensibly looking for proof that he had treated wounded NUFF warriors and other types who could not be attended to at the hospitals and health centres. Sampath estimates that between May 1971 and 1975 the police searched 3,000 homes.

25. David Millette, "Guerrilla war in Trinidad", *The Black Power Revolution*: 625–60. What Millette's narrative does establish is that there was conspiracy in Trinidad and that NUFF did draw upon the resources of a network which predated their insurrection.

26. Ryan, *Revolution and Reaction*: 21.

27. *Crisis*, edited by Owen Baptiste (Port of Spain: Inprint 1976): 10.

28. *Crisis*: 37.

29. *Crisis*: 35.

30. One suspects that this phrase may have been coined by Lloyd Best who revels in the naming game. It may have first appeared in print in Adrian Espinet and Jacques Farmer, "Pussonal nonarchy – The paradox of power in Trinidad", *Tapia*, 16 November 1969: 6.

31. Selwyn Ryan, "Dr Eric Williams, the People's National Movement and the independence experience: a retrospective", *Trinidad and Tobago: The Independence Experience* 1962–1987 edited by Selwyn Ryan with the assistance of Gloria Gordon (St Augustine, Trinidad: ISER, UWI 1988): 151.

32. 1960 *Census of Trinidad and Tobago* (*Bulletins No 1 and 2*) quoted in Ivar Oxaal, *Black Intellectuals and the Dilemmas of Race and Class in Trinidad and Tobago* (Cambridge, Mass.: Schenkman 1981): 22.

33. Pantin, *Black Power Day*: 25–28.

34. Jack Harewood, "Racial discrimination in employment in Trinidad and Tobago (Based on data from the 1960 census)" *Social and Economic Studies* vol. 20.3(3 September 1971): 267–93; Acton Camejo, "Racial discrimination in employment in the private sector in Trinidad and Tobago: a study of the business elite and the social structure", *Social and Economic Studies* 20.3 (3 September 1971): 294–317.

35. Lloyd Best, "The nine political tribes of Trinidad and Tobago", *Social and Occupational Stratification in Contemporary Trinidad and Tobago*, edited by Selwyn Ryan (St Augustine, Trinidad: ISER, UWI 1991): 145–46.

36. Oxaal, *Black Intellectuals Come to Power*: 85.

37. Propriety decrees gloss. S. Hylton Edwards, *Lengthening Shadows: The Birth and Revolt of the Trinidad Army* (Port of Spain: Inprint 1982): 93 comments simply that, "The Minister must have had his own reasons for retiring Serrette and these he kept to himself."

Yet, in reproducing at length the decision of the Appeal Court to reverse the judgement against the mutineers, he demonstrates that the officers and gentlemen of the court martial were privy to the celebrated public secret but gallantly shielded pillars of race, class and sex even at the expense of erring in law. See *Lengthening Shadows*: 129–59.

38. Pantin, *Black Power Day*: 89; McCree, "Joffre Serrette", 526–27.

39. Hylton Edwards, *Lengthening Shadows*: 128–49.

40. "1970, according to David Bloom", *Express*, 6 April 1986: 3 criticises the account given by Lt Commander Mervyn Williams in *People*, 9 February 1986: 3 and contradicts that of Major Julien Spencer in *Sunday Guardian*, 20 April 1986: 5.There are many other accounts of gallantry and decisiveness most of which differ in critical detail.

41. "The violence which shook Tobago", *Express*, 8 April 1970: 1.

42. Zeno Constance, *Valentino, Poet and Prophet: Blues and Rebellion* (Trinidad: privately printed, 1984): 8.

43. Esther Le Gendre, "Life is a stage", *Tapia* vol. 3.7, 18 February 1973: 2.

44. Constance, *Valentino, Poet and Prophet*: 10.

45. Valentino (Emrold Phillip), personal interview, 23 January 1991. Valentino recalls a ceremony of 'baptism' at which rum was poured on his head and he was solemnly renamed "The Lord Valentino", Kitchener being sponsor and other Revue calypsonians the witnesses. For some years Valentino lived at Kitchener's house.

46. Kambon, *George Weekes*: 210. *Nation* 11.38, 7 June 1968: 1 charged Weekes with plagiarism. Williams, The *Nation* recalls, was the one who first used the term "Parliament of the People".

47. Eric Williams, "Revolution and dignity", *Forged from the Love of Liberty* 162–67; Eric Williams, "The Black Power Disturbances", *Forged from the Love of Liberty*: 167–71.

48. Teddy Belgrave quoted in Brian Meeks, "The development of the 1970 revolution in Trinidad and Tobago" (MSc thesis, UWI, Mona, Jamaica 1976): 277.

49. Eric Williams, "National Reconstruction", *Forged from the Love of Liberty*: 171–79. The term had been used before by Tapia spokesmen, namely Syl Lowhar, "Black Power and national reconstruction", *Tapia*, April 1970 and Lloyd Best "Tapia diary", *Tapia*, 20 December 1970.

50. Harold Mc Collin [Rocky], *The Lord Brynner: His Life and Times* Radio 7.30 AM, Port of Spain, February 1985.

51. Louis Regis, *Black Stalin: The Caribbean Man* (Trinidad: privately printed 1987): 9–10.

52. Squibby [Stanley Cummings], a close friend of Maestro, says that the latter distrusted Granger. He did not say why.

53. Adolphus Parmassar, an associate of Abdul Malik, turned state witness against his former employer and his evidence contributed to the verdict against Malik and later against Stanley Abbott and Edward Chadee. These murder trials of the early 1970s were highly sensational media events and received more than a fair share of coverage in the calypso, certainly more than the courts martial.

54. Louis Regis, *Maestro: The True Master* (Trinidad: privately printed *c.* 1981): 3.

55. Eric Williams "*Massa Day Done*": A *Masterpiece of Political and Sociological Analysis* (Port of Spain: PNM Publishing Co 1961).

56. Lennox Grant, "PNM loves me", *Tapia* 2.8, 26 November 1972: 11; Keith

Smith, "A reply to Johnny King", *Express*, 6 January 1985: 26. Smith quotes Chalkie's self-definition as a "Black Power Catholic".

57. Raoul Pantin, "Fête like bush at PNM Rally Expression '71", *Express*, 26 January 1971: 10.

58. "God help our gracious king", *Tapia* vol. 16, 23 May 1971: 1.

59. Hollis Liverpool, *Kaiso and Society* (St Thomas: Virgin Islands Commission on Youth 1986): 49.

60. "Chalkie: I feel so unwanted", *Express*, 10 February 1985: 35. Chalkdust remembers that Williams "laughed for so" when he heard "Let the Jackass Sing".

61. "God help our gracious king", *Tapia*: vol 16, 23 May 1971: 8.

62. Pantin, *Black Power Day*: 89 quotes Hudson-Phillips as saying, even 20 years after the 'fact', that, "They stuck a rifle up my ass." Karl Hudson-Phillips, "1970 – A betrayal of the hopes and aspirations of 1956", *The 1970 Black Power Revolution*: 621 denies this emphatically. Raffique Shah, "Reflections on the mutiny and trial", *The 1970 Black Power Revolution*: 517 supports Hudson-Phillips' statement.

63. Clevon Raphael, "Meet Kamal the songwriter", *Trinidad Guardian*, 21 August 1972: 3.

64. Carl Parris, "Trinidad and Tobago – September to December 1973", *Social and Economic Studies* 30. 3 (September 1981): 42–59. Parris thought the whole affair an exercise in legitimation. Selwyn Ryan, *Revolution and Reaction*: 4–32 thought that Williams was sincere in his earlier decision but that he changed his mind and then stage managed his return.

65. "Pegasus show to aid Brynner", *Express*, 3 November 1968: 3

66. "Choko, Bomb lose to ANR", *Express*, 19 January 1973: 1.

67. "Goddard refused to sign", *Sunday Guardian*, 26 February 1974.

68. Winston Mahabir, *In and Out of Politics: Tales of the Government of Dr Eric Williams Taken from the Notebooks of a Former Minister* (Port of Spain: Inprint 1978): 52–53.

69. Therese Mills, "Shorty charged with indecency", *Trinidad Guardian*, 8 March 1973: 1.

70. Gordon Rohlehr, "'Man talking to man': Calypso and social confrontation in Trinidad 1970–1984", *My Strangled City and Other Essays* (Port of Spain: Longman Caribbean 1992): 330.

71. David Millette, "Guerrilla war in Trinidad 1970–1974", *The Black Power Revolution*: 625–60.

72. Andrew Camacho, a popular UWI lecturer, met his death in mysterious circumstances while chauffeuring along a beach road in Mayaro. Gordon Rohlehr, "The dilemma of the West Indian academic in 1970", *The Black Power Revolution*: 396–97 briefly discusses the Camacho Affair.

73. Gordon Lewis, "He never played second fiddle . . . for Will was the superstar of them all", *Trinidad and Tobago Review* vol. 4.7, 1981.

74. Pantin, *Black Power Day*: 106.

75. Gordon Rohlehr, *Pathfinder: Black Awakening in The Arrivants of Edward Kamau Brathwaite* (Tunapuna, Trinidad: Gordon Rohlehr 1981): 22.

76. Frank Arlen, "Was Shorty paying for Chalkdust's pudding?" *Express*, 18 March 1973: 13; Syl Lowhar, "The hospital, the jail or the cemetery", *Tapia* 3.11, 18 March 1973: 12.

77. Constance, *Valentino, Poet and Prophet*: 24.

Chapter 5

1. Rudolph Ottley, *Calypsonians from Then to Now Pt 1* (Arima, Trinidad and Tobago: Rudolph Ottley 1995): 65. Shorty had said the same thing to Sookram Ali in an interview on Radio 105 FM in August 1994.

2. Roger Wallis and Krister Malm, *Big Sounds from Small Peoples: The Music Industry in Small Countries* (London: Constable 1984): 244.

3. Zeno Constance, "'Dem whey dread': a study of the Rastafari through the eyes of the calypsonian", (typecript *c.* 1985).

4. Gordon Lewis, *The Growth of the Modern West Indies* (New York: Modern Readers Paperbacks 1968): 212.

5. Keith Subero, "19 Calypsoes banned on air", *Sunday Express*, 26 January 1975: 32. According to this report, a rumour had circulated that the prime minister's office had ordered state-owned NBS Radio 6.10 and TTT not to broadcast Chalkdust's "Watergate Scandal", a calypso which alleges that Nixon fell over Watergate because he lacked the instruments and agencies of cover-up and control which Williams employed optimally in Trinidad and Tobago. Reporters investigating the rumour discovered that Radio 6.10 had in fact banned the following 18 calypsoes: Conqueror's "Fork Off"; Crazy's "Handyman" aka "The Electrician" and "Licks in '75"; Dougla's "Doctor"; Duke's "Cock of the Rock"; Funny's "Tantie"; Hawk's "Lady"; Kitchener's "Local Wood"; Maestro's "Jake and Blake"; Rose's "Mr Frenchie"; Shorty's "How to Kill a Cat"; and "Love the Hi Falutin' Way"; The Sparks' "Cricket Game"; Sparrow's "Wine Back", "Wife and Boat" and "Poopsin"; Squibby's "The Chook"; and Wonder's "Ashford Party", 18 suggestive and/or smutty songs. Radio 6.10, however, announced that there was no directive on Chalkdust's "Watergate Scandal" but that it was unlikely to be aired.

6. Louis Regis, *Black Stalin: The Caribbean Man* (Trinidad: privately printed 1987): 12.

7. Errol Pilgrim, "Blakie blames CDC for tent problems", *Trinidad Guardian*, 30 January 1976: 1.

8. "Anti corruption: big rats still at large", *Liberation* 6 (September 1977). This article asks: "Does any idiot believe that after 20 years of Oil and Gas that Williams only have that lil bit of money in the bank?" The answer is that many *need* to believe this, their last political illusion.

9. Selwyn Ryan, *The Disillusioned Electorate: The Politics of Succession in Trinidad and Tobago* (Port of Spain: Inprint 1989): 11.

10. Carl Parris, "Trinidad and Tobago – September to December 1973", *Social and Economic Studies* 30.3 (September 1981): 50–51.

11. Raoul Pantin, *Black Power Day: The 1970 February Revolution: A Reporter's Story* (Santa Cruz, Trinidad: Hatuey 1990): 109–10.

12. "Dr Williams' $50m welcome speech at Piarco", *Trinidad Guardian*, 4 August 1976: 23.

13. Mrs Beritha Downes, one of Stalin's primary school teachers at San Fernando Boys' RC, recalls that he was so poor that he had to be outfitted for classes by the Infant Department.

14. Information supplied by Mrs Donna Coombes-Montrose, OWTU librarian.

15. Selwyn Ryan, *Race and Nationalism in Trinidad and Tobago: A Study of Decolonisation in a Multiracial Society* (St Augustine, Trinidad: ISER, UWI 1974): 137.

16. Ranjit Kumar, *Thoughts and Memories of Ranjit Kumar* (Port of Spain: Inprint 1981): 236.

17. "Jamaica P.M. admits he said it: but I did not mean to offend Trinidad", *Trinidad Guardian*, 30 January 1980: 1.

18. Rosina Wiltshire-Brobder, "Trinidad and Tobago foreign policies 1962–1987: an evaluation", *Trinidad and Tobago: The Independence Experience 1962–1987*, edited by Selwyn Ryan with the assistance of Gloria Gordon (St Augustine, Trinidad: ISER, UWI 1987): 293.

19. "Gov't to gov't arrangements: a $5 billion illusion", *Trinidad Guardian*, 18 June 1982: 1. Selwyn Ryan, *The Disillusioned Electorate: The Politics of Succession in Trinidad and Tobago*: 14–27 reviews the history of the ill-conceived adventure.

20. Government of the Republic of Trinidad and Tobago, Ministry of Finance and Planning, *Report of the Review Team to Enquire into the Malabar 2,200 Housing and the Centralised Racing Complex Projects* (Port of Spain: Government Printery, July 1981).

21. *Report of the Review Team*: 31–32.

22. Eric Williams, *"The Caribbean Man": Address of the Political Leader of the PNM at the 21st Annual Convention* (Port of Spain: PNM Publishing Co 1979): 4.

23. "Look what they've done to our song", *Express*, 14 August 1981: 12.

24. Bro. Resistance (Roy Lewis}, "'Kaiso gone dread': Black Stalin, the Caribbean man in cultural perspective" (Caribbean Studies thesis, UWI, St Augustine 1980).

25. Courtenay Bartholomew, interview with Ken Gordon, "My professional relationship with Dr Williams", *Express*, 4 April 1981: 21.

26. *Sunday Express*, 10 February 1985: 15.

27. Clevon Raphael, "Lord Shorty: nothing serious", *Trinidad Guardian*, 8 January 1971: 10.

28. Regis, *Black Stalin*. Regis accepts uncritically several of Stalin's autobiographical statements,

especially those relating to the songs which Stalin chose to forget because they were inconsistent with his post-1970 image.

29. Williams, "*The Caribbean Man*".

30. *Bomb*, 21 January 1972 cited in Glen Roach, "Calypso and politics 1956–1972" (Caribbean Studies thesis, UWI, St Augustine 1972): 16.

31. Sparrow is handy with public relations statements. At the annual OYB-Revue clash of 3 February 1975, he outraged some patrons by advising hecklers to "Kiss my black Grenadian arse!" Months later, *Trinidad Guardian*, 6 July 1975: 3 quotes him as saying: "I have nothing against the Trinidadian community. And those people who have been following me around inciting me to the point of letting them know how I feel, they're probably from outside communities." Sparrow of the mid 1970s may have been feeling the need to stress how much he belonged to Trinidad and may have chosen to do so by pointing to his closeness to the Father of the Nation.

32. "PM praises Sparrow's inspiration", *Express*, 6 January 1980: 3.

33. *Juba Publications Presents Eric Eustace Williams: Through the Eyes of the Calypsonian*, programme notes, 10 December 1981.

34. Hollis Liverpool, *Kaiso and Society* (St Thomas: Virgin Islands Commission on Youth 1986): 49.

35. Peter Harper, "So you think calypso is dying", *Express*, 5 January 1971: 11. Harper wrote: "If what Chalkie was telling his smiling audience was all true, Dr Williams certainly did not allow his facial expressions to agree or object. He simply sat motionless and appeared to be marvelled by the wealth of information 'Chalkie' had,

either true or false." Harper did not consider that Williams, forewarned, may have simply switched off his hearing aid.

36. "PM summons Chalkie", *Sunday Punch*, 4 June 1989: 5.

37. Raoul Pantin, *Black Power Day: The 1970 February Revolution: A Reporter's Story* (Santa Cruz, Trinidad: Hatuey 1990): 101–2 tells of an attempt by Williams to charm him into compliance.

38. It is widely known that Erica Williams had urged her father to give it all up. He reinforced this in his retirement speech of 1973. No one is saying what exactly passed between them when he chose instead to remain as Father of the Nation, but she flew out of the country, and, it seems, out of his life. He did not even attend her wedding in Florida, and characteristically offered no reason for not doing so.

39. Khafra Kambon, *For Bread, Justice and Freedom: A Political Biography of George Weekes* (London: New Beacon Books 1988): 307.

40. Eric Williams, "Message to the youth of the nation", *Forged from the Love of Liberty: Selected Speeches of Dr Eric Williams*, ed. by Paul Sutton (Port of Spain: Longman Caribbean 1981): 328–29.

41. Ric Mentus, "Why has the ONR upset the PNM and George Chambers?", *People* (November 1981): 44–45.

42. According to Glen Roach, personal interview, 17 January 1991, Sparrow's new friends were also his business partners. His recordings were financed by Jet Age Furniture and appeared under that label in the early 1980s. Roach also claims that the proprietors of Jet Age Furniture – he did not name them – were strong members of the ONR.

43. The first incident took place in 1959 and perhaps inspired "Ten to One Is Murder" (1960). This calypso is fictional and does not explain the incident of 1959.

44. See note 31 to this chapter.

Chapter 6

1. Government of the Republic of Trinidad and Tobago, Ministry of Finance and Planning, *Report of the Review Team to Enquire into the Malabar 2,200 Housing and the Centralised Racing Complex Projects* (Port of Spain: Government Printery, July 1981).

2. John O'Halloran, popularly thought to be the prime personification of PNM corruption, was granted a diplomatic passport which enabled him to flee prosecution.

3. "Firm admits $3.3m in payments in report", *Trinidad Guardian*, 8 August 1982: 1.

4. "$3,000 for four million dollars: Amar freed for illegal money export", *Sunday Guardian*, 20 June 1982: 1.

5. Terrence Farrell, "The development of the non-bank financial institutions in Trinidad and Tobago 1973-1987", *Trinidad and Tobago: The Independence Experience 1961–1987*, ed. Selwyn Ryan with the assistance of Gloria Gordon (St Augustine, Trinidad: ISER, UWI 1988): 90–91.

6. See chapter 2, pages 25–29.

7. See chapter 2, page 27.

8. Political Reporter, "PM promises to deal with 'Sinking Ship'", *Trinidad Guardian*, 27 January 1986: 1.

9. *Trinidad Guardian*, 6 February 1986: 3.

10. Title of chapter 15 of Eric Williams' *Inward Hunger: The Education of a Prime Minister* (London: Deutsch 1969): 118–27.

11. "'Vote Dem Out' came from the heart says calypsonian Deple", *Sunday Guardian*, 25 January 1987: 26.

12. "Deple still singing 'Vote Dem Out'," *TnT Mirror*, 21 October 1987.

13. Ruth Finnegan, *Oral Literature in Africa* (London: Clarendon Press 1970): 283.

14. "Tesoro – The Trinidad success story that almost wasn't", *Sunday Express*, 15 March 1987: 6; Norris Solomon, "The Tesoro story," *Sunday Guardian*, 15 March 1987: 5; "It all started with an 'arrangement' some 18 years ago", *Sunday Guardian*, 22 March 1987: 9.

15. John Eckstein, "Corruption: What is the truth?" *Trinidad Guardian*, 9 September 1988: 9. Eckstein here claims that McGraw Hill, publishers of *Platt's Oilman*, had apologised for a 1982 statement reproducing an allegation that Chambers had received illegal payments from the Tesoro Petroleum Corporation.

Chapter 7

1. Roy Mitchell, "The quest for independence and the Making of Makandal Daaga", *Trinidad and Tobago Review* vol. 9.11 & 12, 10.1, September–October n/y. This extract, which was sold on the streets by NJAC members, is the source for all the information in this paragraph.

2. See chapter 6, pages 164-65.

3. Tapia member, Dennis Pantin, informed the concourse of students assembled to hear the matter discussed that the garment was in fact an African *kanga*. He also faulted Aimey for lending credibility to the *Bomb*. See *Embryo* (St Augustine: Guild of Undergraduates 1973), 5.8: 11.

4. "'Indrani' is no insult", *Express*, 3 April 1973: 4.

5. Ramesh Deosaran, "'The Caribbean man': a study of the psychology of perception and the media", *India in the Caribbean*,

ed. David Dabydeen and Brinsley
Samaroo (London: Hansib 1987): 81.

6. "'Om Shanti' puts Goddard on spot",
Express, 27 January 1979.

7. "Another kaiso kicked out by radio and
TV", *Express*, 13 February 1980: 24.

8. *Trinidad Guardian*, 12 March 1985: 9.

9. "Chalkdust in trouble: 'Grandfather'
calypso too racial, officials say", *Sun*,
28 January 1985: 1.

10. Ken Ali, "Funny cheated", *Sunday Punch*,
30 August 1987.

11. Hollis Liverpool, "Who is to judge this
judge?" *Sunday Guardian*, 29 March
1987: 10.

12. "Duke: Chalkdust deserved 2nd in
calypso monarch race", *Express*, 15
March 1987: 5. Keith Smith, "What is
Calypso?" *Sunday Express* 1 February
1987: 21, quotes Chalkdust as charging
that "Because of its metaphorical
language 'Calypso Music' will only find
an audience in intelligent people – he's
singing calypso for UWI."

13. *Express*, 18 January 1971: 10. Duke
threatened a boycott of the CDC tent
by Chalkdust and himself, alleging
preferential treatment to "yesterday's
calypsonians". To this Lion replied that
Duke was the highest-paid performer,
after Chalkdust (emphasis added). See
Express, 19 January 1971: 11.

14. Angela Fox, "I picked the finalists",
Sunday Punch, 23 August 1987: 9.

15. Angela Fox, "Winning song no good for
schools", *Sunday Punch*, 30 August
1987:7.

Chapter 8

1. Ruth Finnegan, *Oral Poetry: Its Nature,
Significance and Social Context* (London:
CUP 1977): 26.

2. Leopold Sedar Senghor quoted in
Janheinz Jahn, *Muntu: An Outline of the
New African Culture* (New York: New
Grove Press 1961): 94.

3. C.L.R. James, *Party Politics in The West
Indies* (Port of Spain: Inprint 1984):
footnote to 172.

4. Max Ifill, *The Solomon Affair: A Tale of
Immorality in Trinidad* (Port of Spain:
People's Democratic Society, vol. 1
1964): 2.

5. Elodie Jourdain, "Creole – A folk
language", *Caribbean Quarterly* vol. 3.1
(n/d): 29.

6. S. Hylton Edwards, *Lengthening Shadows:
Birth and Revolt of the Trinidad Army* (Port
of Spain: Inprint 1982): 69. British-born
Hylton Edwards, a former commander
of a rifle company in the regiment,
notes with surprise that snakes evoked
particular terror in his soldiers.

7. R.D. Abrahams, "The shaping of folklore
traditions in the British West Indies",
*Journal of Inter-American Studies and World
Affairs* 9 (1967): 456–57.

8. Winston Mahabir, *In and Out of Politics:
Tales of the Government of Dr. Eric Williams
Taken from the Notebooks of a Former Minister*
(Port of Spain: Inprint 1978): 54 records
that Williams met queries from his
cabinet colleagues about his 1958
marriage with stony silence.

9. "'Chalkie was disrespectful' say women,"
Sunday Guardian, 11 March 1973: 1.

10. Hollis Liverpool, *Kaiso and Society* (St
Thomas: Virgin Islands Commission on
Youth 1986): 49.

11. "Chalkie: I feel so unwanted" *Express*, 10
February 1985: 35.

12. Short Pants (Llewelyn McIntosh),
interview with William Tanifeani, *Black
Scholar* (Fall 1988): 71.

13. Eric Roach, "Chalkdust the political
swordsman of calypso", *Trinidad
Guardian*, 29 January 1974: 4.

14. Gordon Lewis, *The Growth of the Modern
West Indies* (New York: Modern Readers
Paperbacks 1968): 213.

15. Eric Williams, *Inward Hunger: The Education of a Prime Minister* (London: Deutsch 1969): 160.

16. Zeno Constance, *Valentino, Poet and Prophet: Blues and Rebellion* (Trinidad: privately printed 1985): 31.

17. Monty Williams, son of legendary musician John Buddy Williams, and former leader of the popular dance band, the Casanovas, committed suicide in a New York subway. It is said that his death had something to do with cocaine abuse.

18. M. Mauricette, "Some Trinidadian attitudes through the calypso of Sparrow", *Kokeeoko* 1.12 (July 1970): 4.

19. James George Frazer, *The Magic Art and the Evolution of Kings* 1 (London: MacMillan 1980): 235–36.

20. Bridget Brereton, *A History of Modern Trinidad 1783–1962* (Kingston: Heinemann 1981): 48. The song is translated on 51.

21. Samuel Ebeneezer Elliot (1900–1968), better-known as Papa Nizer, was perhaps the best-known shaman of his day.

22. Selwyn Ryan, *Race and Nationalism in Trinidad and Tobago: A Study of Decolonisation in a Multiracial Society* (St Augustine, Trinidad: ISER, UWI 1974): 141–42.

23. Ryan, *Race and Nationalism*: 154. According to Ryan, *Race and Nationalism*: 157, the *Trinidad Guardian* compared Williams to Hitler. Gordon Rohlehr, *Calypso and Society in Pre-Independence Trinidad* (Port of Spain: Gordon Rohlehr 1990): 310 remarks that, "The notion of Hitler's godlessness was one of the most frequently expressed condemnations of the German leader."

24. Denis Forsythe, "Charisma West Indian Style", *Tapia*, 19 November 1972: 7.

25. Sir Isaac Hyatali was a High Court Judge who had made himself free with a negative verdict of Chalkdust's calypso singing in 1968; Karl is Karl Hudson-Phillips of Public Order Bill fame; Shorty is the proud composer/performer of "The Art of Love Making", a song whose inclusion in the Dimanche Gras show of 1973 Chalkdust – and others – had contested; Abdul Malik is the international scoundrel who committed two murders in Trinidad for which he was executed; Azard Ali was a beauty queen show organiser notorious for his 'sexploitation' of black beauty.

26. Rohlehr, *Calypso and Society*: 307–08. Caresser's "Not so, Carolina" (1939) was censored for suggesting that one could find *obeah* at the Abbey of Mount St Benedict.

27. *Express*, 18 February 1985: 8.

28. NJAC of the 1980s and 1990s reverted to Pegasus style operations seeking the patronage of respectable middle class Afro-Trinidadians for their annual Calypso Awards Ceremony. In 1990 NJAC spokespersons revealed – implausibly – that NJAC had merely tolerated the myth of a Black Power concept in 1970.

29. Selwyn Ryan, *The Disillusioned Electorate: The Politics of Succession in Trinidad and Tobago* (Port of Spain: Inprint 1989): 11.

30. See notes 9 and 10 of this chapter.

Appendixes

Appendix 1

This is a glossary of local terms as understood by use in this book. No discussion of orthography, morphology or semantics is attempted.

bacchanal	carousal complete with rum, food, song and dance	*douennes*	mythological creatures, the spirits of unbaptised children, who lure children to their doom
badjohn	street fighter, often given to boasts and threats		
balisier	a variety of the shrub Heliconia Bihar	*dolak*	percussion instrument in Indian music
bobol	shady or underhand dealings	*doolahin*	young Hindu woman
		dougla	person of mixed ancestry, usually of Afro-Indo parentage
callaloo	a broth made of the leaf of the dasheen bush and including assorted vegetables. It is very difficult to guess what is in a callaloo by just looking at it	*extempo*	apocopation of extemporaneous
		fateeg	jokes against the person
		freeco	entertainment without charge
chantuelle	singing leader of stickfighting band	*jamette*	loose woman of the urban underclass
cokieoko	piggyback ride	*jingay*	magical charm or incantation
comesse	anything from a minor squabble to a major imbroglio	*kaiso*	perhaps the original name for what is now called 'calypso'. Now a term reserved for a 'true-true' calypso, it is usually a spontaneous acclamation
corbeau	scavenger bird		
cosquel	overdressed		
crapaud	local term for frog or toad		

kalinda	a song-dance complex, universally popular with the New World African
kuchela	a pungent East Indian condiment
la couree	controversy
macafouchette	stale food fit for disposal
mamaguy	flattery: to flatter, to deceive, to trifle with
mapepire	a poisonous snake
mepris	verse form in which singers trade insults
niggergram	colloquialism for rumour
obeah	the theory and practice of homeopathic magic and sympathetic magic
obsoquie	ill-fitting, awkward-looking
orisha	Yoruba for deity
pappyshow	something held up for ridicule, usually in a subtle way
picong	anything from light banter to caustic comment
ratichfeye	any practice from chicanery to skulduggery
ramajay	free-flow expression
rapso	mixture of 'rap' and calypso
sagaboy	idle man about town, usually with macho sex appeal
sans humanité	without mercy. Formula from the recitative calypso of the early twentieth century
tampi	slang for cannabis; also 'weed', 'grass'
zandolie	species of garden lizard

Appendix 2

This attempts to document the calypsoes cited or alluded to in the book. Avoiding all pretensions to being a comprehensive discography, it aims simply to list the singer's sobriquet (where applicable), his legal name (where known), song title and year of tent performance or record release (as far as can be ascertained).

Aimey, Rawle
"The Indo-Saxon" (1973).
Atilla the Hun (Raymond Quevedo)
"No Nationality" (c. 1946).
Baker, Lord (Kent King)
"God Bless Our Nation" (1967).
Bally (Errol Ballantyne)
"Party Time" (1987). B's records: BSR BP 064. 1987.
"School Book" (1987).
Blakie, The Lord (Carlton Joseph aka Carlton Herbert)
"Doctah Ent Day" (1965).
"Don't Dam the Bridge" (1971).
"Message to Granger". Antilliana: A-957. 45 rpm. 1971.
"My Sweet Trinidad" (1967). NSP-10. 45 rpm.
"Twenty Years Too Long" (1976).
Blue Boy, now Super Blue (Austin Lyons)
"Jingay" (1987) Jingay. Rohit International. 1987.
"Soca Baptiste [sic]" (1980). Romey: RS 019. Disco 45. 1979.
Bomber, The Mighty (Clifton Ryan)
"Money Is No Problem, The Problem Is No Money" (1977).
"Political Wonder" (1970).
Brynner, The Lord (Cade Simon)
"Dr Bridge" (1971) Uhuru Harambee: ELPS 1942. 1969.
"Heaven Help us All" (1971).
"Trinidad and Tobago Independence" RCA: 72116.
Cardinal (Elan Baghoo)
"Band of the Year" (1983).
"Productivity" (1983).

Caruso, Lord
"Run the Gunslingers" (1959).
Chalkdust, The Mighty
"Ah Fraid Karl" (1972). First Time Around. Straker: GS 7784. c.1973.
"Answer to Black Power" (1971). Tropico: TS 1109. 45 rpm.
"Badjohn Willie" (1981). Flipside Chalkie. Charlie's Records: CR 253. 1980.
"Black Inventions" (1979). Origins.
"Brain Drain" (1968).
"Bring him In". First Time Around.
"Calypso Drug Report".
"Calypso Cricket". Chalkdust the Master. Straker: GS 2283.
"Chalkdust Gone Mad" (1986).
"Chauffeur Wanted". Total Kaiso. Straker: GS 2298. 1988.
"Clear your Name" (1973). Stay Up. Straker: GS 7789. 1973.
"Devaluation" (1968).
"Eric Williams Dead" (1985). Chalkdust the Master.
"Eric Williams Loves me" (1979).
"Goat Mout' Doc" (1972). First Time Around.
"Grandfather Backpay" (1985). On a Blackboard of Truth. Straker: GS 2263. 1984.
"Juba doo bai" (1973). First Time Around.
"Let the Jackass Sing" (1974). Stay Up.
"The Letter" (1969).
"Massa Day Must Done" (1970).
"Money Ent No Problem".
"National Pride" (1983). Chalkdust with a Bang. Straker: GS 2243. 1982.
"Our Only Hope" (1983).

"Port of Spain Gone Insane" (1986). *Port of Spain Gone Insane*. Straker: GS 2267. 1985.

"Reply to the Ministry" (1969).

"Say Thanks to Daaga" (1979). *Origins*.

"Scapefox" (1987).

"Shango Vision" (1977).

"Silent Speech" (1974).

"Singing Protest" (1977). *Teacher Commoner and King*. Straker: GS 8886.

"Somebody Mad" 919720. *First Time Around*.

"Stay Up" (1973). *Stay Up*.

"They Ent African at All" (1984). *Kaiso with Dignity*. Reynold Howard, RH Prod: TEC-CIII-H. 1983.

"Three Blind Mice" (1976). *Ah Put On Mih Guns Again*. Straker GS 2263. 1984.

"Two Sides of the Shilling" (1971).

"We Blight" (1974). *Stay Up*.

"We Is We" (1972). *First Time Around*.

"White Man's Plan" (1985). *On a Blackboard of Truth*.

"Who Next" (1972). *First Time Around*.

Commentor (Brian Honore)

"Opera of the Midnight Robber" (1976).

"Organised Nazi Rule" (1981). Chantrel: BH 001. 1981.

Composer, The Mighty (Fred Mitchell)

"Black Fallacy" (1970). *This Is Composer*. Telco.

"Blow the Whole Place Down" (1971). *Trinidad, Land of Calypso*.

Antilliana: LPS 1001.

"Different Strokes" (1976).

"True or Lie" (1976).

"Workers' Lament" (1971). *Trinidad, Land of the Calypso*.

Contender

"We Smart" (1982).

Crazy (Edwin Ayoung).

"No Face, No Vote" (1982). *Crazy Crazy*. CLO KSR 004. 1981.

Cristo Lord (Christopher Laidlow)

"Election War Zone" (1962).

"Mad Professor" (1964).

"Mock Democracy" (also known as "Alabama") (1966). SP 10643.

"Sweet Trinidad" (1965).

"Town Gone" (1960).

Cro Cro (Weston Rawlings)

"Botha" (1987).

"Happy Anniversary" (1987).

Crusoe, formerly Crusoe Kid, now Tobago Crusoe (Othneil Bacchus)

"I Eric Eustace Williams" (1982).

"Politicians" (1974).

"Productivity" (1983).

"Wet Yuh House" (1980).

Cypher, The Mighty (Dillary Scott)

"Balisier" (1957).

"Black Power" (1971). Antilliana: A-954. 45 rpm.

"Don't Go, Doctor" (1974).

"Guerrilla" (1974).

"If the Priest Could Play" (1967). NSP 134.

"No Police Ent See" (1965).

"Last Elections" (1967).

"Rhodesia Crisis" (1966).

Dacron

"Sponsorship" (1975).

D'Alberto (Winston Albert)

"Rambo" (1987).

De Fosto, The Original . . . Himself (Winston Scarborough)

"The Flag" (1987).

"Reflections of Our Late Prime Minister" (1982). Cucumba Music: TODH. 006. Disco 45. 1981.

Delamo (Franz Lambin)

"Ah Cyar Wine" Solar: FV 10001.

"Ah Want a Wuk" (1987) Solar: FV 10001.

"Apocalypse" (1981). SDI 24. 1981.

"Armageddon". Isha. 1985.

"Eric Williams' Children" (1983).

"Six Months Hard Labour" (1979). RM 002.

"Sodom and Gomorrah" (1982). Isha Records: SDI 24. 1981.

"Visions" (1987).

Deple (Tyrone Hernandez)

"Vote Dem Out" (1986). Fishe: 001. Disco 45. 1986.

Dougla, The Mighty (Cleitus Ali)

"Independence" (1962).

"Lazy Man" (1961).

"Split Me in Two" (1961).

"Teacher, Teacher" (1961).

Duke, The Mighty (Kelvin Pope)

"Black Is Beautiful" (1969). *Black Is Beautiful.*
Tropico: TSI 2017.

"Little Nation" (1967).

"Lock Them Up" (1970). *Exciting Calypso.*
Tropico: TSI 2022. MAPS 1090.

"Memories of '60" (1961).

"Memories of '70" (1971). *Exciting Calypso.*

"A Point of Direction" (1982). *Over & Over &
Over Again.* B's Records: BSR 1009. 1981.

"Someone Will Have to Pay" (1980). *Harps of
Gold.* Sound Services Prod. Sharc: SS 1079-
1. 1979.

"Teach the Children" (1976). *The Mighty Duke
on Stage.* Camille: LP 9041.

"Trinihard" (1974).

"What Is Calypso?" (1968). *Calypso All Night
Tonight.* TLP 1000.

Eagle (Ewart Isaac)

"Law and Poor" (1984).

Explainer, The Mighty (Winston Henry)

"Caribbean Integration [sic]". *Man from the
Ghetto.* Charlie's records: ECR 421.1981.

"Chambers" (1982). *Man from the Ghetto.*

"Charity Begins at Home".

"Dread" (1979). *Positive Vibrations.* Semp Prod.:
SWH 001. 1979.

"In Parliament They Kicksin". *Positive
Vibrations.*

"Is Grass" (1978). *This Is Explainer.* Umbala:
UPLP 001. 1978.

"Selwyn" (1978). *This Is Explainer.*

"The Table Is Turning" (1980). *Something
Special.* Boaex: BAX 001 1979.

Fluke, Lord (Cecil Duke Taylor)

"Black Power" (1971).

Funny, The Lord (Donrick Williamson)

"Ah Soul Man" (1981). CLO 352. Disco 45.
1981.

"Bacchanal in Hell" (1972).

"How Yuh Feel" (1987).

"Right and Wrong" (1983). Strakers' Records:
GS2743. 1983.

Gibraltar, The Mighty.

"Politics Is a Dirty Game" (1971).

Gypsy (Winston Peters)

"Respect the Calypsonian" (1988). *Life.*
Mayaro Music. 1987.

"The Sinking Ship" (1986). *The Action too High.*
MRS 3386. 1986.

Happy (Gilbert O'Connor)

"Boy George" (1985).

Hepburn, Nap (Randolph Hepburn)

"Discipline, Tolerance and Production"
(1962).

"General Election" (1962).

"The Mad Scientist" (1962). Telco: TW 3113.
45 rpm.

"Political Girl" (1962). Telco: TW 3122. 45
rpm.

Invader, Lord (Rupert Grant)

"Hitler's Moustache"

J., Bro. (Selwyn James)

"The Advice" (1987).

"National Unity" (1987).

The Young Killer

"Is a Policeman" (1964).

King, Johnny (Johnson King)

"Nature's Plan" (1984).

Kitchener, The Lord (Aldwyn Roberts)

"Africa My Home".

"A Bad Impression" (1964). *Kitch.* Tropico:
LPS 3027.

"Black Or White". *Lord Kitchener: Calypsoes Too
Hot to Handle.* Melodisc: MLC 200.

"Black Power" (1971). *Curfew Time.* Trinidad
Records: TRCS 0001. 1971.

"If You are Brown". *Lord Kitchener Sings
Calypsoes.* Songs of the Caribbean SLP
729.

"Jerico" (1974). *Tourist in Trinidad.* Trinidad
Records: TRCS 0004. 1974.

"No freedom" (1973). *We Walk 100 Miles.*
Trinidad Records: TRCS 0003. 1973.

"Not a Damn Seat for Them" (1982). Kam's:
KAM 005. 1981.

"PNM March" (1977). *Kitch Hot and Sweet*. TR CCS-0005. 1976.

"Rain-o-rama" (1973). *We Walk 100 Miles*.

"The Road" (1963).

"Soca Corruption" (1984). *Simply Wonderful*. Trinidad Records: CR 144. 1983.

"Symphony in G" (1979). *Spirit of Carnival*. Trinidad Records: TRCS-007. 1979.

"Tribute to Spree" (1975). *Carnival Fever in Kitch*. Trinidad: TRCS-4000. 1975.

Lester, Lord (Calvin Downes)

"Don't Stop Carnival" (1971).

Leveller, The Mighty (Carlton Roseman)

"How to Stop Delinquency" (1966).

Lion, The Roaring (Rafael de Leon)

"The Visit of His Holiness John Paul II" (1987). Wirl, RL-W 231.

Lutha (Morell Peters)

"Trinbago" (1987).

Maestro, El or Lord (Cecil Hume)

"Black Identity" (1973). Straker: S 117 a. 45 rpm.

"Dread Man" (1977). Kalinda: PKL-150. 45 rpm. 1976.

"Great Inventors" (c. 1969).

"Mr Trinidadian" (1974). *Maestro Live*. Recording Artist. 1981.

"Not Call Them Name" (1977). Anatomy of Soca. KH records: KDS-2914. 1977.

"The Poor Man" (1973). Straker: S 117 B 45 rpm.

"Portrait in Black" (1976).

"Savage" (1977). Kalinda: PKL-150. 45 rpm. 1976.

"Some Came Running" (1976). *Fiery Tempo*. Kalinda: KDS-2007. 1976.

"Tomorrow" (1976).

"To Sir with Love" (1975). *Maestro Live*.

McCarthy, Charmaine.

"Our Native Son" (1980).

Melody, The Lord (Fitzroy Alexander)

"Aphan Jhaat" (1959).

"Dr Make Your Love" (1959). *Again Lord Melody Sings Calypsoes*. Cook: 914.

Merchant, The (Denis Williams Franklyn)

"Come Let Us Build a Nation Together" (1982). Network: 004. Disco 45.

"Let No Man Judge" (1978). Kalinda: KD-562. 45 rpm.

"Pain (Peace)" (1986). *Ah Coming Too*. Straker: 2273.

"Who Squatting?"(1980). "D" Hardest. Kai soca: KSR-453. 1980.

Monkee or Monkey

"Vengeance of Moko" (1980).

"We Cyar Come" (1984).

Montano, Machel

"I Love My Country" (1986). *Too Young to Soca*. Macho music: 24-11-74 B. 1985.

Network Riddum Band, The

"Squatter's Chant" (1981). Network Productions: NP-001. Disco 45. 1981.

Penguin (Seadley Joseph)

"Betty Goaty" (1982). *Life Is a Lollipop*. BE 01. 1981.

"Doggie, Look a Bone" (1981). CLO 355. 45 rpm. 1981.

"Games" (1985). *King on the Move*. IBIS: 009. 1984.

"Look de Devil Dey" (1980). CLO 349. 45 rpm. 1979.

"We Living in Jail" (1984). *Touch It*. IBIS: 003. 1983.

Plainclothes (Clinton Moreau)

"Chambers Done See" (1985). IBIS: 007.

Prince, Calypso.

"Come as You Are Party" (1974).

Pretender, Lord (Aldric Farrell)

"Black Power".

"Don't Stop the Carnival" (1971).

"God Made Us All" (1943). *The Livng Legend*. Riddum Distribution Network: RDN 1256. 1989.

"Our 25th Anniversary" (1987).

Prowler, The Mighty, later The Mystic (Roy Lewis)

"Build More Trade Schools" (1969).

Quazar (Christopher Grant)

"All ah We Tief" (1987). *All ah We Tief*. Sabre.

Rajah, The (Danny Gopaul)
"Is We" (1978). CLO-348 B. 45 rpm. 1979.
Relator, Lord, later Bro. (Willard Harris)
"China Syndrome" (1981).
"Colour Television" (1986).
"Deaf Panmen" (1974).
"Food Prices" (1980). *Relator, the Real Master.*
Makossa: MD 19.
"Our Children Deserve Better" (1981).
"Take a Rest" (1980).
Rio, Trinidad (Daniel Brown)
"We Will Survive" (1987).
Rose, Calypso
"Balance Wheel" (1982). *Mass in California.*
Straker: GS 2234. 1981.
"I Thank Thee" (1978). *Her Majesty Calypso Rose.*
CLO-444. 1977.
"Respect the Balisay" (1977). *Sexy Hot Pants.*
SLP-002.
Rudder, David
"Calypso Music" (1987). *Charlie's Roots. Calypso Music.* Lypsoland: CR06. 1987.
"Hoosay" (1991). *Rough and ready.* Lypsoland: CR 016. 1990.
"Kojak" (1987). *Calypso Music.*
"Madness" (1987). *Calypso Music.*
Scraper
"The More You Live, the More You See" (1974).
Scrunter, The (Owen Reyes Johnson)
"Take the Number" (1980). Keystone Records: KN-002. 45 rpm. 1980.
Shadow, The Mighty (Winston Bailey)
"From Then Til Now" (1987).
"Snakes" (1984). *Return of de Bassman.* SR 009. 1983.
Short Pants (Llewelyn McIntosh)
"Is I" (1979).
"The Law Is an Ass" (1979). MNE 45 rpm.
"Leh We Show" (1987).
Smiley, Lord (Gaston Nunes)
"The Chinee Man" (1973).
"The Law for One Is the Law for All" (1974).

"What Is Wrong with the Negro Man?"
Shorty, Lord, now Ras Shorty I (Gabriel Blackman)
"Art of Making Love" (1973). *Shorty.* S-003. 45 rpm. 1973.
"Endless Vibrations"(1975).
"Indian Singers" (1966).
"Jour Ouvert" (1974). *The Love Man.* Shorty. SLP 1000. 1974.
"Kalo gee bul bul" (1974). *The Love Man.*
"Index of a Nation" (1969).
"Indrani" (1973). *Shorty,* S-002. 45 rpm. 1973.
"Money Eh No Problem" (1979). *Soca Explosion.* Charlie's CR 1004. 1979.
"Oh Trinidad" (1976). *Sweet Music. Shorty.* SLP 1003. 1976.
"PM Sex Probe" (1974). *The Love Man.*
"Sokah: The Soul of Calypso" (1977). *'Sokah': The Soul of Calypso.* Semp. 1977.
"Sweet Music" (1976). *Sweet Music.*
Sniper, The Mighty (Mervyn Hodge)
"Portrait of Trinidad" (1965). T7 2202. 45 rpm.
"A Way to Success" (1968).
Sparrow, The Mighty (Slinger Francisco)
"Ah Digging Horrors" (1975). *Calypso Maestro.* Recording Artist: RA 5050. 1975.
"Badjohns" (1974). *Knock Dem Down.* RA 4020. 1973.
"Balisier" (1962).
"Capitalism Gone Mad" (1983). *Sparrow the Greatest.* Sparrow Hideaway: Jet Age Furniture 1006. 1982.
"Congo Man" (1965). *Sparrow's Carnival* 1965. NLP 5050.
"Drink You Balisier" (1961). *Sparrow: Calypso King.* Tropico: TSI 1097.
"Federation" (1962). *Sparrow Come Back.* RCA: LPS 3006.
"Get to Hell Out" (1965). *Sparrow Calypso King.* RCA: LPB-1097.
"The Gunslingers" (1959). *Sparrow in Hi-Fi.* Balisier: HDF 1009.
"Hangman Cemetery" (1962). *Sparrow Come*

Back. Tropico: TSI 3006.

"Honesty" (1966). *Genius*. Hilary: SP 3001.

"Karl Say" (1981). *The Mighty Sparrow*. Sparrow Hideaway: JAF 1004. 1980.

"Leave the Dam Doctor" (1960). *Sparrow*. RCA: LPB-9035. August 1959.

"Lend a Hand" (1971).

"Marajhin" (1982). *Sweeter Than Ever*. CR: JAF 1005. 1981.

"Marajhin Cousin" (1984). *King of the World*. B's: BSR-SP 002. 1984.

"Marajhin Sister" (1983). *The Greatest*. SH: JAF 1000. 1982.

"Martin Luther King" (1969). *More Sparrow More*. RA 2020.

"Martin Luther King for President" (1963). *The Outcast*. National: NLP 4199.

"Model Nation" *Calypso Sparrow*. Tropico: TSI 3010.

"No, Doctor, No" (1957). *More Sparrow's Greatest Hits*. Tropico: TSI 1086.

"Mr Robinson and Lockjoint" (1964). *The Outcast*. MM0014. 1987.

"Pay as You Earn" (1958). *Sparrow's Greatest Hits*. RCA: LPB-1067.

"Police Get More Pay" (1961).*The Mighty Sparrow*. RCA: LPB-1956.

"Popularity Contest" (1963). *The Slave*. National: NLP 4188.

"Present Government" (1961). *Sparrow the Conqueror*. RCA: LPB-2035.

"The Prophet of Doom and Gloom" (1983). *The Greatest*.

"Robbery with V" (1961). *Sparrow Come Back*. RCA Victor: RD 7156.

"Rose" (1961). *Sparrow: Calypso King*. RCA: LPB-1097.

"Sam 'P'" (1984). *Sparrow: King of the World*. B's: BSR-Sp-002A. 1984.

"Sedition" (1973). *Many Moods of Sparrow*. Bestway: BW 1001. 1972.

"The Slave" (1963). *The Slave*.

"Solomon" (1964). *Congo Man*. NRC: NLP 5050.

"Ten to One Is Murder" (1960). *The Mighty*

Sparrow. RCA: LPB 1056.

"Thanks to the *Guardian*" (1961). *Sparrow the Conqueror*. RCA: LPB 2035.

"Wanted Dead or Alive" (1980). *London Bridge*. Sparrow Music: JAF 001. 1979.

"We Like it So" *Sweeter than Ever*. SH: JAF 1005. 1981.

"We Past That Stage" (1974).

"William the Conqueror" (1957).

"Yuh Mad" (1980). *London Bridge*.

Squibby (Stanley Cummings)

"Distant Drums" (1982). Sunshine Records: SR 1015. 1981.

"Shango" (1979). SDI-005. 1979.

"Steelband Running Wild" (1981).

"Streakers" (1974).

Stalin, formerly The Mighty, now Black (Leroy Calliste)

"Breakdown Party" (1980). *Just for Openers*. Makossa: MD 905. 1980.

"Burn Dem" (1987). *I Time*. B's: BSR-BS-061.

"Caribbean Unity" (1979). *To the Caribbean Man*. Wizards: Nilsta music. 1978.

"In ah Earlier Time" (1982) *In Ah Earlier Time*. Hulu records: HC 8001. 1980.

"Leave the Doctor alone" (1966).

"Make Them Alright" (1983). *You Ask for It*. Ebonel Kalico Records. 1984.

"The Immortal Message of Martin Luther King" (1969).

"Money" (1980). *Just for Openers*.

"More times" (1979). *To the Caribbean* Man.

"National Reconstruction" (1971).

"New Portrait of Trinidad".

"No Politics for Carnival" (1971).

"Not That Man" (1982). *In ah Earlier Time*.

"Nothing Ent Strange" (1975).

"Now is the Time" (1974).

"De Ole Talk" (1974).

"Piece of the Action" (1976).

"Plan Your Future" (1980).

"Show Your Works" (1984). *You Ask for It*.

"That Is Head " (1983).

"United Africa" (1963).

"Vampire Year" (1981). *In ah Earlier Time.*
"Wait Dorothy" (1985).
"What Consciousness?" (1971).
Striker, The Mighty (Percy Oblington)
"Don't Blame the PNM" (1958).
"The United Indian" (1959).
Swallow, The Mighty (Rupert Philo)
"Don't Stop the Party" (1979). *Don't Stop the Party.* Clarke's Records: CR 247. 1979.
"Trinidad, The Caribbean Godfather". *Trinidad, The Caribbean Godfather.*
Superior, formerly Lord, now Brother (Andrew Marcano)
"Why I Left, Why I Returned" (1974).
Terror, The Mighty (Fitzgerald Henry)
"Madness" (1981).
Tiger, The Growling (Neville Marcano)
"Don't Touch Them" (1964).
"The Doc's Secret Wedding" (1959).
"Workers' Appeal" (1936).
"Workers' Appeal" (1965).
Valentino, formerly Lord, now Brother (Emrold Phillip)
"Barking Dogs" (1973). *Third World Messenger.* S 012.
"Bills and Acts" (1976).
"Dis Place Nice" (1975). *Third World Messenger.*
"Every Brother Is Not a Brother" (1978). Taurus: CGPI-002. 1978.
"I Salute You" (1987).
"The Invitation" (1972).
"Liberation" (1973). Straker Records: S-0099. 45rpm.
"Life Is a Stage" (1972).
"Mad Cure" (1971). Straker Records: S-0023. 45rpm.
"Mad, Mad World" (1973). Straker Records: S-0099. 45rpm.
"No Revolution" (1971).
"Recession" (1983). VP-RRI: VP002. 1983.
"The Roaring Seventies" (1986).
"Third World" (1972). Straker: S 0022. 45rpm.
"Trini Gone Through in They Consciousness" (1984).

"Victim of Society" (1974). Straker: GS 133. 45rpm.
"Where We Going" (1977).
Valiant, Prince
"Don't Spoil This Country" (1971).
Warrior (Wilfred Sylvester)
"Killer Bees" (1979). Taurus: CGPI 003. 1978.
"No, No, Tony May".
Watchman (Wayne Hade)
"Attack with Full Force" (1991).
Wilson, Natasha
"One Day" (1987).
"Reincarnation Wish" (1985).
Zebra, The Mighty (Charles Harris)
"Rhodesia: Calypso Commentary" (1969).

Appendix 3

This is a listing by year of calypso song books. Privately printed and published in Port of Spain, these provide the lyrics of calypsoes performed in a given year, except for those books compiled by Terror which sometimes include classics from earlier years.

1956   *Calypso Souvenir of* 1956. OYB. Melody.

1957   *Authentic Calypsoes*. Compiled by Dictator.

1959   *Calypso Souvenir* 1959. Compiled by Small Island Pride.

1959   *The Hummingbird Carnival.*

1959   *Trinidad Calypso Book*. Compiled by Carl Roach.

1960   *The Hummingbird Carnival.*

1960   *Kaiso (Calypso)*. Compiled by Invader.

1960   *Trinidad Calypso Book.*

1960   *Trinidad Carnival and Calypsoes* 1960: *What's On?* Compiled by Nathaniel Roberts.

1960   A *Souvenir of Calypsoes* 1960. Published by Theophilius Woods.

1961   *The Hummingbird Carnival.*

1962   *Trinidad and Tobago Calypso and Carnival.*

1962   *Trinidad Carnival and Calypso* 1962: *What's On?* Compiled by Nathaniel Roberts.

1963   *Trinidad Calypso Book*. Compiled and published by Pat Chokolingo.

1963   *Trinidad Carnival and Calypso* 1963: *What's On?* Compiled by Nathaniel Roberts.

1964   *Trinidad Calypso Booklet* 1964. Compiled by The Growling Tiger.

1965   *Trinidad Calypso Booklet '65.* Compiled by The Growling Tiger.

1965   *Trinidad Carnival '65: Calypsoes.* Compiled by Kenneth Wynne.

1966   *Trinidad Calypso Book*. Compiled by Carl Roach.

1966   *Trinidad Carnival and Calypso* 1966: *What's On?* Compiled by Nathaniel Roberts.

1967   *Trinidad and Tobago Calypsoes.* Compiled by Lord Observer.

1967   *Trinidad Calypso Book*. Compiled by Carl Roach.

1967   *Trinidad Carnival and Calypso* 1967: *What's On?* Compiled by Nathaniel Roberts.

1968   *Calypso '68.* Compiled by Carl Roach.

1968   *Carnival Calypso Spectacular:* 1968 *Souvenir.* Compiled by Felix Maynard.

1968   *Trinidad and Tobago Calypso Hits* 1968. Compiled by Leroy Williams.

1968   *Trinidad and Tobago Carnival and Calypso* 1968: *What's On?* Compiled by Nathaniel Roberts.

1968   *Trinidad and Tobago Carnival and Calypso* 1969: *What's On?* Compiled by Nathaniel Roberts.

1970   *Carnival Calypsoes from Trinidad and Tobago.* Compiled by Leroy Williams.

1970   *Trinidad Calypso.* Compiled by Carl Roach.

1970   *T&T Carnival and Calypso* 1970: *What's On?* Compiled by Nathaniel Roberts.

1971 *Calypso Revue 1971.*
1971 *Carnival and Calypso Spectacular 1971.*
1971 *Carnival '71 Calypsoes.* Compiled by Leroy Williams.
1971 *Trinidad Calypso 1971.* Compiled by Carl Roach.
1971 *T&T Calypso Journal.* Compiled by The Mighty Terror.
1971 *Trinidad and Tobago Carnival and Calypso: What's On?* Compiled by Nathaniel Roberts.
1972 *Calypso '72.* Published by Unique Services.
1972 *Calypso and Carnival Spectacular.* Compiled by Rampersad.
1972 *Trinidad and Tobago Calypso Callaloo '72.* Compiled by Terror.
1972 *Trinidad and Tobago Carnival and Calypso 1972: What's On?* Compiled by Nathaniel Roberts.
1972 *'72 Calypsoes.* Compiled by Leroy Williams.
1973 *Original Regal: Regally Yours Calypso Hits '73.*
1973 *Trinidad and Tobago Carnival and Calypso: What's On?* Compiled by Nathaniel Roberts.
1974 *T&T Carnival '74 Calypsoes.* Compiled by Leroy Williams.
1974 *Trinidad and Tobago Carnival and Calypsoes: What's On?* Compiled by Nathaniel Roberts.
1975 *Calypsoes for Carnival '75.* Compiled by Leroy Williams.
1975 *TnT Calypso Callaloo.* Compiled by Terror.
1976 *Calypso 1976.* Compiled Leroy Williams.
1976 *T&T Carnival and Calypso 1976: What's On?* Compiled by Nathaniel Roberts.
1977 *Calypso 1977.* Compiled by Leroy Williams.
1977 *Trinidad Calypso 1977.* Compiled by Carl Roach.
1979 *'79 Carnival Calypsoes.* Compiled by Leroy Williams.
1980 *Carnival Calypsoes '80.* Compiled by Leroy Williams.
1981 *Calypso Callaloo 1981.* Compiled by Terror.
1981 *Trinidad Calypso Souvenir '81.* Compiled by Carl Roach.
1982 *Carnival and Calypsoes.* Compiled by Leroy "Fathead" Williams.
1983 *Trinidad Carnival and Calypsoes 1983.* Compiled by Leroy "Fathead" Williams.
1984 *Carnival and Calypsoes.* Compiled by Leroy "Fathead" Williams.
1986 *TnT Carnival and Calypsoes.* Compiled by Leroy "Fathead" Williams.
1987 *Calypso Souvenir.* Compiled by Carl Roach.
1987 *Trinidad and Tobago Calypso Callaloo 1987.* Compiled by Terror.
1987 *Trinidad and Tobago Carnival and Calypsoes.* Compiled by Leroy "Fathead" Williams.

Bibliography

Selected Bibliographic and Oral Sources

Interviews

Aimey, Rawle. Personal interviews, May 1991.
Composer [Fred Mitchell]. Personal interview.
Bro. J. [Selwyn James]. Personal interview, 26 July 1991.
Roach, Glen. Personal interview, 17 January 1991.
Short Pants [Llewelyn McIntosh]. Personal interview .
Sparrow [Slinger Franciso]. Personal interview, 24 January 1991.
Valentino [Emrold Phillip]. Personal interview, 23 January 1991.

Radio Programmes

The Lord Brynner: His Life and Times. Scripted by Harold "Rocky" McCollin. Radio 7.30 AM, February 1985.
Cristo: The Man, His Time and His Music. Scripted by Harold "Rocky" McCollin. Radio 7.30 AM, January 1985.
From Atilla to the Seventies. A 26-part radio series researched, scripted and narrated by Gordon Rohlehr. Government Broadcasting Unit, Port of Spain, January–July 1973.
Indian Soca. Scripted and presented by Sookram Ali. Radio 95 FM, 31 August–1 September 1989.
Shorty: Then and Now. Presented by Sookram Ali. Radio 105 FM, August 1994.

Trinidad and Tobago Newspapers and Magazines

The *Bomb*
Express, *Sunday Express*, The *Sun*
Trinidad Guardian, *Sunday Guardian*

Liberation (organ of the NJAC)
Daily Mirror, Sunday Mirror
TnT Mirror
Moko
The Nation (organ of the PNM)
Sunday Punch
People
Tapia (organ of the Tapia House Party)
Trinidad and Tobago Review
Vanguard (organ of the OWTU)

Articles and Books

Abrahams, R.D. 1967. "The shaping of folklore traditions in the British West Indies". *Journal of Inter-American Studies and World Affairs*, 9: 456–80.

Adonis, Naomi. 1989. "The image of Dr Eric Williams in the calypso". Caribbean Studies thesis, Dept of English, UWI, St Augustine.

Anthony, Michael. 1989. *Parade of the Carnivals of Trinidad 1839–1939*. Port of Spain: Circle Press.

Arlen, Frank. 1973. "Was Shorty paying for Chalkdust's pudding?" *Express* (18 March): 13.

Arnold, Matthew. 1971. Preface to the 1853 Edition of Poems. In *Critical Theory since Plato*, edited by Hazard Adams, 576–83. New York: Harcourt.

Babb, John. 1987. "Scott drug report made public". *Trinidad Guardian* (7 February): 1.

Baptiste, Owen, ed. 1975. *Crisis*. Port of Spain: Inprint.

Bartholomew, Courtenay. Interview with Ken Gordon. "My professional relationship with Dr Williams". *Express* (24 April): 20.

ben Jochannan, Josef A.A. 1976. *The Saga of the "Black Marxists" versus the "Black Nationalists": a Debate Resurrected*. 3 vols. New York: J. ben Jochannan.

Best, Lloyd. 1970. "'70: year of revolution". *Tapia* (20 December): 9.

Best, Lloyd. 1991. "The nine political tribes of Trinidad and Tobago". In *Social and Occupational Stratification in Contemporary Trinidad and Tobago*, edited by Selwyn Ryan, 145–46. St Augustine, Trinidad: ISER.

Brathwaite, Edward. 1975. *The Arrivants: A New World Trilogy*. London: OUP.

Brereton, Bridget. 1981. *A History of Modern Trinidad 1783–1962*. Kingston: Heinemann.

Cadogan, Glenda. 1986. "Our singers losing ground". *Sunday Punch* (2 February): 16.

Calder-Marshall, Arthur. 1939. *Glory Dead*. London: Michael Joseph.

Camejo, Acton. 1971. "Racial discrimination in employment in the private sector in Trinidad and Tobago: a study of the business elite and the social structure". *Social and Economic Studies*. 20, no. 3: 294–317.

Cleaver, Elridge. 1970. *Soul on Ice*. London: Panther.

Constance, Zeno. *c*. 1984. *Valentino, Poet and Prophet: Blues and Rebellion*. Trinidad: privately printed.

Constance, Zeno. *c*. 1985 "Dem whey dread: a study of the Rastafarian through the eyes of the calypsonian". Manuscript.

Constance, Zeno. 1991. *Tassa, Chutney & Soca: The East Indian Contribution to the Calypso*. Trinidad: privately printed.

Constance, Zeno. 1996. *De Roaring 70s: An Introduction to the Politics of the 1970s*. Fyzabad, Trinidad: Zeno Obi Constance.

Craig, Susan. 1982. "Background to the 1970 Confrontation in Trinidad and Tobago". In *Contemporary Caribbean: a Sociological Reader*, vol. 2, edited by Susan Craig, 385–423. Port of Spain: Susan Craig.

Daily Mirror. 1964. "This Young Killer is a bit nervous". *Daily Mirror* (6 February): 12.

Darbeau, Dave. 1970. "Black students on trial in racist Canada". *Vanguard* (7 March): 3.

Dean, Darryl. 1987. "Sex scandal in Tesoro case". *Trinidad Guardian* (13 March): 1.

deFour, Linda Claudia. 1993. *Gimme Room to Sing: Calypsoes of the Mighty Sparrow: a Discography*. Port of Spain: Linda Claudia deFour.

DeLeon, Rafael. 1988. *Calypso from France to Trinidad: 800 Years of History*. Trinidad: privately printed.

Deosaran, Ramesh. 1987. "The Caribbean man: a study of the psychology of perception and the media". In *India in the Caribbean*, edited by David Dabydeen and Brinsley Samaroo, 81–117. London: Hansib.

de Verteuil, Anthony. 1984. *The Years of Revolt: Trinidad 1981–1988*. Port of Spain: Paria.

Douglas, Karl. 1963. "In this calypso, the psychology of the slave mind". *Sunday Guardian* (20 January): 8.

Elder, J.D. 1996. "Evolution of the traditional calypso of Trinidad and Tobago: a socio-historical analysis of song change". Dissertation, University of Pennsylvania, Ann Arbor.

Epstein, Dena. 1977. *Sinful Tunes and Spirituals: Black Folk Music to the Civil War*. Urbana, Chicago: University of Illinois Press.

Espinet, Adrian, and Jacques Farmer. 1969. "Pussonal nonarchy – the paradox of power in Trinidad". *Tapia* (16 November): 6.

Express. 1968. "Teacher by day – kaisonian by night". *Express* (24 January): 7.

Express. 1968. "Regiment warned of Marxists". *Express* (24 October): 1.

Express. 1968. "Pegasus show to aid Brynner". *Express* (3 November): 1.

Express. 1970. "The violence which shocked Tobago". *Express* (8 April): 1.

Express. 1973. "Choko, Bomb lose to A.N.R.". *Express* (19 January): 1.

Express. 1980. "PM praises Sparrow's inspiration". *Express* (6 January): 3.

Express. 1985. "Chalkie: I feel so unwanted". *Express* (10 February): 35.

Express. 1987. "'Ministers prefer blondes': T&T official named in US$b Tesoro lawsuit". *Express* (13 March): 1.

Farrell, Terrence. 1988. "The development of non-bank financial institutions in Trinidad and Tobago 1973–1987". In *Trinidad and Tobago: The Independence Experience 1962–1987*, edited by Selwyn Ryan with the assistance of Gloria Gordon, 81–96. St Augustine, Trinidad: ISER, UWI.

Finnegan, Ruth. 1970. *Oral Literature in Africa*. London: Clarendon Press.

Finnegan, Ruth. 1977. *Oral Poetry: its Nature, Significance and Social Context*. London: CUP.

Fox, Angela. 1987. "I picked the finalists". *Sunday Punch* (23 August): 9.

Fox, Angela. 1987. "Winning song no good for schools". *Sunday Punch* (30 August): 7.

Forsythe, Denis. 1972. "Charisma West Indian style". *Tapia* (19 November): 7.

Frazier, James George. Republished 1980. *The Magic Art and the Evolution of Kings*. Vol 1. London: Macmillan.

Gibbons, Rawle. 1991. *Sing de Chorus*. Directed by Louis McWilliams (January–February). Canboulay Productions, Queen's Hall, Port of Spain.

Gibbons, Rawle. 1994. *No Surrender: a Biography of The Growling Tiger*. Tunapuna, Trinidad: Canboulay Productions.

Government of the Republic of Trinidad and Tobago, Ministry of Finance and Planning. 1981. *Report of the Review Team to Enquire into the Malabar 2,200 Housing and the Centralised Racing Complex Projects*. Port of Spain: Government Printery.

Grant, Lennox. 1972. "PNM loves me". *Tapia* (26 November): 11.

Greene, Evans. 1987. "Burroughs freed. Judge accepts no-case plea by the defence". *Trinidad Guardian* (15 January): 1.

Grimes, John. 1961. "Tonight is the night for calypsonians. Who will be '61's king?". *Sunday Guardian* (12 February): 21.

Harewood, Jack. 1971. "Racial discrimination in employment in Trinidad and Tobago (based on data from the 1960 census)". *Social and Economic Studies* 20, no. 3: 267–93.

Harper, Peter. 1971. "So you think calypso is dying". *Express* (5 January): 11.

Harvey, George. 1964. "A job for Solomon: 'I have the power', PM tells Arima crowd". *Trinidad Guardian* (21 September): 13.

George Harvey. 1986. "The 1970 mutiny – Part I: a soldier remembers". *Sunday Guardian* (20 April): 5.

George Harvey. 1987. "The NAR campaign that devastated the PNM". *Sunday Guardian* (11 January): 15.

Henry, Ralph. 1988. "The state and income distribution in an independent Trinidad and Tobago". In *Trinidad and Tobago: the Independence Experience 1962–1987*, edited by Selwyn Ryan with the assistance of Gloria Gordon, 471–92. St Augustine, Trinidad: UWI, ISER.

Henry, Zin. 1988. "Industrial relations and the development process". In *Trinidad and Tobago: the Independence Experience 1962–1987*, edited by Selwyn Ryan with the assistance of Gloria Gordon, 47–56. St Augustine, Trinidad: UWI, ISER.

Herbert, Carlton [Blakie], as told to Aldwin Primus. 1990. "The Doc would give us $3,000 of his own when we were broke". *Bomb* (15 June): 11.

Hill, Sydney, comp. and ed. 1986. *Bibliography*. St Augustine, Trinidad: ISER., UWI.

Hudson-Phillips, Karl. 1995. "The betrayal of the spirit of 1956". In *The Black Power Revolution 1970: a Retrospective*, edited by Selwyn Ryan and Taimoon Stewart, with the assistance of Roy McCree, 617–24. St Augustine, Trinidad: ISER, UWI.

Hylton Edwards, Stewart. 1982. *Lengthening Shadows: the Birth and Revolt of the Trinidad Army*. Port of Spain: Inprint.

Ifill, Max. 1964. *The Solomon Affair: a Tale of Immorality in Trinidad*. Port of Spain: People's Democratic Society.

ISER/UWI Calypso Research Project. 1986. Papers from seminar on the Calypso, 6–10 January 1986. St Augustine, Trinidad: ISER, UWI.

Jacobs, Carl. 1969. "Now Birdie speaks his mind". *Sunday Guardian* (2 March): 13.

Jahn, Janheinz. 1961. *Muntu: an Outline of the New African Culture*. New York: Grove Press.

James, C.L.R. 1984. *Party Politics in the West Indies*. Port of Spain: Inprint.

Jourdain, Elodie. n.d. "Creole – a folk language". *Caribbean Quarterly* 3, no. 1.

Juba Publications Presents Eric Eustace Williams: through the Eyes of the Calypsonian. 10 December 1981. Programme notes.

Kambon, Khafra. 1995. "Black Power in Trinidad and Tobago: February 26–April 21 1970". In *The Black Power Revolution 1970: a Retrospective*, edited by Selwyn Ryan and Taimoon Stewart, with the assistance of Roy Mc Cree, 215–42. St Augustine, Trinidad: ISER, UWI.

Kambon, Khafra. 1988. *For Bread, Justice and Freedom: a Political Biography of George Weekes*. London: New Beacon Books.

Kumar, Ranjit. 1981. *Thoughts and Memories of Ranjit Kumar*. Port of Spain: Inprint.

LeGendre, Esther. 1973. "Life is a stage". *Tapia* (18 February): 2.

Lewis, Gordon. 1968. *The Growth of the Modern West Indies*. New York: Modern Readers Paperbacks.

Lewis, Roy. 1980. "Kaiso gone dread: Black Stalin, the Caribbean man in cultural perspective". Caribbean Studies thesis, UWI, St Augustine.

Liberation. 1977. "Anti-corruption big rats still at large". *Liberation* (6 September): 8.

Liverpool, Hollis. 1973. "From the horse's mouth: an analysis of certain aspects in the development of the calypso and its contribution to contemporary society as gleaned from personal communication". Caribbean Studies thesis, UWI, St Augustine.

Liverpool, Hollis. 1985. "Resistance and protest in carnival art forms of Trinidad and Tobago 1783–1981". MA thesis, UWI, St Augustine.

Liverpool, Hollis. 1986. *Kaiso and Society*. St Thomas: Virgin Islands Commission on Youth.

Mahabir, Winston. 1978. *In and Out of Politics: Tales of the Government of Dr Eric Williams Taken from the Notebooks of a Former Minister*. Port of Spain: Inprint.

McCree, Roy. 1995. "Joffre Serrette: Black man on a white horse?" In *The Black Power Revolution 1970: a Retrospective*, edited by Selwyn Ryan and Taimoon Stewart, with the assistance of Roy McCree, 523–41. St Augustine, Trinidad: ISER, UWI.

Mentus, Ric. 1981. "Why has the ONR upset the PNM and George Chambers?". *People* (November): 44–45.

Millette, David. 1995. "Guerilla war in Trinidad: 1970–1974". In *The Black Power Revolution 1970: a Retrospective*, edited by Selwyn Ryan and Taimoon Stewart, with the assistance of Roy McCree, 625–60. St Augustine, Trinidad: ISER, UWI.

Millette, James. 1995. "Towards the Black Power Revolt of 1970". *The Black Power Revolution 1970: a Retrospective*, edited by Selwyn Ryan and Taimoon Stewart, with the assistance of Roy McCree, 59–96. Trinidad, St Augustine: ISER, UWI.

Mills, Therese. 1973. "Shorty charged for indecency". *Trinidad Guardian* (8 March): 1.

Mitchell, Roy. "The quest for independence and the making of Makandal Daaga". *Trinidad and Tobago Review*.

"Mr Q". 1995. "A Politician Recalls 1970". In *The Black Power Revolution 1970: a Retrospective*, edited by Selwyn Ryan and Taimoon Stewart with the assistance of Roy McCree, 579–606. St Augustine, Trinidad: ISER, UWI.

Nation. 1964. "The uses of adversity". Editorial. *Nation* (18 September): 6.

Nation. 1969. "Dear Mr Prime Minister". Editorial. *Nation* (2 May): 1.

Ngubane, Jordan. *Ushaba*. 1974. Washington: Three Continents Press.

Obika, Nyahuma. n.d. *Gene Miles: Our National Heroine*. Point Fortin, Trinidad: Caribbean Historical Society.

Obika, Nyahuma. 1983. *An Introduction to the Life and Times of Tubal Uriah Buzz Butler*. Point Fortin, Trinidad: Caribbean Historical Society.

Ottley, Rudolph. 1995. *Calypsonians from Then to Now Pt 1*. Arima, Trinidad and Tobago: Rudolph Ottley.

Oxaal, Ivar. 1968. *Black Intellectuals Come to Power: The Rise of Creole Nationalism in Trinidad and Tobago*. Cambridge, Mass.: Schenkman.

Oxaal, Ivar. 1977. *Race and Revolutionary Consciousness* . Cambridge, Mass.: Schenkman.

Oxaal, Ivar. 1981. *Black Intellectuals and the Dilemmas of Race and Class in Trinidad and Tobago*. Cambridge, Mass.: Schenkman.

Pantin, Raoul. 1971. "Fete like bush at PNM rally Expression '71". *Express* (26 January): 10–11.

Pantin, Raoul. 1990. *Black Power Day: The 1970 February Revolution: A Reporter's Story*. Santa Cruz, Trinidad: Hatuey.

Parmasad, Ken. 1971. "The Indian problem". *Pelican*, 17–20. St Augustine, Trinidad: UWI Guild of Undergraduates.

Parmasad, Ken. 1995. "Ancestral impulse, community formation and 1970: Bridging the Afro-Indian divide". In *The Black Power Revolution 1970: a Retrospective*, edited by Selwyn Ryan and Taimoon Stewart, with the assistance of Roy McCree, 309–17. St Augustine, Trinidad: ISER, UWI.

Parris, Carl. 1981. "Trinidad and Tobago – September to December 1973". *Social and Economic Studies* 30, no. 3: 42–49.

Pilgrim, Errol. 1976. "Blakie blames CDC for tent problems". *Trinidad Guardian* (30 January): 1.

Quevedo, Raymond [Atilla the Hun]. 1983. *Atilla's Kaiso: A Short History of Trinidad Calypso*, edited by Errol Hill. Port of Spain: UWI Department of Extra Mural Studies.

Raphael, Clevon. 1971. "Lord Shorty: nothing serious". *Trinidad Guardian* (8 January): 10.

Regis, Louis. 1987. *Black Stalin: the Caribbean Man*. Trinidad: privately printed.

Regis, Louis. 1981. *Maestro: the True Master*. Trinidad: privately printed.

Richardson, Leigh. 1982. "Requiem for a mad(?) scientist". *Sunday Guardian* (7 February): 8.

Riviere, Bill. 1971. "Black Power, NJAC and the 1970 Confrontation in the Caribbean: an historical interpretation". Manuscript, UWI, St Augustine.

Roach, Eric. 1967. "Chalkdust, the political swordsman of calypso". *Trinidad Guardian* (7 February): 7.

Roach, Glen. 1973. "Calypso and politics 1956–1972". Caribbean Studies thesis, UWI, St Augustine, Trinidad.

Robinson, Patricia. 1986. Interview with Wayne Brown. *People* (20 July): 3.

Rodney, Walter. 1969. *The Groundings with My Brothers*. London: Bogle L'Overture.

Rohlehr, Gordon.1970. "Political calypsoes". Manuscript, Department of English, UWI, St Augustine, Trinidad.

Rohlehr, Gordon. 1990 "Sparrow and the language of calypso". *Savacou* (September) 1–2.

Rohlehr, Gordon. 1975. "Sparrow as poet". In *David Frost Introduces Trinidad and Tobago*, edited by Michael Anthony and Andrew Carr. London: Deutsch.

Rohlehr, Gordon. 1981. *Pathfinder: Black Awakening in* The Arrivants *of Edward Kamau Brathwaite.* Tunapuna, Trinidad: Gordon Rohlehr.

Rohlehr, Gordon. 1990. *Calypso and Society in Pre-Independence Trinidad.* Port of Spain: Gordon Rohlehr.

Rohlehr, Gordon. 1991. "Apocalypso and the soca fires of 1990". *The Shape of That Hurt and Other Essays.* Port of Spain: Longman.

Rohlehr, Gordon. 1992. "Literature and the folk". *My Strangled City and Other Essays.* Port of Spain: Longman.

Rohlehr, Gordon. 1992. "'Man talking to man', calypso and social confrontation in Trinidad 1970–1984", *My Strangled City and Other Essays.* Port of Spain: Longman.

Rohlehr, Gordon. 1992. "The problem of the problem of form", *The Shape of That Hurt and Other Essays.* Port of Spain: Longman.

Rohlehr, Gordon. 1995. "The dilemma of the West Indian academic in 1970". In *The Black Power Revolution 1970: a Retrospective,* edited by Selwyn Ryan and Taimoon Stewart, with the assistance of Roy McCree, 381–402. St Augustine, Trinidad: ISER, UWI.

Ryan, Selwyn. 1974. *Race and Nationalism in Trinidad and Tobago: a Study of Decolonisation in a Multiracial Society.* St Augustine, Trinidad: ISER, UWI.

Ryan, Selwyn. 1989. *The Disillusioned Electorate: The Politics of Succession in Trinidad and Tobago.* Port of Spain: Inprint.

Ryan, Selwyn. *Revolution and Reaction: Parties and Politics in Trinidad and Tobago 1970–1981.* St Augustine, Trinidad: ISER, UWI.

Ryan, Selwyn, ed. 1991. *Social and Occupational Stratification in Contemporary Trinidad and Tobago.* St Augustine, Trinidad: ISER, UWI.

Ryan, Selwyn, and Taimoon Stewart, et al., eds. 1995. *The Black Power Revolution 1970: A Retrospective.* St Augustine, Trinidad: ISER, UWI.

Ryan, Selwyn, ed. 1988. *Trinidad and Tobago: The Independence Experience 1962–1987,* edited with the assistance of Gloria Gordon. St Augustine, Trinidad: ISER, UWI.

Sampath, Martin. 1961. "Dangerous influence deplored in the words of some calypsoes". Letter to the editor. *Trinidad Guardian* (27 February): 8.

Sampath, Martin. 1976. *Search and Destroy.* Siparia, Trinidad: Arawak.

Scott Drug Report: Report of the Commission of Enquiry into the Extent of the Problem of Drug Abuse in Trinidad and Tobago. 1987. San Fernando, Trinidad: Unique Services.

Shah, Raffique. 1995. "Reflections on the mutiny and trial". In *The Black Power Revolution 1970: a Retrospective,* edited by Selwyn Ryan and Taimoon Stewart, with the assistance of Roy McCree, 509–22. St Augustine, Trinidad: ISER, UWI.

Short Pants |Llewelyn McIntosh|. 1984. *"Things Going thru Mih Mind": Kaiso Souvenir.* Port of Spain: privately printed.

Shorty |Garfield Blackman|. 1979. Interview with Roy Boyke. "Shorty, man of the mantra". *Trinidad Carnival.* Port of Spain: Key Caribbean.

Singh, Rickey. 1987. "Report says get rid of all cops involved in drug deals". *Trinidad Guardian* (4 February): 1.

Smith, Keith. 1985. "A reply to Johnny King". *Express* (6 January): 26.

Smith, Keith, ed. 1986. *Sparrow the Legend.* Port of Spain: Inprint.

Solomon, Norris. 1987. "The Tesoro story". *Sunday Guardian* (15 March): 5.

Solomon, Patrick. 1981. *Solomon: an Autobiography*. Port of Spain: Inprint.

Sparrow [Slinger Francisco]. 1963. *120 Calypsoes to Remember*. Port of Spain: National Recording Company.

Stewart, Taimoon. 1995. "The aftermath of 1970: transformation, reversal or continuity?" In *The Black Power Revolution 1970: a Retrospective*, edited by Selwyn Ryan and Taimoon Stewart, with the assistance of Roy McCree. St Augustine, Trinidad: ISER, UWI.

Subero, Keith. 1975. "19 calypsoes banned on air". *Sunday Express* (26 January): 32.

Sunday Express. 1987. "Duke: Chalkdust deserved 2nd in Calypso Monarch race". *Sunday Express* (15 March): 5.

Sunday Express. 1987. "Tesoro – the Trinidad success story that almost wasn't". *Sunday Express* (15 March): 6.

Sunday Guardian. 1960. "Calypsonians complain of propaganda". *Sunday Guardian* (24 January): 10.

Sunday Guardian. 1973. "Hindu group asks PM to ban 'Indrani'". *Sunday Guardian* (9 March): 3.

Sunday Guardian. 1973. "'Chalkie was disrespectful' say women". *Sunday Guardian* (11 March): 1.

Sunday Guardian. 1974. "Goddard refused to sign". *Sunday Guardian* (26 February): 7.

Sunday Guardian. 1987. "'Vote Dem Out' came from the heart says calypsonian Deple". *Sunday Guardian* (25 January): 26.

Sunday Guardian. 1987. "It all started with an 'arrangement' some 18 years ago". *Sunday Guardian* (22 March): 9.

Sunday Punch. 1989. "PM summons Chalkie". *Sunday Punch* (4 June): 5.

Tanifeari, William. 1988. "Interview with Short Pants". *The Black Scholar*.

Tapia. 1971. "God help our gracious king". *Tapia* (23 May): 8.

Tennyson, Alfred. 1989. "The lotus eaters". In *Tennyson: a Selected Edition*, edited by Christopher Rich. Essex: Longman.

TnT Mirror. 1987. "Deple still singing 'Vote Dem Out'". *TnT Mirror* (21 October): 23.

Trinidad Chronicle. 1958. "Dr Williams is married". *Trinidad Chronicle* (5 December): 1.

Trinidad Guardian. 1959. "Tiger quits over 'secret marriage'". *Trinidad Guardian* (10 January): 1.

Trinidad Guardian. 1961. "Sparrow runs for police". *Trinidad Guardian* (31 January): 10.

Trinidad Guardian. 1964. "Minister took prisoner away". *Trinidad Guardian* (10 September): 1.

Trinidad Guardian. 1964. "Sparrow's calypso on Dr Solomon". *Trinidad Guardian* (30 September): 3.

Trinidad Guardian. 1968. "Ministry queries Chalkie's dual role". *Trinidad Guardian* (16 February): 1.

Trinidad Guardian. 1982. "Gov't to Gov't arrangements a $5 billion illusion". *Trinidad Guardian* (18 June): 1.

Trinidad Guardian. 1982. "Firm admits $3.3 m on payments in report". *Trinidad Guardian* (8 August): 1.

Trinidad Guardian. 1987. "PM sees scandal in drug report". *Trinidad Guardian* (1 January): 1.

Trinidad Guardian. 1987. "A budget of sacrifices". *Trinidad Guardian* (24 January): 1.

Vincent-Brown, Kenneth. 1964. "Solomon back again". *Sunday Guardian* (11 October): 1.

Wallis, Roger, and Krister Malm. 1984. *Big Sounds from Small Peoples: the Music Industry in Small Countries*. London: Constable.

Warner, Keith. 1982. *Kaiso: The Trinidad Calypso – a Study of the Calypso as Oral Literature*. Washington, DC: Three Continents Press.

Warner-Lewis, Maureen. 1986. "The influence of Yoruba music on the minor-key calypso". Seminar on the calypso, 6–10 January 1986. ISER/UWI Calypso Research Project, St Augustine, Trinidad.

Wight, Gerald. 1961. "Sir Gerald sees danger ahead". *Sunday Guardian* (8 January): 1.

Williams, Eric. 1961 "*Massa Day Done*": *a Masterpiece of Political and Sociological Analysis*. Port of Spain: PNM Publishing Co.

Williams, Eric. 1969. *Inward Hunger: the Education of a Prime Minister*. London: Deutsch.

Williams, Eric. 1979. "*The Caribbean Man*": *Address of the Political Leader of the PNM, 21st Annual Convention*. 28 September 1979. Port of Spain: PNM Publishing Co.

Williams, Eric. 1981. *Forged from the Love of Liberty: Selected Speeches of Dr Eric Williams*, compiled by Paul Sutton. London: Longman Caribbean.

Wiltshire-Brodber, Rosina. 1988. "Trinidad and Tobago foreign policy 1962–1987: an Evaluation". In *Trinidad and Tobago: The Independence Experience 1962–1987*, edited by Selwyn Ryan with the assistance of Gloria Gordon, 281–302. St Augustine, Trinidad: ISER, UWI.